Windows Forensic
Analysis Toolkit

Windows Forensic Analysis Toolkit

Advanced Analysis Techniques for Windows 7

Harlan Carvey

Technical Editor
Jennifer Kolde

AMSTERDAM • BOSTON • HEIDELBERG • LONDON
NEW YORK • OXFORD • PARIS • SAN DIEGO
SAN FRANCISCO • SINGAPORE • SYDNEY • TOKYO
Syngress is an imprint of Elsevier

ELSEVIER

Acquiring Editor: Chris Katsaropoulos
Development Editor: Heather Scherer
Project Manager: Jessica Vaughan
Designer: Alisa Andreola

Syngress is an imprint of Elsevier
225 Wyman Street, Waltham, MA 02451, USA

Library of Congress Cataloging-in-Publication Data
Carvey, Harlan A.
  Windows forensic analysis toolkit advanced analysis techniques for Windows 7 / by Harlan Carvey.
     p. cm.
  Includes bibliographical references.
  ISBN 978-1-59749-727-5
  1. Computer crimes—Investigation—United States—Methodology. 2. Microsoft Windows
(Computer file)—Security measures. 3. Computer networks—Security measures. 4. Internet—
Security measures. 5. Computer security. I. Title.
  HV8079.C65C3726 2012
  363.25'968—dc23

                                                                                    2011043150

British Library Cataloguing-in-Publication Data
A catalogue record for this book is available from the British Library

ISBN: 978-1-59749-727-5

Printed in the United States of America

11 12 13 14 15   10 9 8 7 6 5 4 3 2 1

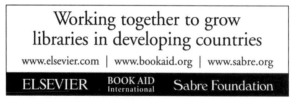

Working together to grow
libraries in developing countries

www.elsevier.com | www.bookaid.org | www.sabre.org

ELSEVIER   BOOK AID International   Sabre Foundation

For information on all Syngress publications, visit our website at www.syngress.com.

To Terri and Kylie—you are my light and my foundation.

Contents

Preface

I am not an expert. I have never claimed to be an expert at anything (at least not seriously done so), least of all an expert in digital forensic analysis of Windows systems. I am simply someone who has found an interest in my chosen field of employment, and a passion to dig deeper. I enjoy delving into and extending the investigative process, as well as exploring new ways to approach problems in the field of digital forensic analysis. It was more than 13 years ago that I decided to focus on Windows systems specifically, in large part because no one else on the team I worked with at the time did so. We had folks who focused on routers and firewalls, as well as those who focused on Linux; however, almost no effort, beyond enabling configuration settings in the vulnerability scanner we used, was put toward really understanding Windows systems. As I moved from vulnerability assessments into incident response and digital forensic analysis, understanding what was happening "under the hood" on Windows systems, understanding what actions could create or modify certain artifacts, became a paramount interest. I am not an expert.

When I sat down to write this book, I wanted to take a different approach from the second edition; that is, rather than starting with the manuscript from the previous edition and adding new material, I wanted to start over completely and write an entirely new book, creating a companion book to the second edition. As I was writing the second edition, Windows 7 was gaining greater prominence in the marketplace, and there has been considerably more effort dedicated toward and developments as a result of research into Windows 7 artifacts. Even now, as I write this book (summer 2011), Windows 8 is beginning to poke its head over the horizon, and it likely won't be too awfully long before we begin to see Windows 8 systems. As such, there's a good deal more to write about and address, so I wanted to write a book that, rather than focusing on Windows XP and looking ahead now and again to Windows 7, instead focused on Windows 7 as an analysis platform and target, and refer back to previous versions of Windows when it made sense to do so.

Therefore, regardless of the title, this book is not intended to replace the second edition, but instead to be a companion edition to be used alongside the second edition. Let me say that again—if you have the second edition of *Windows Forensic Analysis*, you will not want to get rid of it and replace it with this book. Instead, you'll want to have both of them (as well as *Windows Registry Forensics* and *Digital Forensics with Open-Source Tools*) on your bookshelf or Kindle (or whichever ebook platform you're using). In fact, if you have just purchased this edition, you will want to also purchase a copy of the second edition, as well.

I will say upfront that there are some things not covered in this book. When writing this book, I did not want to reiterate some of the information available in other media, including previous editions of *Windows Forensic Analysis*. As such, while mentioning how physical memory can be collected from a Windows system, this book does not go into detail with respect to memory analysis; truthfully, this is a topic best covered in a book of its own. In this book, we also discuss malware detection within an acquired image, but we do not discuss malware analysis, as this topic has been addressed extremely well in its own book.

INTENDED AUDIENCE

This book is intended for anyone with an interest in developing a greater understanding of digital forensic analysis, specifically of Windows 7 systems. This includes digital forensic analysts, incident responders, students, law enforcement officers, and researchers, or just anyone who's interested in digital forensic analysis of Windows 7 systems. Even system administrators and hobbyists will get something useful from this book. I've tried to point out how the information in this book can be used, by both forensic analysts and incident responders alike.

In reading this book, you'll notice that there are several tools described throughout that were written in the Perl scripting language. Don't worry, you don't need to be a Perl expert (after all, neither am I) to use these scripts; not only are the scripts very simple to use, but in most cases, they are accompanied by Windows executables, "compiled" using "Perl2.exe" (found at *http://www.indigostar.com/perl2exe.php*). While some programming capability would be beneficial if you want to develop your own RegRipper plugins, several folks with little to no Perl programming skill have written working plugins for that particular tool. Others have rewritten tools like RegRipper in other languages, because again, it's not about the tool you use to solve the problem, it's about solving the problem.

ORGANIZATION OF THIS BOOK

This book consists of eight chapters.

Chapter 1: Analysis Concepts

This chapter addresses the core investigative and analysis concepts that I've found to be so critical to what we do, yet somehow glaringly absent from many books and discussions. As professionals within the digital forensic analysis community, there are a number of concepts that are central to what we do, and while (at this time) there isn't a centralized authority to mandate and manage this sort of information, I've found these concepts to be absolutely critical to the work I've been doing. Further, whether presenting at a conference or discussing analysis with someone one-on-one, I see "the light come on" when talking about these concepts.

These concepts are vitally important because we cannot simply load an acquired image into a forensic analysis application and start pushing buttons; this really gets us nowhere. What do we do when something doesn't work or gives us output that we didn't expect? How do we handle or address that? Do we move on to another tool, documenting what we're doing? I hope so—too many times I've seen or heard of analysts who've accepted whatever the tool or application has provided, neglecting to conduct any critical thought, and moved on to their findings. Operating systems and targets may change, but the core concepts remain the same, and it's imperative that analysts understand and employ these concepts in their analysis.

Chapter 2: Immediate Response

In this chapter, we discuss the need for immediate response once an incident has been identified. Often, an organization is notified by another entity (e.g., bank, law enforcement agency, etc.) that they've been compromised, and an external third-party consulting firm that provides incident response services is immediately contacted. Once contracting issues have been addressed, consultants are sent onsite, and once they arrive, they need to gather further information regarding what was identified, as well as the "lay of the land" with respect to the network infrastructure. All of this takes additional time, during which information that could prove to be very critical to addressing the inevitable questions faced by the potentially compromised organization is fading and expiring (this says nothing about sensitive data that may continue to flow from the infrastructure). Processes complete, deleted files get overwritten, and new Volume Shadow Copies are created as old ones are deleted. Windows systems are surprisingly active even when supposedly sitting idle; therefore, it is paramount that response activities begin immediately, not whenever someone from outside the organization, who isn't familiar with the infrastructure, can arrive onsite.

Chapter 3: Volume Shadow Copies

The existence of Volume Shadow Copies (VSCs) is relatively well known within the digital forensics community, but means by which analysts can exploit their forensic value are not. As much of the digital forensic analysis occurs using images acquired from systems, this chapter addresses how analysts can access the wealth of information available in VSCs without having to interact with the live system, and without having to purchase expensive solutions.

Chapter 4: File Analysis

This chapter addresses not only the analysis of some of the usual files available on Windows systems, but also files and data structures that are new to Windows 7 (or Vista) and have been identified and better understood through research and testing. Some files available on Windows 7 systems have changed formats, while others are simply new, and both need to be understood by analysts. For example, jump lists are new to Windows 7 systems, and some of them use the compound document binary format (popular in MS Office documents prior to version 2007 of the office suite), in conjunction with the SHLLINK format most often seen in Windows shortcut files. As such, jump lists can contain considerable information (including metadata) that can be very valuable during an investigation.

Chapter 5: Registry Analysis

This chapter addresses some of the information provided through other sources, most notably *Windows Registry Forensics*, and takes that information a step further, particularly with respect to Windows 7 systems. Rather than reiterating the information available in other sources, this chapter uses that information as a foundation, and presents additional information specific to the Windows 7 Registry.

Chapter 6: Malware Detection

Oddly enough, this chapter does not contain the word "analysis" in the title, because we're not going to be discussing either static or dynamic malware analysis. Instead, we're going to discuss a specific type of analysis that is becoming very prominent within the digital forensic community; that is, given an image acquired from a Windows system, how can we go about detecting the presence of malware within that image? Professionally, I've received quite a number of images with the goal being to determine if there was malware on the system. Sometimes, such a request is accompanied by little additional information, such as the name of a specific malware variant, or specific information or artifacts that can be used to help identify the malware. Given that malware authors seem to be extremely adept at keeping their code hidden from commercial antivirus scanning applications, analysts need other tools (preferably a process) in their kits for detecting malware within an acquired image.

Chapter 7: Timeline Analysis

The idea of timeline analysis, as applied to digital forensic analysis, has been around for quite a while. Rob Lee of SANS fame discussed performing a limited version of timeline analysis as far back as 2000. Over time, we've seen how a considerable amount of time-stamped information is tracked by the Windows operating systems, and all of this can potentially be extremely valuable to our analysis. Also, much of this time-stamped information is contained in artifacts that persist even after applications and malware have been removed from the system, and can be revealed through timeline analysis. In addition, incorporating multiple data sources of time-stamped data into a timeline will provide considerably more value to an examination.

Chapter 8: Application Analysis

This chapter discusses a number of concepts and techniques that are usually associated with dynamic malware analysis, but takes a more general approach. There are a number of applications that analysts run into during an examination, and many times the question that needs to be answered (i.e., the goal of the analysis) is to determine whether a particular artifact is the result of default application behavior or specific user activity.

ONLINE CONTENT

There is no DVD that accompanies this book; instead, the code that I've written and described in this book is provided online at the WinForensicAnalysis Google Code site (*http://code.google.com/p/winforensicaanalysis/downloads/list*). Updates to the provided code will be discussed and described via the WindowsIR blog (*http://windowsir.blogspot.com*).

Acknowledgments

I'd like to begin by thanking God for the many blessings He's given me in my life, the first of which has been my family. I count having the interest, ability, and heart for writing this book, as well as the others, as one of those blessings. I try to thank Him daily, but I find myself thinking that that's not nearly enough. A man's achievements are often not his alone, and in my heart, being able and afforded the environment to write books like this is a gift and a blessing in so many ways. My hope is that this effort benefits many more than just those who purchase and use the books.

I'd like to thank my true love and the light of my life, Terri, and my stepdaughter, Kylie. Both of these wonderful ladies have put up with my antics yet again (intently staring off into space, scribbling in the air, and of course, there are my excellent imitations taken from some of the movies we've seen), and I thank you both as much for your patience as for being there for me when I turned away from the keyboard. It can't be easy to have a nerd like me in your life, but I do thank you both for the opportunity to "put pen to paper" and get all of this stuff out of my head.

I'd like to thank Jennifer Kolde, my technical editor, yet again. I say "again" because this isn't the first time that Jennifer and I have worked together. Going through the process of working on my very first book with you has left an indelible mark on how I have approached and written books since then. Over the years we have had a number of opportunities to engage and exchange thoughts and ideas, and that has really been very beneficial for me. I'm sure when I've sent you chapters for this book, you've alternatively laughed and cried at my prose, but I do thank you so much for your invaluable insight and input.

I've said it before and I'll say it again … I miss working with Cory Altheide. Cory and I exchanged emails several years ago and published some research with respect to tracking USB removable storage devices across Windows systems. At one point, Cory and I had an opportunity to work together, and while employment at that organization ultimately didn't work out for either of us, I'm going to be entirely selfish and say simply that when we did have an opportunity to work together, it was a blast! We collaborated on *Digital Forensics with Open-Source Tools*, in so much as it was Cory's idea and he was by far the primary author. So, if you have a copy of *DFwOST*, do not refer to it as "Harlan's book," and always make sure Cory signs it first and biggest. I'm sure trading him an autograph for a beer will leave everyone involved satisfied.

I want to be sure to thank everyone who has written tools—commercial or open-source—that I mentioned in this book. Christopher Brown of Technology Pathways, LLC, has graciously granted me a license for ProDiscover since version 3, and I've a great deal of fun working with this application and seeing it grow over time. By the time this manuscript was submitted to the publisher, ProDiscover was at version 7.0.0.8. I'd like to thank Matt Shannon for all the fantastic work he's done on F-Response, as that is a tool that has really done a lot to change how incident response should be done. It has also been interesting to see how this tool has developed over time, as Matt comes from an incident response and digital forensics background, so this is a tool for practitioners, designed and written by a practitioner. I'd also like to thank the guys at Kyrus Tech, Inc. for developing Carbon Black. They have a quote from me on one of their web pages, stating that "Carbon Black changes the dynamics of incident response." I stand by that statement, because I believe it. I've seen their demo, and even worked with it in my own small lab, and found myself looking back over the previous 10 years and wishing that the customers that I'd interacted with had had something like Carbon Black installed. I'd like to thank Mark Woan and Mark McKinnon for providing and sharing their tools, as well as anyone else I may have missed. I think that in a community that really has a lot to learn with respect to sharing, anyone who is writing and sharing tools is really way out in front of the pack.

I'm sure at this point I've missed some folks, so please accept my sincerest apologies and "thank you" if I engaged with you or read something you wrote, and came away with something that became the seed of an idea that ended up in this book.

Finally, I'd like to thank the Syngress staff, especially Heather Scherer, for their patience throughout this process. I'm sure it can't be easy if your job is publishing books, but for those writing the books, authoring is not their primary job, and sometimes not their primary focus.

About the Author

Harlan Carvey (CISSP) is vice president of Advanced Security Projects with Terremark Worldwide, Inc. Terremark is a leading global provider of IT infrastructure and "cloud computing" services, based in Miami, FL. Harlan is a key contributor to the Engagement Services practice, providing disk forensics analysis, consulting, and training services to both internal and external customers. Harlan has provided forensic analysis services for the hospitality industry, financial institutions, as well as federal government and law enforcement agencies. Harlan's primary areas of interest include research and development of novel analysis solutions, with a focus on Windows platforms.

Harlan holds a bachelor's degree in electrical engineering from the Virginia Military Institute and a master's degree in the same discipline from the Naval Postgraduate School. Harlan resides in northern Virginia with his family.

About the Technical Editor

Jennifer Kolde is a technical analyst and researcher supporting computer intrusion investigations for the federal government. Prior to her current position, she spent nearly 10 years as a defense contractor, providing network and system administration, network security, incident response, forensics, and malware analysis for the U.S. Navy. Her experience includes managing information security and incident response on a 10,000-node research and development network, geographically distributed from the U.S. east coast to the Asian Pacific rim.

Jennifer received her undergraduate degree from the University of Michigan and her MS in Computer Science and Information Security from James Madison University. She is a former SANS instructor and director of the GIAC certification program, and has edited several technical books for various publishers.

Analysis Concepts

CHAPTER OUTLINE

INFORMATION IN THIS CHAPTER

- Analysis Concepts
- Setting Up an Analysis System

INTRODUCTION

If you've had your eye on the news media, or perhaps more appropriately the online lists and forums, over the past couple of years, there are a couple of facts or "truths" that should be glaringly obvious to you. First, computers and computing devices are more and more a part of our lives. Not only do most of us have computer systems, such as desktops at work and school, laptops at home and on the go, we also have "smart phones," tablet computing devices, and even smart global positioning systems (GPSs) built into our cars. We're inundated with marketing ploys every day, being told that we have to get the latest-and-greatest device, and be connected not just to WiFi, but also to the ever-present "4G" (whatever that means ...) cellular networks. If we don't have a phone-type device available, we can easily open up our laptop or turn on our tablet device and instantly communicate with others using instant messaging, email, Twitter, or Skype applications.

The second truth is that as computers become more and more a part of our lives, so does crime involving those devices in some manner. Whether it's "cyberbullying" or "cyberstalking," identity theft, or intrusions and data breaches that result in some form of data theft, a good number of real-world physical crimes are now being committed through the use of computers, and as such, get renamed by prepending "cyber" to the description. As we began to move a lot of the things that we did in the real world to the online world (e.g., banking, shopping, filing taxes, etc.), we became targets for cybercrime.

What makes this activity even more insidious and apparently "sophisticated" is that we don't recognize it for what it is, because conceptually, the online world is simply so foreign to us. If someone shatters a storefront window to steal a television set, there's a loud noise, possibly an alarm, broken glass, and someone fleeing with their stolen loot. Cybercrime doesn't "look like" this; often, something isn't stolen and then absent, so much as it's copied. Other times, the crime does result in something that is stolen and removed from our ownership, but we may not recognize that immediately, because we're talking about 1s and 0s in cyberspace, not a car that should be sitting in your driveway.

These malicious activities also appear to be increasing in sophistication. In many cases, the fact that a crime has occurred is not evident until someone notices a significant decrease in an account balance, which indicates that the perpetrator has already gained access to systems, gathered the data needed, accessed that bank account, and left with the funds. The actual incidents are not detected until well after (in some cases, weeks or even months) they've occurred. In other instances, the malicious activity continues and even escalates after we become aware of it, because we're unable to transition our mindset from the real world (lock the doors and windows, post a guard at the door, etc.) to the online world, and effectively address the issue.

Clearly, no one and no organization is immune. The early part of 2011 saw a number of high-visibility computer security incidents splashed across the pages (both web and print) of the media. The federal arm of the computer consulting firm HBGary suffered an embarrassing exposure of internal, sensitive data, and equally devastating was the manner in which it was retrieved. RSA, owned by EMC and the provider of secure authentication mechanisms, reported that they'd been compromised. On April 6, Kelly Jackson Higgins published a story (titled "Law Firms Under Siege") at *DarkReading.com* that revealed that law firms were becoming a more prevalent target of advanced persistent threat (APT) actor groups. The examples are numerous, but the point is that there's no one specific type of attack that is used in every situation, or victim that gets targeted. Everyone's a target.

To address this situation, we need to have responders and analysts who are at least as equally educated, armed, and knowledgeable as those committing these online crimes. Being able to develop suitable detection and deterrence mechanisms depends on understanding how these online criminals operate, how they get in, what they're after, and how they exfiltrate what they've found from the infrastructure. As such, analysts need to understand how to go about determining which systems have been accessed, and which are used as primary jump points that the intruders use to return at will. They also need to understand how to do so without tipping their hand and revealing that they are actively monitoring the intruders, or inadvertently destroying data in the process.

In this book, we're going to focus on the analysis of Windows computer systems—laptops, desktops, servers—because they are so pervasive. This is not to exclude other devices and operating systems; to the contrary, we're narrowing our focus in order to fit the topic that we're covering into a manageable volume. Our focus throughout this book will be primarily on the Windows 7 operating system (OS), and much of the book after Chapter 2 will be tailored specifically to the analysis of forensic images acquired from those systems.

In this chapter, we're going to start our journey by discussing and understanding the core concepts that set the foundation for our analysis. It is vitally important that responders and analysts understand these concepts, as it is these core concepts that shape what we do and how we approach a problem or incident. Developing an understanding of the fundamentals allows us to create a foundation upon which to build, allowing analysts to be able to address new issues effectively, rather than responding to these challenges by using the "that's what we've always done" methodology, which may be unviable.

ANALYSIS CONCEPTS

Very often when talking to analysts—especially those who are new to the field—I find that there are some concepts that shape not only their thought processes but also their investigative processes and how they look at and approach the various problems and issues that they encounter. For new analysts, without a great deal of actual experience to fall back on, these fundamental analysis concepts make up for that lack of experience and allow them to overcome the day-to-day challenges that they face.

Consider how you may have learned to acquire images of hard drives. Many of us started out our learning process by first removing the hard drive from the computer system, and hooking it up to a write-blocker. We learned about write-blockers that allowed us to acquire an image of a hard drive to another, "clean" hard drive. However, the act of removing the hard drive from the computer system isn't the extent of the foundational knowledge we gathered; it's the documentation that we developed and maintained during this process that was so critical and foundational. What did we do, how did we do it, and how do we know that we'd done it correctly? Did we document what we'd done to the point where someone else could follow the same process and achieve the same results, making our process repeatable? It's this aspect that's of paramount importance, because what happens when we encounter an ecommerce server that needs to be acquired but cannot be taken offline for any reason? Or what happens when the running server doesn't actually have any hard drives, but is instead a boot-from-SAN server? Or if the running laptop uses whole disk encryption so that the entire contents of the hard drive are encrypted when the system is shut down? As not every situation is going to be the same or fit neatly into a nice little training package, understanding the foundational concepts of what you hope to achieve through image acquisition is far more important than memorizing the mechanics of how to connect source and target hard drives to a write-blocker and perform an acquisition. This is just one example of why core foundational concepts are so critically important.

Windows Versions

I've been told by some individuals that there are three basic computer operating systems that exist: Windows, Linux, and Mac OS X. That's it, end of story. I have to say that when I hear this I'm something a bit more than shocked. This sort of attitude tells me that someone views all Windows versions as being the same, and that kind of thinking can be extremely detrimental to even the simplest examination. This is due to the fact that there are significant differences among Windows versions, particularly from the perspective of a forensic analyst.

The differences among Windows versions go beyond just what we see in the graphical user interface (GUI). Some of the changes that occur among Windows versions affect entire technologies. For example, the Task Scheduler version 1.0 that shipped with Windows XP is pretty straightforward. The scheduled task (.job) files have a binary format, and the results of the tasks running are recorded in the Task Scheduler log file (i.e., "SchedLgU.txt"). With Vista and Task Scheduler version 2.0, there are significant differences; while the Task Scheduler log file remains the same, the .job files are XML format files. In addition (and this will be discussed in greater detail later in the book), not only do Vista and Windows 7 systems ship with many default scheduled tasks, but information about the tasks (including a hash of the .job file itself) is recorded in the Registry.

On Windows XP and 2003 systems, the Event Log (.evt) files follow a binary format that is well documented at the Microsoft web site. In fact, the structures and format of the .evt files and their embedded records are so well documented that open-source tools for parsing these files are relatively easy to write. Beginning with Vista, the Event Log service was rewritten and the Windows Event Log (.evtx) framework was implemented. Only a high-level description of the binary XML format of the logs themselves is available at the Microsoft site. In addition, there are two types of Windows Event Logs implemented; one group is the Window Logs and includes the Application, System, Security, Setup, and ForwardedEvent logs. The other group is the Application and Services logs, which record specific events from applications and other components on the system. While there are many default Application and Services logs that are installed as part of a Windows 2008 and Windows 7, for example, these logs may also vary depending on the installed applications and services. In short, the move from Windows XP/2003 to Vista brought a completely new logging format and structure, requiring new tools and techniques for accessing the logged events.

From a purely binary perspective, there is no difference among the Registry hive files of the various Windows versions, from Windows 2000 all the way through to Windows 7 (and even into Windows 8). In some cases, there are no differences in what information is maintained in the Registry; for the most part, information about Windows services, as well as the contents of the USBStor key, continue to be similar for versions between Windows 2000 and Windows 7. However, there are significant differences between these two Windows versions with respect to the information that is recorded regarding USB devices, access to wireless access points, and a number of other areas. Another example of a difference in what's recorded in the Registry is that with Windows XP, searches that a user performed through the Explorer shell (e.g., "Start→Search") are recorded in the ACMru key. With Vista, information about searches is moved to a file, and with Windows 7, user searches are recorded in the WordWheelQuery key.

Other differences in Windows versions are perhaps unintentional. In December 2010, there was a question posted to an online forum asking about the purpose of the Microsoft\ESENT\Process Registry key within the Software hive on a Windows XP system. During the ensuing exchange, various respondents included references to Google searches that indicated that there were some versions of malware that modified the contents of that key. For example, one reference at the *ThreatExpert.com* site indicated that a Trojan associated with online games modified this key when installed. Ultimately, with the assistance of Troy Larson (senior forensic investigator at Microsoft), it was determined that the key should only exist on Windows XP systems, as Windows XP shipped with a debug or "checked build" of "esent.dll." This indicated that the dynamic link library (DLL) had been compiled to generate additional information for debugging purposes, and then had not been recompiled for "production" delivery, and the debug version of the DLL was shipped with the operating system installation. In checking the software hives on several available test systems, as well as within acquired images of Vista, Windows 2003/2008, and Windows 7 systems I had access to, I didn't find any indication that the key existed on any other system than Windows XP.

Some differences among versions of the Windows operating system can be subtle, while others can be covert and not visible to the casual user or administrator. However, the fact remains that, as a forensic analyst, what you look for (based on your examination goals) and what you see, and how you access and interpret it, will be impacted significantly by the Windows version that you're examining. Troy Larson has been putting considerable effort toward highlighting many of the new technologies within Windows 7 and identifying possible sources of forensic artifacts, and discussing these areas in presentations. There are a number of other presentations available (via searching) online that discuss similar findings, indicating that there are those, in the forensic community as well as within academia, who feel it's important to identify as many of the new potential sources of forensic artifacts or "evidence" as possible.

Documenting all of the differences among the various Windows versions would simply be an enormous task. Throughout the rest of this book, as different topics are discussed, I will attempt to point out the differences among Windows versions, where this is pertinent to the understanding of the topic. The point, however, is to understand that "Windows" is not simply "Windows," and the Windows version (XP or Windows 7, 32- or 64-bit, etc.) will have a significant impact on the tools used and the investigative approach used.

Analysis Principles

Many times when discussing forensic analysis with other folks, particularly new analysts, it seems that when someone gets into this business, the primary focus of their training (and therefore, their investigative approach) is on tools. So when they're given an image to analyze, analysts' first thought is to open up the commercial forensic analysis application that they're familiar with or were trained on. However, if you were to take that application away, where would they be? What would they be left with, and what would they be able to do? I ask this, because I have heard analysts state, "I need [insert application name]" when given an examination.

Many of the principles and concepts discussed throughout the rest of this chapter will likely be familiar to many analysts. You may have seen them in my blog, or you may have heard another analyst or responder discuss them in a presentation at a conference. Chris Pogue's *Sniper Forensics* presentations cover many of these ideas; Chris and I worked at IBM together, and spent time discussing many of these concepts. I'm presenting the principles again here because they're important, and I really feel that analysts need to understand them, or at least have a familiarity with them.

Goals

The goals of our analysis are perhaps the most important aspect of what we do. Without having goals for our analysis, we'd likely end up spending weeks or months combing through a few images, finding all manner of potentially "bad stuff." But to what end? Analysts and consultants in the private sector most often work under the auspices of a contract that specifies a set number of hours. The same is true for law enforcement examiners, although any limits or constraints may often be more of a resource issue than from a contract.

When handed a drive image, the first question that should come to every analyst's mind is, "What question am I trying to answer?" Locate and identify malware? Locate indications of access to (or attempts to access) specific files? Locate indications of attempts to hide activity? Determine if a user accessed specific web sites or remote computer systems? Without having some kind of concise, achievable goal for analysis, a small stack of hard drives (or images acquired from them) can easily engage an analyst for a significant (perhaps inordinate) amount of time. But to what end? At the end of, say, two weeks of dedicated analysis, what is the final result? What does the report look like, if a report can be written at all? What are the analyst's findings and conclusions? Without a destination, how do you know when you get there?

As such, "find all bad stuff" is *not* a goal of forensic analysis. I know of an analyst who acquired an image of a desktop hard drive and was told to "find all bad stuff." Accepting that as a goal, the analyst returned to his lab and began analysis, and found quite a bit of "bad stuff." However, it turned out that the employee whose system had been imaged was tasked with "hacking" activities to protect the company web site; once that context was added to the examination, it was clear that all of the work that had been done had simply found the tools that the employee used in his job.

Developing goals for an examination can be pretty straightforward. When I was in the military, I had a company commander who told me that if I couldn't sum up an issue in a couple of bullet statements on a 3×5 index card, I didn't know enough about that issue. At the time, I didn't think that I had a very good idea of what he was talking about, but over time, I learned the wisdom of what he'd said. Let's say that you're tasked with examining an image of a system; do you know why that system was acquired in the first place? What was the event that occurred that caused someone to acquire an image of that system? Did a pop-up appear on the desktop reporting a virus? Was some sort of network traffic observed emanating from or going to the system that triggered an intrusion detection system alert, or caught an security operations center (SOC) analyst's attention? Were there some unusual firewall logs or domain name service (DNS) requests that indicated a possible issue with the system? If this is what happened, then the goals of the examination go from "find bad stuff" to something a bit more specific and achievable, such as "determine if malware was present on the system that could have caused or resulted in the observed event/traffic."

The goals of an examination can be important for other reasons, as well. Back in 2000, I was working as the network security engineer at a now-defunct telecommunications company. At one point, the security manager was considering having some forensic analysis performed, and we'd heard that another group within the company had worked with a particular vendor that provided forensic analysis services. When we asked some of the members of this group about the vendor, we were told that they didn't do a very thorough analysis of one drive in particular, as they had missed a hidden DOS partition. That was it … no mention of the reason the vendor had been hired or what the goal of the analysis was, just this one negative comment. When we spoke to the vendor, he was prepared for our questions, and brought a copy of the contract that specified the goal of the analysis, which was to determine if the system had the SubSeven Trojan installed. There was nothing in the contract that specified the need to determine if there were any other partitions, particularly hidden ones, although the analyst did see the partition and noted it. The issue of the hidden DOS partition was a distraction, and aside from that, the vendor had fulfilled the terms and conditions of the contract; they'd met the goals of the examination that they'd been given. Regardless of any personal or professional issues that the company employee may have had, the forensic analyst for the vendor had remained focused on the goals of the analysis.

Another important aspect of your goals is that they can often help you scope and better define an incident. For example, in data breach investigations, the primary question that needs to be answered is, "What data, if any, left the infrastructure?" Various state notification laws or mandates set forth by regulatory bodies may come into play, and may result in significant costs and negative press exposure for the organization. Most incident responders know that to definitively answer this question, you need full packet traffic captures from the time when the data actually left the systems and the infrastructure. However, understanding what data may have left the infrastructure and been exposed then leads responders to those systems that may be involved in the incident, including where the data were stored (e.g., database server) or may have been processed (e.g., back office payment processor server, user's workstation, etc.).

Tools Versus Processes

When it comes to analysis, too many times we seem to focus on tools rather than the process. This is a trap that new analysts often fall into, as their initial introduction and training is often focused on developing familiarity with one tool (e.g., a commercial forensic analysis application) to get them up and running as quickly as possible. However, even more experienced analysts can find themselves focusing on a specific tool or application rather than the overall process.

Consider the implementation of the Volume Shadow Copy Service (VSS) in Windows systems beginning with Vista (VSS had actually been implemented in Windows XP, but in a somewhat limited manner). Long after this technology was implemented (Vista was released in November 2006), most commercial forensic analysis applications had not provided a means for easily accessing Volume Shadow Copies (VSCs, discussed in detail in Chapter 3) within acquired images. For example, ProDiscover, from Technology Pathways, was the first commercial forensic analysis application to allow easy access to VSCs in the spring of 2011. However, as will be described in detail in Chapter 3, there are a number of methods for accessing VSCs within an acquired image that do not require the purchase of a commercial product. The point is that by focusing on specific tools ("My tool can't do that, so I can't answer that question"), analysts often lose sight of the process and what's really required to meet their goals ("What tool or method is most appropriate for obtaining the data I need?"). By understanding what it is you hope to achieve, as well as the technology you're faced with, you can understand the overall process you need to follow to achieve your goals. After all, if all you have is a hammer, every problem becomes a nail.

Locard's Exchange Principle

This is an analysis concept that has been addressed and discussed in a number of resources; I'm including it here because no discussion of analysis concepts would be complete without it. In short, Locard was a French scientist who postulated that when two objects came into contact, material from each was transferred to the other. We see this mentioned quite often in TV crime shows, like *CSI*, when analyst Nick Stokes declares, "… possible transfer."

Okay, so how does this principle apply to digital forensic analysis, you ask? That is an excellent question. In short, any interaction between two entities (one being the computer operating system) results in the transfer or creation of data. For example, when a user logs into a system, even when auditing of logins is not enabled, artifacts of the login, as well as the user's activities, are created. When a user interacts with the system, there are traces of this activity, whether the user logs in locally or accesses the system remotely. Whenever a program runs within the operating system, there is a "transfer" or creation of data of some kind. The data or artifacts may vary in how persistent they are (this is known as the *order of volatility*), but they will be created. Many of these artifacts will exist only for a short time, and some may persist until the system is rebooted. Other artifacts will persist well after the system is shut down and rebooted. But the thing to remember is that artifacts will be created.

Avoiding Speculation

Whether working as an incident responder or as a digital forensics analyst, we need to be sure that we don't fall into the trap of filling in gaps in our information with guesses, and answering questions through speculation. This is also an issue (perhaps even more so) for information technology (IT) staff attempting to scope or deal with a computer security incident, but doing so without the benefit of the training and experience of skilled incident responders. The fact is that many times we simply don't know what we don't know, and we fill in the gaps in our information with speculation rather than facts. This most often results with incorrect information being provided to decision makers higher up the corporate ladder.

One of the things I used to hear a lot that really made me cringe was when an analyst would say, "If I had been the hacker, I would have done this." I'm not entirely sure I see how that applies during an examination, other than to provide some possible avenues of investigation that can (and should be, possibly even before the statement is made) quickly be run down. More often than not, these statements develop into avenues of reason and pseudo-fact, and can lead the incident response completely off-track.

Don't get me wrong—during incident response or even forensic analysis, brainstorming can be good, and a valuable tool. Throwing out ideas to be discussed, run down, or refuted can be an excellent exercise. Probative questions like "what if …" and "why did you …" can lead to some pretty interesting findings. Where this goes wrong is when assumptions are made and used to move the examination forward, without those assumptions being verified, and facts are not used (rather than the assumptions) to fill in gaps in the analysis. This is something that we all have to be careful of, as it happens to all of us at one time or another; we'll make an assumption about how an artifact is created or modified without performing any research or verification, and our analysis will progress based on that assumption, however incorrectly. Unchecked, this can lead us down the road of incorrect findings and conclusions, or worse, lead us down a rabbit hole of confusion.

One way to avoid using assumptions to replace facts is to correlate multiple facts to support your findings. This concept is discussed in greater detail in Chapter 7, when we dig into the specifics of timeline creation and analysis; however, the basic idea is to look at your analysis and determine where it is based on a single arti-fact or finding, and then attempt to locate additional artifacts that support (or refute) your conclusions. An example of this might be an application file that you found on a system; you think that this application (remote-access program, etc.) may be critical to the incident, but you find that the file appears to have been created on the system several years prior to the actual incident; in fact, the creation date of the file appears to correspond with other files copied over from the installation media. So, with this finding, what do you do? Do you accept the creation date as legiti-mate and simply rule the application out from being associated with the incident? I would hope not; file system creation dates are trivial to modify. Or, do you attempt to determine whether the creation date was modified to disguise the file's presence on the system?

There are a number of artifacts that you could use to quickly validate the crea-tion date finding, such as additional attributes from the file's entry in the master file table (MFT, discussed in greater detail in Chapter 4). With respect to launch-ing the application, is there a Prefetch file, or any indication in the user's Registry hive that they launched the application? Are there any other artifacts that can be directly associated with the application having been executed? Some tools, such as the Cain & Abel password collection and cracking tool, produce a series of output files when run. These artifacts of execution may be used to better determine when a file or application had been added to a system; why would it have been added to the system in 2008 but not executed until 2011? How likely would that be? It would be far more likely that the application had been added to the system in relative close proximity to the first execution of the application, particularly during a compromise or breach.

The key concept to understand here is that filling in gaps in information with speculation can be very misleading, and ultimately detrimental to an organization attempting to respond to an incident. Whenever possible, seek out multiple support-ing artifacts, particularly if those artifacts are found in network or firewall logs, or on other systems not associated with the system being examined. Regardless of whether a cluster of artifacts are all found within or external to the system being examined, a knowledgeable analyst will be able to correlate them quickly and efficiently, as they understand not only the system being examined, but also their analysis goals.

Direct and Indirect Artifacts

Generally, there are two types of artifacts that you can expect to find when per-forming an examination: direct and indirect. Some analysts might not make a clear distinction between the two, but when I've been looking for something new or undefined (e.g., the request is to "find the malware" or "find the bad stuff"), it helps to look to where the indirect artifacts tend to collect to see if there are any indica-tions of anything new.

A *direct artifact* is something that is the direct result of an incident, such as a malware infection or an intrusion. These are usually things like files that are added or copied to a system, and any modifications made by the intrusion or compromise, such as Windows services or other Registry keys and values being created on the system. Other direct artifacts include files produced as a result of the infection or addition of malware, such as keystroke captures or the output of native commands (e.g., ipconfig, "net start," etc.).

When I was working data breach examinations, I ran across a set of malicious programs that constituted a "memory scraper"; that is, one program would collect the contents of virtual memory for any of eight specifically named processes, and then another would comb through the memory dump for track data (the stuff in that magnetic stripe on the back of your credit card). The program that looked for the track data was a Perl script that had been "compiled" with Perl2Exe (*http://www.indigostar.com/perl2exe.php*) so that the script could be run as a standalone executable, and not require that Perl be installed on the compromised system. Besides the program files themselves, the direct artifacts for this incident included the Windows service that was created when the files were installed (along with the associated Registry keys) and the files created every time the malware was run (i.e., the memory dump file, the archive of extracted track data, and the DLLs extracted from the "compiled" Perl script as a result of the use of Perl2Exe).

An *indirect artifact* is something that is the result of the ecosystem or environment in which the incident occurs, and is not a direct result of the incident. Sounds kind of fancy, I know, but the simple fact is that there's a lot that occurs on Windows systems when a program or a process is launched, regardless of whether it's for a legitimate application or for malware or malicious activity of some kind. Some of these things that go on, we never see—they just happen in the background. For example, if you use Microsoft's Process Monitor (the use of which will be demonstrated later in the book) and look at what Registry keys are accessed when any program is started, you'll begin to notice that there's one (the Image File Execution Options key) that is read whenever you launch a program. This is not something that the malware does, it's what the operating system does when a program is launched.

Other indirect artifacts include application prefetch files and entries in the "index.dat" file. Prefetch files are created by default on Windows XP, Vista, and 7 whenever an executable file is run on Windows. The prefetch file contains information about the files loaded by the executable, and is used to optimize execution of the program. Prefetch files are indirect artifacts because, while they are not the direct result of an incident, they may be created by applications executed during the course of an incident. "Index.dat" files are created by Windows applications (e.g., Internet Explorer) that use the WinInet application programming interface (API) for off-system communication. Entries in an "index.dat" file are not the direct result of an incident, but may be created by applications used in an incident that leverage the API (e.g., malware that uses the API to connect to an external site).

TIP

Internet History

"Index.dat" files are most often associated with a user's Internet history; when performing analysis on a system and attempting to discern what the user had been up to, an analyst will often look to the contents of the "index.dat" file, particularly if the user used the Internet Explorer web browser.

However, malware authors may make use of the same API to exfiltrate data from systems or allow their malware to communicate with a command and control (C2) server, and in doing so, will leave similar traces. What can be very telling about this kind of malicious use of the WinInet API is when the malware is running with system privileges, such as within a Windows service. In such instances, the LocalService or Default User (depending on the specific privileges employed by the malware) account will suddenly have indications of Internet activity populated in the "index.dat" file in that profile.

Another example of an indirect artifact is the entries for Windows services beneath the Enum\Root key in the Registry hive. This artifact is a result of the function of the operating system, and will be addressed in greater detail in Chapter 5.

WARNING

ZeroAccess

In November 2010, Giuseppe Bonfa wrote a series of articles (available at the InfoSecInstitute web site, found online at *http://resources.infosecinstitute.com/author/giuseppe/*) describing his findings in reverse engineering the ZeroAccess/Max++ crimeware rootkit. One of the things he found was that the rootkit was installed on a Windows system as a service, and when the service was started, it would delete not only its entry in the Services key, but also the relevant entries beneath the Enum\Root key. This is an indication of someone who is taking great pains to not only remain undetected on systems, but to also subvert deep forensic analysis of compromised systems.

Another way to look at this is that direct artifacts are those that only exist as a result of the incident occurring (e.g., SQL injection statements in web server logs, malicious executable files and log files being created on the compromised system, etc.), whereas indirect artifacts are those artifacts that would be generated—by design—as the result of any action (legitimate or malicious) occurring on the system. For example, with Windows services, administrators can install applications that create services (e.g., web server, antivirus applications, etc.) and the same artifacts would be generated if a malicious service were installed. Again, an indirect artifact is not a direct result of the incident or malicious action, but instead the result of the interaction within environment.

Remember that earlier we discussed the fact that different Windows versions employ different implementations of technologies such as Task Scheduler,

Windows Event Log, etc.? Well, this has an effect on the indirect artifacts that are available to an analyst. If the system you're examining doesn't have application prefetching enabled (either by default, or because it was purposely disabled), then you shouldn't expect to see any prefetch files. The same holds true for other technologies, as well, including but not limited to the Task Scheduler, System Restore Points, Volume Shadow Copies, etc. The artifacts that you can expect to find can be dependent not just on how the system is configured, but which Windows version you're analyzing.

So by now you're probably wondering why I've presented all of this. Well, the point is that there are a lot of ways to compromise, do mischief, and remain persistent on a system. That is to say, there is not a simple, short list of artifacts to look for when examining a system or an image, and as such, we often have to look for indirect artifacts as indicators of the incident. Because often we don't really know what we're looking for, identifying indirect artifacts of the incident may lead us back to the direct artifacts. When performing your analysis, pursue and stay open to the indirect artifacts, as they will often provide clear indicators to the direct artifacts that we would not otherwise have observed or found.

NOTE

Absence of an Artifact

All this discussion of direct and indirect artifacts, as well as using multiple artifacts to support your findings, should lead you to one inevitable conclusion; that is, *the absence of an artifact where you would expect to find one is in itself an artifact*.

Wait ... what? What does this mean? Let's say that you're paranoid because you think someone's been going through your home while you're gone, and before leaving for work in the morning, you place a small piece of scotch tape over the door jamb. You then leave through the garage. Later that day, you return home and find what you think may be indicators that someone's been in your house, and you assume that they only way they could get in was through the front door. However, there are no fingerprints on the exterior doorknob, there are no indications that the door was forced open, and the piece of tape you left is still intact. Are there other artifacts that would indicate that someone came in through the front door? Or is the real issue that the absence of these specific artifacts instead indicates that access was *not* achieved through the front door?

Okay, so how does this apply to digital forensic analysis? Quite a lot, actually. The absence of artifacts demonstrating, for example, a user logging in and using the web browser on the system may indicate that the user never performed these actions, or that specific steps were taken to hide or destroy these artifacts. Either way, there will likely be other artifacts that indicate either of these (or other) scenarios.

Let's say that you're attempting to determine whether a user logged into a system from the console or via Terminal Services. One of the first artifacts you might look for is a record of the login in the Event Logs. If you don't find such a record, is it because auditing of logins wasn't enabled? Had the Event Logs been cleared? We sometimes don't think about these things, but many times when we don't find an artifact or series of artifacts that we would expect to find, this can tell us as much as (or more than) if we had found those artifacts.

Least Frequency of Occurrence

Back in the early days of the Internet, and even as late as the turn of the century, malware could and did run rampant across the Internet. One of the side effects of worm infections was that when a worm got into an infrastructure, it would often spread like wild fire, infecting and reinfecting systems over and over again. System A would become infected and then infect systems B, C, and D, which would then each infect the other systems over and over again, ad infinitum, ad nauseum. The result was that in fairly short order, systems would become so massively infected that they'd cease to function altogether, as the repeated infections consumed all available resources on the system. This was bad for the victim, and for the most part, bad for the attacker, because if the infected systems were offline or simply couldn't be accessed, what good were they to anyone? To address this issue and allow access to infected systems, malware authors began adding a throttling mechanism to their programs so that once systems were infected, they wouldn't be reinfected. Some created and checked for the existence of specific files, some used specific Registry keys or values, but the most prevalent method appears to have been to create a unique mutual exclusion in memory.

The end result of this, from a responder/analyst perspective, was that a malware infection became the least frequent activity to occur on a system. As malware authors and intruders began taking specific steps to ensure that their actions became less noticeable and "flew beneath the radar," these actions became more difficult to detect, as the infections did *not* result in massive amounts of file activity or memory consumption. Pete Silberman, an analyst with the consulting firm Mandiant, was the first in our community that I heard use the expression "least frequency of occurrence" to describe this phenomenon.

The same often applies to intrusions. With the exception of turning a compromised server into a "warez server" (essentially a repository of pirated movies, etc.), most intruders appear to take very conscious and specific steps to remain undetected, and avoid drawing attention to their activities by loading massive numbers of files on to the victim system, running a large number of programs, etc. Why copy an archive of tools and utilities over to a compromised system when the system itself has plenty of native tools that can be readily used for the same purpose?

One of the things I see quite often is analysts who create timelines (timeline creation and analysis will be discussed in Chapter 7) of activity on systems, and then attempt to locate indicators of malicious activity by looking for spikes in that activity. What most analysts don't seem to understand is that Windows systems are inherently "noisy" when it comes to activity on the system, particularly file system activity. During normal day-to-day operations, most users read and compose email, surf the Web, maybe create reports and spreadsheets; however, a great deal of activity occurs automatically, under the hood. Consider Windows XP systems as an example; by default, a System Restore Point is created every 24 hours. This all occurs with no other interaction from the user beyond simply turning the system on. This also means that now and again, some System Restore Points are deleted. In addition, by default, a limited defragmentation process is run on the system every three days.

We also need to keep in mind that in many instances, Windows Updates are set to run automatically, and many applications (e.g., Adobe Reader, Apple QuickTime and iTunes, Java, etc.) have their own update processes that run in the background. In short, just turning a Windows system on and walking away from it can lead to a great deal of activity over time, even with no user interaction with the system at all. So is it then any wonder that a malicious email attachment that is opened by the user, which then downloads malware that provides an attacker with remote access to the system, is, in the grand scheme of things, often the least frequent activity on a system?

Documentation

In short, documentation is the bread and butter of what we do. There, I said it. And I said it knowing full well that technically oriented people (nerds) hate, more than anything else, to document anything.

But without documentation, where are we? If we didn't document our analysis goals, how do we make sure that we remain on track throughout our analysis, and actually achieve those goals? If we don't document our analysis, our reports would be nothing more than simply a 3×5 index card with a couple of handwritten findings (which may not answer the customer's questions, because we didn't document our goals). In short, if you didn't document it, it didn't happen.

Documentation needs to be a core, central aspect of everything we do. From the point where an incident is detected, we need to begin documentation (we'll touch on this more in Chapter 2). Most organizations have some sort of regulatory body that they need to report to particularly during or following an incident, and without clear, concise documentation along the way, responders go off-track, systems get missed, and leaders and managers make bad decisions, all of which can lead to fines and a significant detrimental impact on the organization's brand name.

From the perspective of a consultant, documentation needs to start the instant that a customer contacts you. Most consulting firms have a list of questions (a "triage worksheet," if you will) that they use as a sort of script or guideline when talking to customers, and completing this worksheet serves as the initial documentation. Contracts are then written based on information collected during the initial call, and responders begin collecting and documenting information as soon as they arrive onsite (often before). Consider an incident requiring that data and images be collected from a large number of systems within a data center, or in multiple locations. If you aren't documenting your activities, how likely do you think it would be that you either miss some systems or collect data from the same system twice or more?

Finally, without documentation, how do we learn and grow as analysts or as a community? Throughout our analysis, we may find something that we hadn't seen before, or we may have a question about the function of a specific tool or application. If we don't maintain documentation, we miss significant opportunities to improve our own processes, as well as to provide other analysts with the benefit of our experiences. Say you're on a team with 10 other analysts, and after 8 hours of analysis, you find something that neither you nor any of the other analysts had seen before. Assuming all things (and analysts) being equal, if you don't document and share what you found (and how you found it), this is now going to cost your organization 80 hours for everyone to have that same experience and level of knowledge. However, if you were to document and share it with the other analysts during, say, a "brown bag" or catered working lunch, you've now reduced that time to less than an hour. Documenting and sharing our findings in this way allows us to learn from the past and for a group of analysts to quickly expand their knowledge and capabilities.

Maintaining documentation is relatively straightforward and simple. While there are applications available that were specifically designed for maintaining analyst case notes (e.g., Forensic CaseNotes, *http://www.qccis.com/forensic-tools*), I've found that the simplest way to maintain case notes and analysis documentation is to start by opening MS Word. Word allows the analyst to create tables, outlines, and modify formatting so that notes are easier to read and understand, and also allows the analyst to insert pictures and diagrams that vastly improve the documentation. Many analysts (and their customers) have access to MS Word through their employer, and free and open-source office suites such as OpenOffice (*http://www*
.openoffice.org/) can be used to read and edit Word documents. If you're looking for a word processing application with a wide range of capabilities and portability, MS Word or Writer from OpenOffice are options to consider.

Convergence

Convergence refers to the fact that what we do in what appears to be vastly different aspects of our profession—the actual *work* we do—really isn't all that different. Here's what I mean. In June 2010, I attended the Open Source Conference that Brian Carrier (the author of *File System Forensic Analysis* and the TSK tools, although I'm sure he's famous for other things, as well) put on. While there, I was speaking to a member of law enforcement and he told me, "We do child pornography and fraud cases; you do intrusion investigations and malware cases." When I heard this, my response was that people like me—that is, consultants—dealt with problems, and that the folks who called us for assistance had intrusion and malware problems. Hey, I thought that was a pretty witty and well-considered response. However, the more I thought about it, the more I discovered how off-base the original statement (that as a consultant, I dealt with "problems") really may have been.

Okay, you're probably thinking, "Wait … what?" After all, what the law enforcement officer (LEO) said was pretty much on target with respect to his particular case load, right? Well, what happens during a case involving illicit images? After verifying that there were, in fact, the federally mandated number of contraband images and/or movies on the hard drive, the next thing that the LEOs can expect to hear is, "It wasn't me, it was a virus." That's right, the "Trojan Defense," used in 2003 when then-19-year-old Aaron Caffrey was accused of hacking into computer systems and claimed that a Trojan had been installed on his system, allowing someone else to perform the acts of which he was accused (he was acquitted). At that point, LEOs must then examine the acquired image and determine if there was some form of malware installed on the system, and if so, was it capable of the actions that the defense claims. Well, doesn't the case then become a malware examination?

Or, if the claim is made that some unauthorized person gained access to the system and placed the contraband files on the system, doesn't the case then become an intrusion investigation? And wouldn't both also hold true for fraud cases, if those same claims were made?

We're at a point where there really isn't as much of a divergence between what various investigators do on a daily basis as some would like us to think. Yes, some analysts operate in vastly different environments, and with different requirements. But at the end of the day, we're using a lot of the same tools and processes, and ultimately looking for some of the same artifacts, to answer a lot of the same questions. Rather than divergence, what we do has reached a point of convergence, and as such, analysts from one aspect of our community (such as law enforcement, or the military or government) would likely benefit greatly from engaging with and sharing information with another aspect of the community (such as those in the private sector). And the reverse would be equally true, as well.

No, I'm not talking about sharing case information, or details of investigations. What I am referring to is this: Many analysts who are consultants in the private sector receive cases where the goal is to locate malware that *may be* on a system. As such, those analysts tend to develop detailed step-by-step processes and procedures for performing malware detection (see Chapter 6 for a more detailed discussion of this topic), but these processes and procedures have to be automated to some degree. In addition, the work these analysts do is often based on a contract with a set number of hours. As such, analysts who haven't encountered such examinations before, or don't encounter them often, would likely benefit from engaging with and learning from the private sector analysts.

This is just one example of how the digital forensic community can take advantage of this convergence phenomenon and grow as a community, rather than requiring all analysts to learn all of the same lessons.

Virtualization

Virtualization can have a significant impact on an investigation in a number of ways. If someone were to run a virtual system on their physical system, there's the issue during an examination of where the artifacts would be located. For example, several versions of Windows 7 (Professional, Ultimate, and Enterprise) allow users to download, install, and run Virtual PC (Microsoft's virtualization platform for PCs) and a Windows XP virtual machine (referred to as XPMode). The purpose of this is to allow users to continue to run applications that ran perfectly well on Windows XP but are not supported by Windows 7. However, it's relatively easy for the user to access and run applications from within the virtual machine, such that the artifacts of that activity would not appear within the confines (i.e., files, Registry, etc.) of the host system. With the Virtual PC application installed, users can also run other virtual machines, as well. Analysts who are not familiar with virtualization and what to look for can be left looking for artifacts that they may never find, unless they were to discover and access the actual virtual machine.

While an associate professor at the University of Advancing Technology (UAT), Diane Barrett gave a presentation titled "Virtual Traces." This presentation was the latest in which she addressed the use of virtualization on desktop systems, and described artifacts left on a Windows system following the use of MojoPac (*http:// www.mojopac.com/*) and MokaFive (*http://www.mokafive.com/*), both of which are personal, portable environments that can allow users to take their favorite desktop applications, utilities, and even games with them wherever they go, and run them from any Windows system. Diane also mentioned the MetroPipe Portable Virtual Privacy Machine virtual environment, which is based on Damn Small Linux and purports to allow users to maintain their privacy while Web surfing. These virtual systems, as well as innumerable others that are available, can be run on a live system and leave minimal traces of having been used. Someone can walk up to a computer system, plug in an iPod or thumb drive, run their virtual system, perform any number of activities (legal or otherwise), then disconnect the device and walk away. While there may be indications that the virtual environment was run on the host system, indicators of the malicious activity itself may remain embedded in the virtual machine that the user took with them.

Now, consider *cloud computing*. This term, much-touted in the media, includes such offerings as infrastructure-as-a-service (IaaS), platform-as-a-service (PaaS), and software-as-a-service (SaaS), and aside from these terms it also poses significant challenges to incident responders and forensic analysts. After all, how does one respond to an incident where the system of interest existed at one point, but was deleted and the sectors it consumed were overwritten? In a cloud environment, which is based on virtualization, how does a responder determine where those sectors are? Even if the responder is able to determine where the CPU and memory resources were "located," how does she address the issue of storage, when that storage can be in or spread across systems in another country?

TIP

It's About Implementation

The question of how responders and law enforcement address cloud environments is a valid one, for the reasons discussed in this chapter. The simple fact is that it comes down to implementation; how is the infrastructure designed, architected, and implemented? If you're considering moving into a "cloud" environment, and have to meet legal or regulatory requirements, be sure to get detailed information about the environment and implementation. Further, if you're promised some security measures, or need them to meet compliance, be sure that they're included in your contract.

However, virtualization can be very helpful to an analyst, as well. For example, virtual systems can be used for application and malware testing. As we will see later in the book, virtualization can not only assist the analyst "seeing what the user saw" by allowing them to boot the acquired image as if it were a live system, but also assist the analyst in accessing some data sources to which they might not otherwise have access. For example, being able to boot the system would give the analyst access not only to physical memory from the system, but also the ability to interact with the system just as the user did.

SETTING UP AN ANALYSIS SYSTEM

Another topic that we need to discuss before completing this chapter and moving into the rest of this book is more operational and less conceptual in nature; that is, setting up a system from which you can perform your analysis. I've used desktops, workhorse laptops, and at one point (while I was a member of the ISS Emergency Response Services, or ERS team), I even used a Mac OS X server system with Mac OS X and Windows XP installed via BootCamp. From my perspective and experience, the best way to develop skills in analyzing Windows systems is to use those systems, which is why I tend to opt for Windows as an analysis platform (I also use Windows as my work/admin platform, as well). This is not to say that you couldn't build a complete analysis platform using Linux; Rob Lee has done a great job putting together such a system in the SANS Investigative Forensic Toolkit (SIFT) version 2.0 virtual machine (VM), which is Linux-based and includes a number of very useful tools. However, my personal experience has shown me that to *really* analyze a Windows XP system (and the same thing applies to Windows 7) is to use that platform on a daily basis. As such, my recommendation for an analysis system would be something capable of running the 64-bit version of Windows 7, preferably the Ultimate or Professional editions.

NOTE

SIFT

I have used the SANS SIFT v2.0 Workstation virtual machine, as it can be very useful. In attempting to develop a solution to something of a unique issue, I downloaded (via the SANS Portal) and set up the SIFT VM, and then before starting it up, I added the .vmdk virtual disk file from a Windows XP VM that I already had available. I did this through VMWare Workstation, so I added the VM as an independent, nonpersistent disk. When I booted the SIFT VM, I could "see" the Windows XP VM (via *fdisk*), and could not only mount the device read-only, but (with a little help from Rob Lee himself) also use the TSK tool *icat* to get a copy of the MFT from the device. This can be a very useful approach to data collection and analysis.

As far as a hardware platform goes, I have found great success using Dell Latitude laptops; they're on the beefier end of the spectrum, but still portable enough to carry around if you need to do so. If you're going to be primarily stationary in a lab, then getting a powerful desktop system would be the way to go, if you can afford it. In the end, it comes down to what you prefer and what you can afford. If you don't get a beefy system with a powerful processor (or four) and good amount of RAM, then things will just take a bit longer.

What about the operating system for our analysis platform? Well, I've spent a number of years working with Windows XP and I'm very comfortable with it, having become familiar with some of its nuances; however, over time, I've found that using Windows 7 provides me with a great deal more functionality, particularly when it comes to Volume Shadow Copies and Windows Event Logs (we'll be discussing both of these in greater detail later in the book), which are available on Vista, Windows 2008, and Windows 7. As we'll see later in the book, having access to the necessary OS APIs can be extremely beneficial when you're trying to access data and conduct analysis. Using a 64-bit version of Windows 7 also ensures that I have the necessary capability to address analyzing both 32- and 64-bit editions of Windows (although that shouldn't be an issue when simply accessing specific files).

Now we're up to the point where we can discuss the software we'll be using. First, I want to make one thing clear: I'm not biased against commercial forensic analysis applications. Heck, I've even used some of them. I've used AccessData's FTK as well as Guidance Software's EnCase product, to include various versions of both. I like to use ProDiscover from Technology Pathways, in part because the built-in ProScript scripting language is based on Perl, and due in no small part to the fact that Christopher Brown has been kind enough to provide me with a license since version 3.0. However, I don't use many of the commercial tools on a regular basis simply because I don't need to—most of the things I do during analysis I cannot easily do, or do at all, using commercial forensic analysis applications. This is not to say that commercial forensic analysis applications do not have their place, as they do. In fact, they can be extremely useful. For example, I've used ProDiscover for running keyword searches (for files by name, or file contents) against images, after extracting timeline data so that I can conduct analysis while the search progresses.

However, like any tool, a commercial forensic analysis application is only as strong or as valuable as the analyst who is using it, and what I tend to do as a major aspect of my analysis is produce a timeline of system activity (which is discussed in detail in Chapter 7) from a variety of data sources from the system, and the commercial tools do not include the inherent capability for creating a timeline of system activity from these data sources. Very often I will conduct a complete and thorough analysis using nothing more than open-source and freely available tools, and a file viewer. Remember, analysis isn't about the tools you use; it's about the goals and your process.

> **TIP**
>
> Open-Source Tools
>
> Cory Altheide (of Google) and I coauthored *Digital Forensics with Open Source Tools*, which was published by Syngress Publishing, Inc., in April 2011. The book focuses primarily on open-source tools used for forensic analysis of Linux, Mac OS X, and Windows platforms. In addition, the book provides several scenarios describing how the tools are used, and also presents and discusses some free, albeit not open-source, tools. In previous editions of this book, I also spend a great deal of time discussing a number of open-source and freely available tools.

So what tools should you use? Well, it all depends on what to do. One of the first tools I start off with is 7Zip (*http://www.7-zip.org*), a freely available archive utility that recognizes and unpacks files compressed via a number of compression algorithms (including gzip and tar). Next, I often look to the programming languages Perl and Python that are the foundation for many open-source tools (including my own RegRipper). Distributions for both are freely available from ActiveState (*http://www.activestate.com*). From there, you want to make sure that you have hex and text editors available for viewing file contents, as well as programming, if necessary. There are a number of freely available editors that you can find via searches on the Internet, and the ones you choose will likely primarily depend on personal preference. For example, UltraEdit (not free, but available from *http://www.ultraedit.com*) is usually my script editor and file viewer of choice; however, the Crimson Editor (*http://www.crimsoneditor.com/*) also appears to be a good choice for creating and editing Perl scripts, while the HxD hex editor (*http://mh-nexus.de/en/hxd/*) makes a suitable hex viewer.

AccessData provides FTK Imager as a freely available download, and not long ago released version 3.0 of the tool, which not only allows you to acquire images, but also mount acquired images on your system as read-only volumes. As we'll discuss later in the book, this capability can greatly extend the range of your analysis. Loading an acquired image into FTK Imager allows you to quickly verify the integrity of the file system, view and extract files, extract a volume or partition, or even convert an image from either expert witness (EWF, also known as EnCases E0x format) or VMWare virtual disk (.vmdk) format to a raw, dd image.

Version 7.0 of ProDiscover Basic Edition (BE) is freely available from Technology Pathways (*http://www.techpathways.com/DesktopDefault.aspx?tabindex=7&tabid=14*) and provides basic functionality for populating the Registry, Event Log, and Internet History Viewers, as well as conducting searches across the image. In addition, you can also extract files from the image, view the formatted contents of Recycle Bin Info2 or $I files, and view a directory via the Gallery View. This is a considerable amount of functionality available in a free tool.

Other tools you may want to install at this point include the version of "strings .exe" available from the Microsoft/SysInternals site, as well as BinText (a GUI version of a "strings" tool) available from the McAfee/Foundstone site (found online at *http://www.mcafee.com/us/downloads/free-tools/bintext.aspx*). Both of these tools can be used to list strings found in files, including both "regular" files and files that consist of unstructured data, such as a pagefile. This functionality can also be used as the basis for greater investigative capabilities.

Most of the tools and programs mentioned to this point provide basic functionality to an analyst, and will allow you to get started conducting analysis quickly and easily. This list should not be considered all-inclusive; throughout this book, I will be addressing and demonstrating the use of a number of other tools, so I won't present them all here.

SUMMARY

Throughout this chapter, I've attempted to lay the foundation for your analysis by presenting some core analysis concepts, as well as provide some initial, first-step tools that can be installed on an analysis system. Both of these will provide the foundation for the rest of the book; we will not only be building on the analysis concepts throughout the following chapters, but we will also be discussing and demonstrating a number of additional tools that will assist us in our analysis.

Immediate Response

INFORMATION IN THIS CHAPTER

- Being Prepared to Respond
- Data Collection

INTRODUCTION

Much of what we read regarding incident response is that computer security incidents are a fact of life when we employ IT resources. It's long been said that it's not a matter of *if* your organization will experience a computer security incident, but *when* that incident will occur. If the media has made anything clear at all during the first half of 2011, it's that no organization is immune to computer security incidents, whether that's a web page defaced, sensitive corporate emails exposed, or sensitive financial data compromised.

Most books on incident response discuss and demonstrate a variety of tools and techniques that are helpful (or even critical) in preparing for and responding to an incident, so these procedures should be both common knowledge and common practice. In reality, this is often not the case. When an incident does occur, responders—whether internal IT, incident response staff, or third-party consultants—only have access to the data that are actually available. If a company has not prepared appropriately, they may not have access to critical data, may not know where sensitive information is stored, and may not know how to collect key time-sensitive data following the detection of an incident. This is true when internal staff is responsible for incident response, but is even more critical in cases where a company hires a third-party consulting firm to provide incident response services.

In such cases it can often take several days for the contracting process to run its course and for the responding consultants to actually get on a plane and travel to the customer's site. Once they arrive, they usually have to go about determining the layout of the infrastructure they're responding to, the nature of the incident, etc. Now, all of this occurs while the upper-level management of the organization is anxiously awaiting answers.

Given all of this, it behooves an organization to prepare for an incident and to be prepared to perform some modicum of response when those inevitable incidents are identified. In this chapter, we will discuss how organizations can better prepare themselves to respond to incidents, from the perspective of a consultant who has responded to incidents. The purpose of this is to ensure that response personnel—whether internal staff or third-party responders—have data that allow them to resolve the incident in a satisfactory manner. This chapter will not address overall infrastructure design, development of a complete computer security incident response plan (CSIRP), or "best practices" for network and system configuration, as all of these can require considerable thought, effort, and resources to implement in any environment; any book that tries to address all possible factors and configurations will not succeed. Rather, we will discuss some of the things that are easy for the local staff to do that will have a considerable impact on improving incident response and resolution.

BEING PREPARED TO RESPOND

As an incident responder, the vast majority of incidents I have seen have progressed in pretty much the same manner; our team would get a call from an organization that had been notified by an outside third party that an incident had occurred within their infrastructure, and during the initial call, we would ask the point of contact (PoC) a series of questions to determine the nature of the incident as best we could. Many times, those questions were met with the telephonic equivalent of blank stares, and in the extreme cases, due to the nature of the incident, with frantic requests to "Just get someone here as fast as you can!" We would send responders onsite, based on what we knew about the incident, and by the time the responders made it onsite, little if anything had been done to prepare for their arrival.

After introductions, the questions that had been originally asked on the telephone were asked again, and we (i.e., the responders … most often, just one person) had to work with local IT staff to develop an understanding of the network infrastructure and traffic flows, as well as the nature of the incident itself. Many times, much of the information (e.g., network maps, etc.) wasn't available, or the people who knew the answers to the questions weren't available, and considerable time could be spent trying to simply develop a clear and accurate picture of what had been reported or identified, and what had happened. This was never a quick process, and sometimes we would simply have to start arbitrarily collecting and analyzing data. This also takes time and in some cases would prove to be fruitless in the long run, as the systems from which the data were collected were later found to not have been involved in the incident.

While the scenario I've described involved the use of outside consulting help, the situation is not all that different from what might occur with internal responders whenever an organization is not prepared to respond. Sounds pretty bad, doesn't it? So you're probably wondering, what's my point? Well, my point is that the clock doesn't start ticking once an organization becomes aware of an incident; in fact, it's already been ticking by that point, we just don't know for how long, as the incident may have occurred well before it was identified or reported. And when it comes to incident response and digital forensic analysis, a great deal of what can (or can't) be determined about the incident is predicated on time; that is, how much time has passed between when the incident occurred and when pertinent data are collected and analyzed.

Several years ago at a SANS Forensic Summit, Aaron Walters (the creator of the Volatility Framework and a vice president at Terremark WorldWide, Inc.) used the term *temporal proximity* to describe the gap between the incident and response, and really brought to light just how critical time is with respect to incident response. Why is time so important? Consider what occurs on a live Windows system, even when it sits idle; there's actually quite a lot that goes on "under the hood" that most of us never see. Processes complete, and the space (bytes) used by those processes in memory is freed for use by other processes. Deleted files are overwritten by "natural" or "organic" processes that are simply part of the operating system (e.g., the creation and deletion of System Restore Points on Windows XP and Volume Shadow Copies on Vista and Windows 7, etc.). On Windows XP systems, a System Restore Point is created by default every 24 hours, and often one may be deleted, as well. In addition, every three days a limited defragmentation of selected files on the hard drive occurs. On Windows 7 systems, not only are Volume Shadow Copies (VSCs) created and deleted, but every 10 days a backup is made of the main Registry hives.

Windows systems are typically configured to automatically download and install updates; many common desktop applications now provide the same functionality. In short, whether you see it or not, a *lot* of activity occurs on Windows systems even when a user isn't interacting with it. As such, as time passes, information that would give clear indications as to the extent of what occurred begins to fade and be obscured, and is finally simply no longer available. Given this, it is absolutely critical that those most capable of performing immediate incident response actually do so. As it can be some time before the scope of the incident and the need for assistance is really realized, it is critical that the local IT staff be able to react immediately to collect and preserve data.

Questions

When an incident is detected, everyone has questions. Upper-level management most often wants to know how the intruder or malware got into the network, what data were taken, where they went, and the risk to which the organization may be exposed.

The nature of the compromised data—and any legal, regulatory, or reporting requirements associated with them—is often of great concern to legal counsel and compliance staff, as well. It is critical for incident response staff to understand the types of questions that will be asked by key stakeholders in the company, so that the data collection and analysis process can answer those questions, especially when failure to do so may result in significant legal or financial penalties for the organization.

NOTE

Compliance

Regulatory bodies have had a significant impact on incident response over the last five or so years. When my team was conducting payment card industry (PCI) breach investigations, one of the items added to the report was a "dashboard" that gave oversight staff a quick, at-a-glance view of the breach. One of the items in that dashboard was the "window of compromise," or an indication of the time between when the incident actually originated and when the breach was "closed." This was a very critical component of the investigations, as many organizations were able to quantify system uptime not in terms of days or weeks, but in transactions per minute or per hour. Being able to accurately determine when the systems had actually been compromised and when PCI data could have been exposed had significant impact on the number of possibly compromised transactions (as well as notification and any regulatory repercussions), and as time went by, the likelihood of being able to accurately provide this information decreased.

If an outside consulting firm is called to provide emergency incident response, they will also have a number of questions, and how fast they respond and who they send will be predicated on the responses to those questions. These questions are often technical, or the answers that are being looked for are more technical than the point of contact is prepared to provide. Examples of these questions can include such things as how many systems and locations are impacted, what operating systems (e.g., Windows, Linux, AS/400, etc.) and applications are involved, etc. As such, an organization can greatly facilitate both the response time and efficiency by having detailed information about the incident (or the personnel most able to provide that information) available for those preliminary discussions.

TIP

Triage Questions

Wherever I've been an incident responder, I've most often been a consultant. As such, the teams I worked with developed a triage worksheet or questionnaire, which was a list of questions we had written down and documented for each analyst to use for initial contact with a potential client. As calls could come in at any time and any analyst could take the call, I kept a copy of the worksheet (an MS Word document) on my desktop, and had several hard copies printed out and next to my phone for immediate access. The questions were the top dozen or so that we asked for *every* engagement: what is the nature of the incident, when was the incident identified, what systems were involved (and what are their current states), what operating systems were involved, how many locations were involved, had law enforcement been contacted, etc.

Most often, depending on the responses to the questions, combined with our own experiences (every analyst knew that they were to complete the questionnaire as if they would be responding to the incident), we would ask further probing questions. However, the idea of having the questionnaire was to make that initial information collection as efficient as possible, and to give our staff as complete a view of the incident as possible to determine who was to respond, how many analysts and what skill sets would be needed, how long the analysts would be required, etc.

Third-party consulting firms are often contacted to perform emergency incident response for a variety of reasons. Perhaps the biggest reason is that while the internal IT staff is technically skilled, they do not possess the investigative experience and expertise. While they may be able to troubleshoot an MS Exchange server issue or set up an Active Directory, they aren't often called upon to dump physical memory from a live Windows system and determine if there is any malware on the system. Another reason is that any investigation performed by the local IT staff may be viewed as being skewed in favor of the company, in a sort of "fox guarding the hen house" manner. It is important to keep in mind that when a third-party consulting firm is called, they will ask you a number of questions, usually based on their experience responding to a wide range of incidents (e.g., malware, intrusions, data breaches, etc.) in a wide range of environments. And these will often be questions the local IT staff hadn't thought of, let alone experienced before, as they come from an entirely different perspective.

For example, the IT manager may "know" that a system (or systems) is infected with malware or has been compromised by a remote intruder, but the consultant on the other end of the phone is likely going to ask questions to better understand how the IT manager determined her finding. The best thing to do is to ensure that those employees who have the necessary information to accurately respond to these questions are available, and to respond without making assumptions regarding where you think the questions may be leading. If the organization was notified of the incident by an external entity, it is best to have the employee who took the call, as well as any other staff who may have engaged with the caller (e.g., legal counsel, etc.), available to answer questions. For more technical questions regarding the affected systems and the network infrastructure, having the appropriate employees available to respond to questions can be very valuable.

The consulting firm will use your responses to scope the incident. They will also use the responses to determine which skill sets are necessary to respond to the incident, which consultant to send, and how many consultants they will need to send to resolve the incident in a timely manner. If accurate information is not available, too many responders may be sent, incurring additional cost for travel and lodging upfront, or too few responders may be sent, which would incur not only additional costs (e.g., for travel, lodging, labor, etc. for additional responders to be sent on-site) but would also lead to delays in the overall response.

The Importance of Preparation

Did you see the first *Mission: Impossible* movie? After Ethan's (Tom Cruise's character) team is decimated, he makes his way back to a safe house. As he approaches the top of the stairs in the hotel, he takes off his jacket, takes the light bulb out of the fixture in the hallway, crushes the bulb in his jacket, and spreads the shards in the now-darkened hallway as he backs toward the door, covering the only means of approach to his room. Does what he did make sense? He knew that he couldn't prevent someone from approaching his location, but he also knew that he could set up some sort of measures to detect when someone was approaching, because as they entered the darkened hallway, they wouldn't see the glass shards on the floor, and they'd make a very distinctive noise when they stepped on them, alerting him to their presence. And that's exactly what happened shortly thereafter in the movie.

Let's take a look at some examples of how being prepared can affect the outcome of an incident. In my experience as an emergency incident responder, the way the process works has usually been that someone becomes aware of an incident, perhaps does some checking of the information they receive, and then calls a company that provides emergency computer security incident response services for assistance. Many times, they feel that the information they've received could be very credible, and (rightly so) they want someone onsite to assist as soon as possible. From that point, depending on the relationship with the consulting company, it can be anywhere from 6 to 72 hours (or more) before someone arrives onsite.

For example, I've worked with customers in California (I'm based on the east coast) and told them, if you call me at 3 pm Pacific Standard Time, that's 6 pm Eastern Standard Time … the earliest flight out is 6 am the next day, and it's a 6-hour flight. At that point, I wouldn't be on the ground at the remote airport until 18 hours after you called, assuming that there were no issues with contracting. Once I arrive at the airport, I have to collect up my "go kit" (Pelican case full of gear weighing 65 pounds or more), get to the rental car agency, and drive to your location. Once I arrive, we have to get together and try to determine the scope of the incident, hoping that you have the appropriate staff available to address the questions I will have. I have responded to assist organizations that used part-time system administration staff, and the next scheduled visit from the system administrator was two days after I arrived onsite. As you can see, even under ideal conditions, it can be 24 hours or more before any actual incident response activities begin.

Now, most times when I would arrive onsite, considerable work would need to be done to determine the nature and range of the incident and figure out which systems were affected, or "in scope." (Note that this is an essential step, whether performed by outside consultants or your own internal staff.) When the incident involved the potential exposure of "sensitive data" (regardless of the definition you choose), there may have been a strong indication that someone had accessed the infrastructure and gained access to some sensitive data; what this means is that someone with no prior knowledge of the network infrastructure may have accessed it remotely and found these sensitive data (e.g., database or files containing credit card data or transaction information, personally identifiable information, medical records, etc.). As such, when trying to scope the incident, one of the first things I (and most responders) ask is, where does the data in question reside? Very often, this is not known, or not completely understood.

As a result, considerable time can be spent trying to determine the answers to the questions responders ask prior to as well as once they arrive onsite. It is important that these questions be answered accurately and in a timely manner, as responders usually arrive onsite after a contract is signed, and that contract often includes an hourly rate for that responder, or responders. The sooner incident response activities can commence, with accurate information, the less expensive those incident response activities are going to be in the long run. Where internal staff is performing response, these time delays may not translate (directly) into dollars spent on outside help; but any delay will still postpone the identification and collection of relevant data, perhaps to the point where the data are degraded or lost completely.

This is not to say that all organizations I've responded to are not prepared for a computer security incident, at least to some extent. During one particular engagement, I arrived onsite to find that rather than having an active malware infection, the IT staff had already responded to and removed the malware, and the IT manager was interested in having me validate their process. In fact (and I was very impressed by this), the staff not only had a documented malware response process, but they also had a checklist (with checkboxes and everything) for that process, and I was handed a copy of the completed checklist for the incident. Apparently, once the first malware infections were found on several desktops within their infrastructure, the IT staff mobilized and checked other systems, found several infected systems in various departments (e.g., finance, billing, HR, etc.), and removed those infections from the systems. Unfortunately, there were no samples of the malware left to be analyzed, and all we had left was the completed checklist, which included a name used by an antivirus (AV) vendor to identify the malware.

Now, something else that I did find out about this incident was that during a staff meeting following the response to the incident, the IT manager had announced proudly that his team had reacted swiftly and decisively to remove this threat to the infrastructure … at which point, corporate counsel began asking some tough questions. It seems that several of the systems were in departments where very sensitive information was stored and processed; for instance, the billing department handled bank routing information, and the HR and payroll departments handled a great deal of sensitive personal information about the company employees. As such, an infection of malware that was capable of either stealing this information or providing an attacker with access to that information posed significant risk to the organization with respect to various regulatory bodies. In addition, there were legislative compliance issues that needed to be addressed.

It seems that the IT department had put a great deal of effort into developing their malware response process, but had done so in isolation from other critical players within the organization. As such, there was a chance that the organization may have been exposed to even more risk, as many regulatory and legislative compliance policies state that if you can't identify exactly which records (e.g., personally identifiable information, payment card industry information, etc.) were accessed, you must notify that regulatory body that *all* of the records could have been exposed. As the malware had simply been eradicated and no investigation of any kind had been conducted (root cause or otherwise), there was no information available regarding what data could have been accessed, let alone what (if any) data were actually accessed or exfiltrated from the infrastructure.

Now and again, I have had the opportunity to work with an organization that has taken great pains and put a lot of effort toward being prepared for those inevitable incidents to occur. I had another response engagement where as soon as I had arrived onsite and completed my in-brief, I was ushered to a room (yes, they provided me with a place to work without my having to ask!) where there were a dozen drives stacked up on a desk, along with a thumb drive and manila folder. It turns out that while the IT director was calling my team for assistance, his staff was already responding to the incident. They had collected and reviewed network logs and identified 12 affected systems, and replaced the drives in those systems—I was looking at the original drives sitting on the desk. The thumb drive contained the network logs, and the folder contained a printout of the network map (there was a soft copy on the thumb drive). With all of this, I began imaging the provided hard drives and reviewing the logs.

The incident that they'd experienced involved someone gaining unauthorized access to their infrastructure via Microsoft's Remote Desktop Protocol (RDP). They allowed employees to work from remote locations, requiring them to access the infrastructure via a virtual private network (VPN) and then connect to specific systems on the internal infrastructure via RDP. As such, they had VPN and domain authentication logs, as well as logs that clearly demonstrated the account used by the intruder. They had used these logs to identify the 12 systems that the intruder had connected to via the VPN, which corresponded to the 12 hard drives I was imaging. Their response was quick and decisive, and their scoping and analysis of the initial incident was thorough. They had also mapped exactly where, within their infrastructure, certain data existed. In this case, their primary concern was a single file, a spreadsheet that contained some sensitive data that were not encrypted.

The intruder had apparently connected to the VPN and used a single account to access the 12 internal machines using RDP. Once I began analyzing the drive images, it was a relatively straightforward process to map his activities across the various systems. As a result of this analysis, I was able to identify an additional 13 systems that had been accessed internally, via lateral inside the network. As these accesses were internal, indicators were not found within the VPN logs but were visible due to the fact that a profile for the user account the intruder was using was created on each system they accessed (on Windows systems, a user account—either local or a domain account—can be created, but a profile will not be created until the first time the user logs in via that account). I was also able to identify many of the actions that the intruder performed while accessing the various systems and when those actions occurred. These activities included running searches and accessing various files. However, none of the accessed files were spreadsheets, and specifically not the spreadsheet with which the IT director was most concerned. Ultimately, we were able to build a very strong case to present to the regulatory body that indicated that the sensitive data had not been accessed or exposed.

Logs

Throughout this book and in particular in Chapter 4, we will discuss logs that are available on Windows systems, both as part of the operating system and through applications installed on those systems. The two primary concerns during an incident with respect to logs are, where are they located and what's in them—both of which can have a significant impact on the outcome of your incident response activities. Logs often play a significant role in incident response, because as mentioned previously, response happens after an incident occurs, and sometimes this can be a significant amount of time. The state of live systems can change pretty quickly, but logs can provide a considerable historical record of previous activity on the system ... if they are available.

> **TIP**
>
> Device Logs
>
> While we're concerned with logs on Windows systems, much of what is discussed in this section applies to other logs as well, such as those generated by firewalls and other network devices and systems.

One of the challenges of responding to incidents, whether as a consultant or an internal employee, is not having the necessary information to accurately and effectively respond to the questions your customer (or management) has regarding the incident, and therefore not being able to provide an accurate picture of what happened. Most organizations don't maintain full packet captures of what happens on their networks, and even if they did, this would still only be part of the picture, as you would still need to know what happened or what actions were taken on the host. Windows systems have the ability to maintain records of what occurred on the host via the Event Logs (on Vista and Windows 7 systems, this is referred to as "Windows Event Logging"; Event Logs are discussed in more detail in Chapter 4); however, a number of times I have referred to the Event Logs only to find that either the specific events (e.g., logins, etc.) were not being audited, or Event Logging was not even enabled. This limits not just what data are being recorded but also how complete a picture an analyst can develop, and how effectively they can respond and answer the critical questions that are being asked by senior management.

As such, one of the most effective steps in incident preparedness is to understand the logging mechanisms of your systems. A critical step that you can take quickly (and for free) to improve what information will be available when an incident is identified is to ensure that logging is enabled, that appropriate activities are being logged, and that the logs are large enough (or rotated often enough) to ensure sufficient data are available after an incident, which may be identified 6 or 12 months or more after the fact.

> **TIP**
>
> Application Logging
>
> Some applications, in particular AV applications, will record events in the Application Event Log, as well as in text files managed by the application itself. It is important to remember that the Windows Event Logs are often limited to a specific size, and "roll over" to make room for new events. This means that older events may be removed from the Event Log; however, those events should still be available in the log files maintained by the application.

For example, Windows Event Logs have several characteristics that can be modified to enable more effective logging. One characteristic is the file size; increasing the size of the Event Logs will mean that more events will be recorded and available for analysis.

Another characteristic is what is actually being recorded. Recording successful and failed login attempts can be very useful, particularly in domain environments, and on servers or other systems that multiple users may access. In one analysis engagement, we found a considerable amount of extremely valuable data in the Event Log because Process Tracking had been enabled, along with auditing of successful (and failed) login attempts, as illustrated in Figure 2.1.

The actual settings you employ within your infrastructure depend heavily on what makes sense in your environment. Enabling auditing for success and failure Process Tracking events is very useful, as some processes run and complete very

FIGURE 2.1

Windows 7 Audit Policy settings.

quickly, and are no longer visible mere seconds after they were launched. Enabling this auditing capability, as well as increasing the size of the logs (or, better yet, forward the logs from source systems to a collector system, per the instructions for Windows 7 and higher systems found online at *http://technet.microsoft.com/en-us/ library/cc748890.aspx*), will provide a persistent record of applications that have been executed on the system.

Something to keep in mind when enabling this auditing functionality on servers as well as workstations is that, for the most part, there aren't a great number of processes that are launched on a Windows system. For example, once a server is booted and running, how many users log into the console and begin browsing the Web or checking their email? Administrators may log in and perform system maintenance or troubleshooting, but for the most part, once the server is up and running, there won't be a considerable amount of interaction via the console. Also, on workstations and laptops, users tend to run the same set of applications—email client, web browser, etc.—on pretty much a daily basis. As such, enabling this functionality can provide information that is invaluable during incident response.

There are other things you can do to increase both the amount and quality of information available from Windows systems during incident response. Some commercial products may offer additional features such as increased logging capabilities, log consolidation, or log searching. For example, Kyrus Technology, Inc. (*http://www.kyrus-tech.com*) has developed a sensor application called Carbon Black that can be installed on a Windows system and monitors application execution on that system, sending its logs to a server for consolidation. That server can be maintained within the corporate infrastructure, or (for much smaller infrastructures) you can send the logs offsite to a server managed by the vendor.

NOTE

Disclosure

I am providing my recommendation of Carbon Black after having seen a demonstration of the sensor and server, as well as being afforded the opportunity to work with both on my own small virtual network. I installed the sensor, which then reported its logs back to the Carbon Black server, which I installed and had access to on one of my own systems. I received no payment for any review of the application nor for any mention or discussion of it in this book. The simple fact is that I honestly believe that Carbon Black changes the dynamic of incident response, and is something that any organization that uses Windows systems should strongly consider deploying.

Carbon Black is a lightweight (less than 100 kilobytes in size) sensor that you can install on Windows systems that you want to monitor. The sensor monitors the execution of applications, including child processes, file modifications, and loaded modules (as of this writing; future versions of Carbon Black will also record Registry key modifications and network connections). Carbon Black also records the

| | | | | | | 1660 | \device\harddiskvolume1\windows\system32\ipconfig.exe |
| | | | | | | 1712 | \device\harddiskvolume1\windows\system32\cmd.exe |

FIGURE 2.2

Excerpt of logged information available via Carbon Black server.

FIGURE 2.3

Event record for process launched from ADS.

MD5 hash of the executable file, as well as the start and end time for the process, and will also provide a copy of the binary executable file. All of these elements can also be searched within the logged information available via the server. A portion of the information available via the Carbon Black server is illustrated in Figure 2.2.

Again, this information can be extremely useful during incident response. As an example of this, and to get a little more familiar with what the data collected by Carbon Black look like, I logged into a monitored Windows XP system (on my own internal "lab network") and created a "suspicious" application by copying the Solitaire game file ("sol.exe") into an New Technology File System (NTFS) alternate data stream (ADS) attached to a file named "ads.txt." I then launched the game by typing "start .\ads.txt:game.exe" at the command prompt. Having already enabled Process Tracking within the audit policy for the system, I opened the Event Log on the system and found the event record that illustrated the application being launched. This record (event ID 593 indicates that the process has exited) is illustrated in Figure 2.3.

I then logged into the system to which the Carbon Black logs are sent, and accessed the user interface via the Chrome web browser (any web browser could

488	Process Name:	Process MD5:
488	\device\harddiskvolume1\windows\system32\ads.txt:game.exe	373E7A863A1A345C60ED89E20EC32311

FIGURE 2.4

Carbon Black log entry for "suspicious" process.

ads.txt
\device\harddiskvolume1\windows\prefetch\ads.txt:game.exe-02805d6a.pf
\device\harddiskvolume1\windows\prefetch\ads.txt:game.exe-02805d6a.pf

FIGURE 2.5

Results of Carbon Black file modification search.

have been used). I was able to quickly locate the log entry for the "suspicious" process, and even search for it based on the fact that I knew it was a child process of the "cmd.exe" process. The Carbon Black log entry is illustrated in Figure 2.4.

For the process illustrated in Figure 2.4, the exit time (although not displayed) correlated exactly with what is illustrated in the Event Log record in Figure 2.3. Now, this example was a bit contrived, in that it was a test and I knew what I was looking for via the Carbon Black interface. However, an analyst can use regular expressions as well as other search criteria (e.g., times, "new" processes, names of modified files, etc.) to locate potentially suspicious processes. Other search criteria can be used, such as the loaded modules (locate processes that have loaded a specific module, or DLL), MD5 hashes (of processes or loaded modules), and even file modifications. Figure 2.5 illustrates the results of a search for file modifications that include "ads.txt" via the Carbon Black interface.

As you can see, Carbon Black can be a powerful tool for use during incident response, and can be used to very quickly determine the extent and scope of an incident across monitored systems. Using various search criteria, a suspicious process can be found, and its source can quickly be identified; for example, following the parent processes for a suspicious process leads to "java.exe" and then to "firefox.exe" might indicate a browser drive-by compromise. From there, additional searches can reveal any other systems that may have experienced something similar. While Event Logs may "roll over" and new entries push out older ones, the information logged by Carbon Black can be available for a much longer period of time, going back much farther into the past. Once monitoring of network connections has been added to the sensor, an analyst can search across all of the logs to see any other monitored systems that may have attempted to establish connections to a particular IP address, or created a specific Registry key (the significance of this will be a bit more clear once you read Chapter 6). That said, it's important to note that while Carbon Black is a great tool, its functionality and flexibility are based on the fact that logging is configured, appropriate logging is occurring, and log data are being collected and preserved. These same principles apply whether you choose to use an add-on commercial product or native Windows functionality and tools.

Carbon Black (and other logging tools or products) may also have uses beyond incident response. One example of how Carbon Black has been used was in an organization that determined which components of the Microsoft Office Professional suite were being used by its employees, and that information was then used to reduce the overall corporate license for the software suite, saving the organization a significant amount of money on an annual basis.

DATA COLLECTION

In addition to your pre-incident preparation, your response team needs to be prepared to begin collecting critical and/or volatile data once an incident is detected. The main purpose of immediate response is the timely collection of data. It is of paramount importance that IT staff who work with your systems on a regular basis also be trained so that they can begin collecting data from those systems soon after an incident is identified. Processes—particularly malicious processes—often do not run continually on systems. These processes may execute only long enough to perform their designated task, such as downloading additional malware, collecting the contents of Protected Storage from the system, or sending collected data off of the system to a waiting server. Malicious processes that may run on a continual basis include such things as packet sniffers and keystroke loggers.

However, it is unlikely that you will see continuous, ongoing malicious activity on your system. An intruder who has compromised your infrastructure does not go to one system, open a browser, and spend hours surfing the Failblog.org web site. In fact, in a good number of instances, executables may be downloaded to a system, run, the data those processes collect sent off of the system to a waiting server on the Internet, and then the executables and their repository files are deleted. Of course, following this, the first forensic artifacts to decay are the network connections, and then as the system continues to function, MFT entries for the deleted files get reused, as do sectors on the disk that were once part of the files of interest. Therefore, collecting data as soon as the incident is identified can go a long way

---

TIP

Trusted Advisor

If you do not intend to perform your own incident response and analysis, the ideal approach to immediate response is to locate a firm providing incident response services and establish a relationship with them as your "trusted advisor." They can assist you in identifying the appropriate tools, procedures, and documentation for collecting data from your available systems, as well as address issues such as configuration recommendations for future systems. They can also assist you in running drills or "mock incidents" to ensure that the procedures work properly and can be used effectively.

```
G:\>dumpit
  DumpIt - v1.3.2.20110401 - One click memory memory dumper
   Copyright (c) 2007 - 2011, Matthieu Suiche <http://www.msuiche.net>
   Copyright (c) 2010 - 2011, MoonSols <http://www.moonsols.com>


   Address space size:          3716935680 bytes (   3544 Mb)
   Free space size:           100851986432 bytes (  96179 Mb)

     * Destination = \??\G:\OLIVER-20110907-010837.raw

     --> Are you sure you want to continue? [y/n] y
       + Processing...
```

FIGURE 2.6

Example of MoonSol DumpIt use.

toward aiding the follow-on incident response and analysis efforts. In fact, with the proper procedures in place, having specific personnel implement a documented procedure for collecting data can obviate the need to do so later, such as days later (or longer) once the third-party responders arrive onsite.

During immediate response, the first data that you will want to collect are the contents of physical memory. When collecting memory from live Windows systems, perhaps the easiest (and free) approach is the DumpIt utility from MoonSol (*http://www.moonsols.com/ressources/*). DumpIt is a simple-to-employ application written by Matthieu Suiche; simply place a copy of the application on a thumb drive or external USB drive enclosure, and launch the application from the command prompt. You will be asked a confirmation question, and once you respond with "y," a raw dump of memory will be created on the media (therefore, the media needs to be writeable), as illustrated in Figure 2.6.

When the process completes, the work "Success" appears in green following "Processing...." The resulting file (in this example, Oliver-20110907-010837. raw) is named using the system name (Oliver) and the coordinated universal time (UTC) at which the process was initiated; in this case, the date and time in the filename correlate to 9:08 pm on 6 September 2011, Eastern Standard Time. What this means is that physical memory can be collected from multiple systems, or even multiple times from the same system, very easily and without having to use additional media. In fact, it's so easy that all you have to do is have a copy of DumpIt on a couple of USB external drives (or appropriately sized thumb drives) and you're ready to go. The sooner memory is collected after an incident has been identified, the better. Over time, not only do processes complete, but systems can be rebooted, or even taken out of service, and once the memory is gone, it's gone.

Collecting the contents of physical memory is just the start, however. Using other tools such as FTK Imager (*http://accessdata.com/support/adownloads#FTKImager*), you can collect copies of specific files from the system (e.g., Registry hives, Event Logs, etc.), or initiate logical or full physical image acquisition from those systems, in fairly quick order.

NOTE

Spinning Plates

One of the challenges I've faced once arriving onsite is going to a server room or data center and acquiring images from multiple systems. In some cases, each system requires a different approach, particularly if the systems cannot be taken offline for some reason. Live acquisitions can be a challenge when the system has just a USB version 1.0 connector, as you watch the estimated completion time for the acquisition of a 250-gigabyte hard drive start at 2 hours and progress up over 56 hours. I've even encountered a boot-from-SAN system; while the device itself was "in scope," the multiterabyte SAN was not, so we performed a live acquisition of the boot-from-SAN system.

Whenever faced with situations like this, we often try to get as many systems started in the acquisition process as possible, keeping the plates spinning as it were, to reduce the overall amount of time required by using parallel processes. Often, the incident had been going on for several days (or weeks) before we were called, and the contracting process and our (consultant's) travel to get to the site added additional time to the clock. The overall process would have been far better facilitated had the local IT staff followed a documented procedure and initiated the acquisition process immediately.

For example, a great deal of analysis work can be performed rather quickly using a partial acquisition (rather than acquiring a full image) of data from a live system. Installing FTK Imager on a USB external hard drive (often referred to as a "wallet" drive due to the size) will provide suitable storage space for acquired images and files in a small form factor, and when needed the drive can be connected to a system and FTK Imager launched. The IT staff member performing the acquisition can then choose to add either the physical drive of the system, or the logical volume for the C:\ drive (depending on the response plan that's already been established and documented within the organization). From there, a directory listing that includes the last modified, last accessed, and creation dates (from the $STANDARD_INFORMATION attribute in the MFT; see Chapters 4 and 7 for more detail) for all files within the selected volume (as well as their paths) can easily be exported to the storage media using the "Export Directory Listing…" functionality, as illustrated in Figure 2.7.

Once the directory listing has been exported, specific files can then be exported through FTK Imager, allowing for rapid analysis and assessment of the state of the system. These files may include Registry hives, Event Logs, prefetch files, jump lists (Windows 7), application (scheduled task, antivirus, etc.) log files, etc.

FIGURE 2.7

FTK Imager "Export Directory Listing…" functionality.

TIP

F-Response

The acquisition process discussed previously in this chapter requires an IT administrator to physically touch each system to plug the USB hard drive into that system. Depending on the organization and how the infrastructure is designed, this may not be something that can be done in a timely manner. For example, systems may be located in a server room or data center on another floor or in another building within the city, or even in another city. F-Response (*http://www.f-response.com*) is a dongle-based tool designed by Matthew Shannon that provides remote, read-only access to remote systems. Matthew wanted to have a way to perform incident response activities without having to coordinate with his customers to actually get someone physically onsite, and designed F-Response to meet his needs. Using the Enterprise version of F-Response, a responder can sit in a single location with network access to the various systems, deploy the F-Response agent, and connect to each system in read-only mode (all attempts to write to the remote hard drive are dropped by F-Response). From there, the responder can collect specific files or acquire a complete image using their acquisition tool of choice (e.g., FTK Imager). F-Response also provides access to the contents of physical memory on Windows systems.

Another useful aspect of F-Response is that the agent can be deployed on systems ahead of time, as part of incident preparation activities. The agent installs as a Windows service, but by default it is not enabled to run automatically when the system is booted; therefore, it can be installed and waiting to be enabled when needed. The agent can also be installed using a name other than the default, so that it is not obvious that F-Response is installed (although because the service is not started automatically, anyone who logs in to the system and types "net start" at the command prompt will not see the agent listed as a running service anyway).

Training

For employees to perform their jobs effectively, they must be trained. Payroll and accounting staffs within organizations have training to attend, and then return to their organization and begin working in their field. The same is true with a lot of other departments within your business, as well as with professionals in other areas (e.g., emergency medical technicians, police officers, firefighters, doctors, nurses, etc.). Many organizations offer a variety of types of training to their employees, often ranging from the use of office suite applications, to professional development, and even basic first aid.

The same must also be true for those individuals responsible when an incident is identified by the organization. It does no good to have a CSIRP but not have designated staff trained in their activities when the plan needs to be implemented. Several regulatory bodies state that to be compliant (all "compliance vs. security" arguments aside), organizations subject to the regulations must not only have a CSIRP with all response personnel identified within the plan, but they must also receive annual training with respect to the CSIRP and the actions they are to take.

TIP

Mock Incidents

Mock incidents are a great way to test your response plan, either to see what needs to be improved or to simply provide training so that the plan and everyone's role is fresh in everyone's minds. I've provided mock incident and response team training to a number of organizations and seen firsthand just how revealing that first mock incident can be.

During one training event, we found two very interesting items. We'd placed an innocuous bit of software on a system chosen at random that would reach out to the Web every 10 minutes and grab a web page, and then save that web page on the local hard drive in a file with the .dll extension. The first thing that happened during the event was that an incident was declared and the firewall administrator was asked for the firewall logs, and he said that he'd have them to the incident manager in 10 minutes. Half an hour later, the incident manager hadn't received the logs, and when he tried to reach the firewall administrator, it turned out that he'd gone to lunch! When he returned, he said that he had thought that the request for the logs was part of a drill and hadn't actually intended to provide the logs. When he did try to retrieve the logs, we all found out that the logs weren't actually being archived.

The other finding involved the intrusion detection system (IDS). At one point during the exercise, the IDS administrator stated that this wasn't a valid test because, even given the domain and name of the web page being requested, he wasn't seeing anything in the logs. As it turned out, the "malware" had been placed on a subnet not covered by any IDS.

Running an exercise during which the CSIRP is tested or taken for a "shakedown cruise" (please excuse the naval vernacular, as I'm a former Marine officer) should include actually collecting the data that you've decided will be collected. Are you going to collect memory from Windows systems, and if so, how? Will it work? Challenges I've encountered include older systems with USB version 1.0 interfaces, which usually result in processes that should take a short time ultimately taking an inordinate amount of time to complete. How will you address such situations, and have you identified all of the pertinent systems that may have this issue (regardless of the issue)? How will you address virtual systems? How will you collect data from production systems that cannot be "taken down" (e.g., due to service level agreements, transaction processing, etc.)? All of these questions (and likely more) need to be addressed *before* an incident occurs; otherwise, critical, sensitive data will continue to be lost (either exfiltrated or degraded) while managers and staff members try to decide how to react.

SUMMARY

When an incident is identified within an organization, it is critical that local IT staff be trained and knowledgeable in collecting pertinent data from Windows systems. Considerable time (i.e., hours, days, etc.) may pass before third-party consultants arrive onsite to begin performing incident response activities, and even then, the fact that they are not familiar with the organization's infrastructure can extend the overall response time. Being prepared for those inevitable computer security incidents to occur simply by having documentation, as well as network and system data, available will make a significant difference in the ultimate outcome of the incident. This will be true regardless of whether an incident or data breach needs to ultimately be addressed by a compliance oversight body, or by law enforcement interested in intelligence or evidence to pursue prosecution. Properly trained local IT staff can immediately collect data that would otherwise expire or be unavailable hours or days later. Local responders should be able to collect the contents of physical memory, as well as partial, logical, or complete physical images from systems, and have that data ready and documented for the analysis effort that inevitably follows data collection.

Volume Shadow Copies

3

CHAPTER OUTLINE

INFORMATION IN THIS CHAPTER

- What Are "Volume Shadow Copies"?
- Live Systems
- Acquired Images

INTRODUCTION

Every time a new version of the Windows operating system is announced or made public, a collective shudder ripples throughout the forensics community. What new features are going to be available in the next operating system version? What's going to remain the same? What new challenges will we face? Some changes are minor; for example, the binary structure of the Windows Registry hasn't changed among versions, from Windows 2000 all the way through to Windows 7, although how the Registry is used (i.e., where keys are located, what keys and values are created and modified, etc.) by the operating system and applications has changed in many cases. Other changes can be quite significant, such as those that change the very core of how Windows operates. In this chapter, we'll address one of those changes, specifically the introduction of Volume Shadow Copies. However, we will discuss this topic not from the perspective of a developer or programmer, but instead from the perspective of an analyst, and how this technology might be utilized to further an investigation.

WHAT ARE "VOLUME SHADOW COPIES"?

Volume Shadow Copies (VSCs) are one of the new, ominous-sounding aspects of the Windows operating systems (specifically, Windows XP, in a limited manner, and more so with Vista and Windows 7) that can significantly impact an analyst's examination. VSCs are significant and interesting as a source of artifacts, enough to require their own chapter.

With the release of Windows XP, Microsoft introduced the Volume Shadow Copy Service (VSS) to provide functionality for backing up critical system files to assist with system recovery. With Windows XP, users and administrators saw this functionality as System Restore Points, which were created automatically under various conditions (e.g., every 24 hours, when a driver was installed, etc.), and could also be created manually, as illustrated in Figure 3.1.

As illustrated in Figure 3.1, users can not only create Restore Points, but they can also restore the computer to an earlier time. This proved to be a useful functionality, particularly when a user installed something (application, driver, etc.) that failed to work properly, or the system became infected with malware of some kind. Users could revert the core functionality of their systems to a previous state through the System Restore functionality, effectively recovering it to a previous state. However, System Restore Points do not back up everything on a system; for example, user data files are not backed up (and are therefore not restored, either), and all of the data (specifically, the passwords) in the SAM hive of the Registry are not backed up, as you wouldn't want users to restore their systems to a previous point in time and have them not be able to access their systems, as a previous password (which they may not remember) had been restored.

So, while System Restore Points did prove useful when users needed to recover their systems to a previous state, they did little to back up user data and provide access to previous copies of other files. From a forensic analysis, a great deal of historical data could be retrieved from System Restore Points, including backed-up system files and Registry hives. Analysts still need to understand how backed up files could be "mapped" to their original filenames but the fact that the files are backed up is valuable in itself.

To begin, select the task that you want to perform:

◉ Restore my computer to an earlier time

○ Create a restore point

FIGURE 3.1

Windows XP System Restore Point functionality.

With the release of Vista, the functionality provided by the VSS to support services such as Windows Backup and System Restore was expanded. In particular, the amount and type of data captured by System Restore was expanded to include block-level, incremental "snapshots" of a system (only the modified information was recorded) at a given point in time. These "snapshots," known as Volume Shadow Copies, appeared in a different manner to the user. VSCs operate at the block level within the file system, backing up and providing access to previous versions of system and user data files within a particular volume. As with System Restore Points, the actual backups are transparent to the user, but with VSCs, the user can restore previous versions of files through the Previous Versions shell extension, as illustrated in Figure 3.2 (from a Windows 7 system).

Okay, so what does this mean to the forensic analyst? From an analyst's perspective, there is a great deal of historical information within backed-up files. Accessing these files can provide not just historical data (e.g., previous contents, etc.) but additional analysis can be conducted by comparing the available versions over time.

Registry Keys

As you'd expect, there are several Registry keys that have a direct impact on the performance of the VSS, the service that supports the various functions that lead to VSCs. As this is a Windows service, the primary key of interest is:

```
HKLM\System\CurrentControlSet\Services\VSS
```

However, it is important to understand that disabling the VSS may affect other applications aside from just disabling VSCs, such as Windows Backup. As such, care should be taken in disabling this service on production systems. Also, forensic analysts examining Vista and Windows 7 systems that do not appear to have any VSCs available should check this key to see if the service had been disabled prior to the system being acquired.

There's another key within the System hive that affects VSC behavior:

```
HKLM\System\CurrentControlSet\Control\BackupRestore
```

FIGURE 3.2

Windows 7 Previous Versions shell extension.

Beneath this key are three subkeys: FilesNotToBackup, FilesNotToSnapshot, and KeysNotToRestore. The names should be pretty self-explanatory, but just in case, the FilesNotToBackup key contains a list of files and directories that (according to Microsoft; additional information is available at *http://msdn.microsoft.com/en-us/library/bb891959(v=vs.85).aspx*) backup applications should not backup and restore. On a default Windows 7 installation, this list includes temporary files (as in those in the "%TEMP%" directory), the pagefile, hibernation file (if one exists), the Offline Files Cache, Internet Explorer "index.dat" files, as well as number of log file directories. The FilesNotToSnapshot key contains a list of files that should be deleted from newly created shadow copies. Finally, the KeysNotToRestore key contains lists of subkeys and values that should not be restored. It should be noted that within this key, values that end in "\" indicate that subkeys and values for the listed key will not be restored, while values that end in "*" indicate that subkeys and values for the listed key will not be restored from backup, but new values will be included from the backup.

LIVE SYSTEMS

Accessing VSCs on live Vista, Windows 2008, and Windows 7 systems is a relatively simple task, as Windows systems ship with the necessary native system tools

FIGURE 3.3

Sample output of the *vssadmin* command.

to access VSCs. To see the available VSCs for the C:\ drive of the Vista or Windows 7 system that you're logged into, type the following command into a command prompt using elevated privileges (you may need to right-click the command prompt window and choose "Run as Administrator"):

```
C:\>vssadmin list shadows /for=c:
```

Example results of this command are illustrated in Figure 3.3.

As you can see illustrated in Figure 3.3, we can use the *vssadmin* command to gather considerable information about available VSCs on the system.

WARNING

Windows Management Instrumentation (WMI)

The WMI class Win32_ShadowCopy (documentation found at *http://msdn.microsoft.com/en-us/library/aa394428(v=VS.85).aspx*) provides an interface for programmatically extracting much of the same information from Windows systems made available by the *vssadmin* command. However, according to information available at the Microsoft web site (see the "Community Content" section of the previously linked page) at the time of this writing, this class is not supported on the 64-bit version of Windows 2008. Testing using a Perl script indicates that this is also true for Windows 7; the script didn't work at all on 64-bit Windows 7, but ran very well on the 32-bit edition. A sample of what is available via Perl (or other methods for accessing WMI classes) appears as follows:

```
Computer: WIN-882TM1JM2N2
DeviceObject: \\?\GLOBALROOT\Device\HarddiskVolumeShadowCopy1
InstallDate: 20110421125931.789499-240
<snip>
VolumeName: \\?\Volume{d876c67b-1139-11df-8b47-806e6f6e6963}\
```

FIGURE 3.4

ShadowExplorer v0.8 interface.

Don't like the command line approach? Hey, that's okay … it's not for everyone. Head on over to ShadowExplorer.com and get a copy of ShadowExplorer (at the time of this writing, version 0.8 is available). Download and run the setup file on your system to install ShadowExplorer on the system in question. The web site describes ShadowExplorer as being useful to all users, but especially so to users with Windows 7 Home Edition, who don't have access to VSCs by default. Once you install and launch ShadowExplorer, you will see the interface as illustrated in Figure 3.4.

As illustrated in Figure 3.4, you can use the dropdown selector beneath the menu bar to select the date of the VSC you would like access to; unfortunately, ShadowExplorer will only show you the VSCs available within the volume or drive (i.e., C:\, D:\, etc.) on which it is installed. Therefore, if your system has a D:\ drive, you'll need to rerun the installation program and install it on that drive, as well, to view the VSCs on that drive. Navigating through the tree view in the left pane, locate the file for which you'd like to see a previous version, right-click the file, and choose "Export" to copy that file to another location.

Going back to the command prompt, to access the VSCs on your live system and have access to the previous versions of files within those VSCs, you'll need to make a symbolic link to a VSC. To do that, go to the listing for a VSC, as illustrated in Figure 3.3, and select (you'll need to have Quick Edit mode enabled in your command prompt) the VSC identifier, which appears after "Shadow Copy Volume:." Then go back to the prompt and type the following command:

```
C:\>mklink /d C:\vsc
```

Do not hit the Enter key at this point. Once you get that far with command, right-click to paste the selected VSC identifier into the prompt and then be sure to add a trailing slash ("\"), so that the command looks like the following:

```
C:\>mklink /d C:\vsc \\GLOBALROOT\Device\
  HarddiskVolumeShadowCopy20\
```

Remember to add the trailing slash to the command ... this is very important! This is not something that is clearly documented at the Microsoft site, but has been found to be the case by a number of forensic analysts, to include Rob Lee, of SANS fame, and Jimmy Weg, a law enforcement officer from Montana. Now, go ahead and hit the Enter key, and you should see that the symbolic link was successfully created. Now you can navigate to the "C:\vsc" directory, and browse and access the files via the command prompt or Windows Explorer. Once you're done doing whatever you're going to do with these files (e.g., review, copy, etc.), type the following command to remove the symbolic directory link:

```
C:\>rmdir C:\vsc
```

This series of commands is going to be very important throughout the rest of this chapter, so it's important that we understand some of the key points. First, use the *vssadmin* command to get the list of VSCs for a particular volume; note that when you run the command from the command prompt, you do not have to be *in* that volume. For example, if you want to list the VSCs for the D:\ volume, you can do so using the following command, run from the C:\ volume:

```
C:\>vssadmin list shadows /for=d:
```

Once you know which VSC you'd like to access, you can use the *mklink* command to create a symbolic link to that VSC. Remember, you must be sure that the VSC identifier (i.e., *\\GLOBALROOT\Device\HarddiskVolumeShadowCopy20*) ends with a trailing slash. Finally, once you've completed working in that VSC, you remove the symbolic link with the *rmdir* command.

ProDiscover

A number of commercial forensic analysis applications provide access to VSCs within acquired images, and ProDiscover is just one of those applications. However, ProDiscover is also the only commercial forensic analysis application to which I have access. As such, I briefly mention its ability to access VSCs on live systems here. For those who want more detailed information on how to use ProDiscover for this purpose, Christopher Brown posted a five-page PDF-format paper at the Technology Pathways, LLC, web site that describes how to use ProDiscoverIR (the Incident Response Edition) to access and acquire VSCs on remote live systems. This can be very valuable to an investigator who needs to quickly access these resources in another location, or to do so surreptitiously. The paper can be found at *http://toorcon.techpathways.com/uploads/ LiveVolumeShadowCopyWithProDiscoverIR.pdf*.

F-Response

If you're a user of the fantastic F-Response tool from Matt Shannon, particularly the Enterprise Edition (EE), you'll be very happy to know that you can use this product to access VSCs on remote systems. This may be important for a variety of reasons, such as a user within your enterprise environment may have "lost" an important file that they were working on, you may need to access an employee's system surreptitiously, or you may need to quickly acquire data from a system located in another building in another area of the city. While I generally don't recommend acquiring full system images over the network, even over a VPN, you can use tools like F-Response EE, which provides read-only access to the remote system drive, to collect specific information and selected files from remote systems very quickly. This will allow you to perform a quick triage of systems, and potentially perform a good deal of data reduction and reduce the impact of your response activities on your organization by identifying the specific systems that need to be acquired.

That being said, perhaps the best way to discuss F-Response EE's ability to provide access to VSCs is through a demonstration. Before describing the setup I used and walking through this demonstration, I need to make it clear that I used F-Response EE because Matt Shannon was gracious enough to provide me with a copy to work with; this process that I'm going to walk through can be used with all versions of F-Response, including the Consultant and Field Kit editions.

> **TIP**
>
> F-Response VSC Demo Setup
>
> For my demonstration, I don't have a full network to "play with," so I opted to use the tools that I do have available. I booted my 64-bit Windows 7 Professional analysis system, and then started up a 32-bit Windows 7 Ultimate VM (virtual machine) in VMPlayer. I had set the Network Adapter in the settings for the VM to "bridged," so that the VM appeared as a system on the network. For the demonstration, the IP address of the running VM was 192.168.1.8, and the IP address of the host was 192.168.1.5. On both systems, the Windows firewalls were disabled (just for the demonstration, I assure you!) to simulate a corporate environment. Also, it is important to note that Windows 7 ships with the iSCSI initiator already installed, so I didn't need to go out and install it separately.

Again, this demonstration makes use of F-Response EE. (Thanks to Matt Shannon for allowing me the honor to work with this wonderful tool!) Once I logged in to my analysis system, I plugged in my F-Response EE dongle and launched the F-Response License Manager Monitor to install and start the License Manager service. I then launched the F-Response Enterprise Management Console (FEMC), and started by configuring the credentials that I would be using to access

FIGURE 3.5

FEMC Direct Connect user interface.

the remote system. I clicked "File → Configure Credentials…" from the menu bar, and entered the appropriate username/password information to access the remote system (if you're in an Active Directory domain, check the "Use Current User Credentials" option). Next, I clicked "File → Configure Options…" and configured my deployment options appropriately (for this demo, I didn't select the "Physical Memory" option in the Host Configuration section).

As I was going to connect to a specific system, I selected "Scan → Direct Scan" from the menu bar, then entered the IP address of the target system (i.e., 192.168.1.8), and clicked the "Open" button. Once the connection was made, F-Response was installed and started on the target system, as illustrated in Figure 3.5.

From there, I logged into the C:\ volume on the target host, and that host's C:\ drive appeared on my analysis system as the F:\ volume. I then ran the following command on my analysis system:

```
C:\>vssadmin list shadows /for=f:
```

To access the oldest VSC listed (HarddiskVolumeShadowCopy17, created on January 4, 2011), I entered the following command in a command prompt on my analysis system:

```
C:\>mklink /d d:\test \\GLOBALROOT\Device\
    HarddiskVolumeShadowCopy17\
```

This command created a symbolic link on my analysis system called "d:\test" that contained the contents of a VSC created on the target system on January 4, 2011, and allowed me to access all of the files with that directory, albeit via the read-only access provided by F-Response EE.

WARNING

Accessing VSCs on Live Systems

It is very important to remember that when you're accessing VSCs on live systems, that system, whether accessed remotely or locally, is still subject to operating normally. What this means is that if you're accessing the oldest VSC that you found, the system itself is still going about its normal operations, and that VSC could be overwritten to make room for another VSC, as under normal conditions, the VSCs are subject to the first-in-first-out (FIFO) process. This actually happened to me while I was working on some of the demonstrations listed in this chapter. The remote live system continued to operate normally, and the VSC I was accessing was removed simply because I had taken too long to complete the testing (I was just browsing through some of the files). I had to back out of my demonstration and restart it. When I did, I found that the output of the *vssadmin* command was quite a bit different, particularly with respect to the dates on which the available shadow copies had been created.

Another very important aspect of accessing VSCs (and this also applies to accessing VSCs within images) is that you need to be very careful about the files you click or double-click on. Remember, if you double-click a file that is in a VSC on a remote system, your analysis system is going to apply its own rules to accessing and opening that file. This means that if you see a PDF file that you'd like to click on, you should be very sure that it wasn't what led to the remote system being infected in the first place. If it is a malicious PDF, and your system isn't protected (e.g., updated antivirus and PDF viewer, etc.), then your system may become infected, as well.

As I mentioned, there are a number of commercial forensic analysis applications and tools that provide analysts and responders with the ability to access VSCs on remote systems, and what we've discussed here are only a few of your (and my) available options. The application and methodology you choose to use depends largely on your needs, abilities, and preferences (and, of course, which tool or set of tools you can afford).

ACQUIRED IMAGES

Since discussion of VSCs first started, one of the biggest and most often asked questions within the forensic analysis community has been, "How do we access VSCs within acquired images?" First of all, accessing VSCs within images is not the same thing as accessing those on live systems. Figure 3.6 illustrates what the VSCs "look like" within an acquired image.

As illustrated in Figure 3.6, the VSC difference files within the System Volume Information directory are binary files, and we need some means for translating these binary data into accessible information. On live systems, this is usually done through the use of the available API; therefore, one means of accessing the same data on an acquired image would be to boot the image through the use of LiveView and VMWare.

MountPointManagerRemoteDatabase
tracking.log
{218be27a-0609-11df-8044-001c23913ac1}{3808876b-c176-4e48-b7ae-04046e6cc752}
{3808876b-c176-4e48-b7ae-04046e6cc752}
{52802fd5-0488-11df-8bce-001c23913ac1}{3808876b-c176-4e48-b7ae-04046e6cc752}
{52802ff3-0488-11df-8bce-001c23913ac1}{3808876b-c176-4e48-b7ae-04046e6cc752}
{5560ffd4-fbfc-11de-b9c7-001c23913ac1}{3808876b-c176-4e48-b7ae-04046e6cc752}
{992d2118-ff22-11de-b87c-001c23913ac1}{3808876b-c176-4e48-b7ae-04046e6cc752}
{e86fff5b-ffb9-11de-b941-001c23913ac1}{3808876b-c176-4e48-b7ae-04046e6cc752}
{edfa070c-00a2-11df-bfd1-001c23913ac1}{3808876b-c176-4e48-b7ae-04046e6cc752}

FIGURE 3.6

Acquired image of Vista system opened in FTK Imager v3.0.

TIP

LiveView

LiveView, freely available at *http://liveview.sourceforge.net/*, is a Java-based graphical tool developed by a student at Carnegie Mellon University. LiveView creates VMWare configuration files for acquired raw/dd images or physical disks, and supports Windows versions from Windows 98 through Windows 2008 (Windows 7 is not listed among the supported operating systems).

However, even with the ability to "zero out" (not crack, but reset to a new value, possibly using a tool such as ntpwedit, found at the time of this writing at *http://cdslow.webhost.ru/en/ntpwedit/*) the Administrator password so that you can log into the now-running system, this may still not be a viable option. So, the question becomes, with nothing more than an acquired image of a system that may contain VSCs, what are some options for gaining access to the data within those VSCs?

I asked myself this question seriously during the break between Christmas 2010 and the New Year, and I began researching it to find a solution. After all, I'd encountered several systems that contained VSCs, including Windows 7 and even a Vista system. In my case, neither instance required access to the VSCs to complete my analysis, but it was still clear to me that like other analysts, I could fully expect to see more of these systems. Subsequently, I was going to have to come up with a way to access the VSCs.

I began my search by going to Google … of course. I found a number of references to accessing VSCs within acquired images, but in each case the materials included mounting the acquired image using EnCase (from Guidance Software) and the Physical Disk Emulator (PDE) module as part of the process. Well, I don't have access to EnCase, nor to the PDE module, and I thought that there just *had* to be some way to access data within the VSCs of an acquired image without using either one.

For my testing, I had an image acquired from a personal system that was running a 32-bit version of Windows Vista. This was an image of the physical hard drive, and as the system was a Dell laptop, the image contained several partitions including the Dell maintenance partition. As such, I used FTK Imager version 3.0 to extract the active operating system partition from the image, as I wanted to isolate the partition that contained the VSCs. The disk image was called "disk0.001," and the image of the active partition was called "system.001." My analysis workstation was a Dell Latitude E6510 laptop, running a 64-bit version of Windows 7 Professional. On that laptop, I had a copy of FTK Imager version 3.0.0.1443, as well as ImDisk 1.3.1.

VHD Method

A VHD file is a virtual hard disk file used by virtualization software such as Microsoft's Virtual PC or Virtual Server (but can also be used by Oracle's VirtualBox application, as well). The VHD file represents a physical hard disk and can be used by a virtual machine as if it were a physical hard disk. Additional information regarding VHD files can be found at *http://technet.microsoft.com/en-us/library/cc708315%28WS.10%29.aspx*.

As part of my research for this little project, I found "vhdtool.exe" at the Microsoft site (*http://code.msdn.microsoft.com/vhdtool*). I also found that Microsoft's Virtual Server application includes a tool named "vhdmount" (*http://technet.microsoft.com/en-us/library/cc708295%28WS.10%29.aspx*) for mounting VHD files. In reading about "vhdtool.exe," it has an option ("/convert") for converting a raw/dd image file into a fixed-format VHD file. I ran the tool against a copy of the system.001 file (the active OS partition image previously described, on an external USB wallet drive), and although the filename was not changed to ".vhd," the tool reported that it had successfully modified the file (apparently by adding a footer). From there, the next step was to mount the new VHD file; I did this by opening the Computer Management console, selecting "Disk Management" and clicking "Action," then "Attach VHD" from the menu bar. The system.001 file was recognized as a valid VHD file, and the resulting "Attach Virtual Hard Disk" dialog is illustrated in Figure 3.7.

Notice in Figure 3.7 that I had selected the option to mount the VHD file as read-only. Even though I was using a working copy of the image file, and it had

FIGURE 3.7

Windows 7 Disk Manager "Attach Virtual Hard Disk" dialog.

already been modified (via the use of "vhdtool.exe," which I documented), I wanted to be sure to follow best practices in my procedures.

As a result of attaching the VHD file, the Disk Management console showed a 136.46-gigabyte (GB) partition mounted as Disk2, and listed as the G:\ drive/volume, as illustrated in Figure 3.8.

Opening Windows Explorer, I could clearly see the files within in the G:\ volume; I confirmed this using the *dir* command to generate a file listing from the command prompt. The next step was to determine which VSCs were available, if any. To do this, I ran the following command from the command prompt:

```
vssadmin list shadows /for=g:
```

The output of this command indicated that there were a total of seven VSCs available in the image, with creation dates ranging from January 10, 2010 to January 20, 2010. I opted to mount the oldest VSC; to do so, I selected \\?\ *GLOBALROOT\Device\HarddiskVolumeShadowCopy23*, which appeared after "Shadow Copy Volume:" in the output of the previous *vssadmin* command, and right-clicked to copy this string to the clipboard. I then returned to the command prompt and typed in the following command:

```
D:\>mklink /d d:\vsc23
```

FIGURE 3.8

Disk Management console showing G:\ volume.

After typing this command, I right-clicked to paste the \\?\GLOBALROOT... string that I'd copied to the clipboard at the end of the command, and then I made sure to add a closing "\" to the end of the command, and hit the Enter key. The result was that the symbolic link from the VSC to D:\vsc23 was successfully created.

TIP

Final Backslash

The final backslash at the end of the *mklink* command is critically important! Without it, you won't be able to access the mounted VSC properly.

At this point, I had the image file mounted as a VHD file, and the oldest VSC within the image also mounted and accessible from my analysis system (confirmed via the *dir* command). Using "robocopy.exe" (which is native to Windows 7) to preserve file metadata (time stamps), I copied the contents of a user's profile directory (albeit not the subdirectories) from both the mounted VHD file (the imaged Vista operating system partition) and the mounted VSC within the VHD file to run a quick comparison against the NTUSER.DAT files, and in particular the contents of the UserAssist key. I could have run RegRipper (specifically rip.pl or the compiled executable version of the tool, "rip.exe") from the analysis system against the mounted VHD and VSC to obtain the information I was looking for, but copying the files gave me an excuse to run the *robocopy* command (until then, I hadn't ever used the command). To get information from the UserAssist keys from the two copied NTUSER.DAT hive files, I ran the following command:

```
C:\tools>rip.pl -r <path>\ntuser.dat -p userassist2 > output.txt
```

Running the command against each hive file, redirecting the output to the appropriate text file, allowed me to then open the output files in an editor and compare them. From the NTUSER.DAT hive file from the oldest VSC within the image, I found the following entries:

```
Sat Jan 9 11:40:31 2010 Z
UEME_RUNPATH:C:\Program Files\iTunes\iTunes.exe (293)
Fri Jan 8 04:13:40 2010 Z
UEME_RUNPATH:Skype.lnk (5)
UEME_RUNPATH:C:\Program Files\Skype\Phone\Skype.exe (8)
```

Then, from the NTUSER.DAT hive file from the VHD image file itself, I found the following entries:

```
Thu Jan 21 03:10:26 2010 Z
UEME_RUNPATH:C:\Program Files\Skype\Phone\Skype.exe (14)
UEME_RUNPIDL:C:\Users\Public\Desktop\Skype.lnk (1)
Tue Jan 19 00:37:46 2010 Z
UEME_RUNPATH:C:\Program Files\iTunes\iTunes.exe (296)
```

What this clearly demonstrates are the changes that occur between various VSCs and the actual running system, as well as the forensic value of VSCs. As you can see from the previous examples, in the space of 12 days, the user had run the Skype application 6 times, and in about 10 days, had run the iTunes application 3 times. As the UserAssist key records the date and time that the application was most recently run, all we would normally be able to determine from the image of the Vista was that as of January 21, 2010, the Skype application had been run a total of 14 times by the user. However, by accessing the VSCs, we're able to obtain historical information regarding previous times that the user had run the Skype application.

This same concept applies to other Registry keys, as well, particularly those that maintain lists of subkeys and values. Specific keys that may be of interest during an examination may include most recently used (MRU) lists; these keys usually contain a number of values, and the LastWrite time of the key corresponds to the date when the last file was accessed. However, we may be able to use data from hive files within VSCs to determine the dates and times when other files within the MRU list were accessed, as well. Being able to access this type of temporal information allows an analyst to infer certain things about a user's behavior on the system, particularly if (per this example) the fact that the user launched Skype 6 times in the space of approximately 12 days is pertinent to the goals of the examination (additional information regarding the user's activity could then be obtained from the application's log files). It should be clear from this that there is significantly more value to VSCs than simply previous versions of graphic image files.

TIP

Registry Analysis

A more detailed discussion of analysis of the Windows Registry hive files can be found in Chapter 5 of this book, as well as within *Windows Registry Forensics* (Carvey, 2011).

Once I had completed all that I wanted to do (mostly just browsing), I removed the symbolic link that I'd created to the VSC using the following command:

```
D:\>rmdir d:\vsc23
```

As the symbolic link was created to a directory (i.e., "mklink/d"), I needed to treat the symbolic link as a directory to remove it (i.e., *rmdir* or *rd*). I then returned to the Disk Management console (see Figure 3.8), right-clicked on the "Disk 2" box to the left of the G:\ volume (displayed in the lower pane), and chose "Detach VHD" from the context menu.

TIP

Diskpart

The *diskpart* command (a reference for the command, albeit specifically for Windows XP, can be found at *http://support.microsoft.com/kb/300415*) can be used to attach and detach VHD files from the command line. First, you need to simply type "diskpart" at the command prompt to begin working in the *diskpart* shell. To attach a VHD file, use the following commands:

```
selectvdisk file=<path to VHD file>
attachvdisk
```

Using these commands, the VHD file is automatically mounted using the next available drive letter. To detach the VHD file, use the following command:

```
detachvdisk
```

In summary, the process you would follow to access VSCs using this method would be to:

- Convert a working copy of your image file to a VHD file using "vhdtool.exe."
- Attach/mount the newly created VHD file to your Windows 7 analysis workstation, using either the Disk Management console, or "diskpart.exe." Be sure to check the "Read-Only" box (see Figure 3.7) when mounting the VHD file.
- Determine how many VSCs you have available within the image, and for which dates, using "vssadmin.exe" (i.e., *vssadmin list shadows /for=n:*).
- Create a symbolic directory link to the VSC (or VSCs) of interest using "mklink.exe" (i.e., *mklink /d C:\mountpoint\\?\GLOBALROOT\Device\Harddisk VolumeShadowCopyn*). Note: The trailing backslash in the *mklink* command is critically important!
- Perform whatever work is part of your analysis plan (e.g., copy files via robocopy, scan the mounted VSC with antivirus scanners, etc.).
- Remove the symbolic link with the *rmdir* command. When you've completed working with the VHD file itself, detach it via the Disk Management console or "diskpart.exe."

I should note that mounting a working copy of your acquired image as a VHD file can be used for much more than accessing VSCs. For example, all of those tasks we mentioned performing against a mounted/linked VSC (e.g., scanning with AV, performing other malware detection steps, etc.) can be performed on just the mounted VHD file.

VMWare Method

After I figured out how to access the VSCs within an acquired image via the VHD method, I began discussing this with others, and found out that folks like Rob Lee (of SANS and Mandiant fame) and Jimmy Weg (a law enforcement officer from

Montana) have been using VMWare in a very similar manner to access VSCs. Discussing the VMWare method with both of them, I got an idea of the process that they used, and decided to try it on my own to see if I could get it to work. To work through this process you'll need the following:

- The ability to run a VMWare virtual machine, such as VMPlayer (freely available at *http://www.vmware.com/products/player/*) or VMWare Workstation (a 30-day evaluation version is available at *http://www.vmware.com*). Using VMWare Workstation, you can create your own virtual machines.
- A Windows 7 VM (I used a 32-bit Windows 7 Ultimate VM for this demonstration).
- A copy of LiveView or ProDiscover Basic Edition.

The first thing I did was download VMPlayer from the VMWare web site, and get a copy of LiveView. Having only an image in raw/dd format, I needed a way to get the data within the image recognized as a disk or partition by the VMWare tools. LiveView provides that capability by generating a VMWare virtual machine disk format (.vmdk) file that points to the image; however, for this demonstration, I just wanted the .vmdk file, and I didn't necessarily want to boot the virtual machine.

TIP

ProDiscover

The ProDiscover forensic analysis application, from Technology Pathways, LLC, includes functionality for creating VMWare .vmdk files (similar to LiveView). This functionality is included in the Basic Edition (BE), a freely available version of the application. After you've installed ProDiscover BE, open the application, and under the Tools menu option choose "Image Conversion Tools" and then "VMWare Support for "DD" Images..." (see Figure 3.9).

FIGURE 3.9

Selecting "VMWare Support for "DD" Images" in ProDiscover BE.

FIGURE 3.10

ProDiscover BE "VMWare Support for 'DD' Images" dialog.

When the resulting dialog opens, browse for and select the raw/dd image file you're interested in (remember, we're going to use the one named "system.001"), as illustrated in Figure 3.10, and click "OK."

You won't see any progress bar or notification, but a .vmdk file pointing to the raw/dd image file will be created. You can then add the .vmdk file to an existing VM as a hard disk.

Next, launch VMPlayer and select your VM, but do not start it; instead, edit the VM settings to add the newly created .vmdk file to the VM as an additional disk.

WARNING

Nonpersistent Disk

In the following section, we'll be adding an independent, nonpersistent disk to an existing virtual machine via VMWare Workstation. The option to add a new hard disk that is nonpersistent is *not* available in VMPlayer, at least not at the time of this writing. As such, if you choose to use this method to access VSCs, you need to be sure to use a working copy of your image, or use other mechanisms to ensure that the image itself isn't modified.

When the Add Hardware Wizard opens and allows you to select a disk, choose "Use an existing virtual disk" and click "Next," as illustrated in Figure 3.11 (note that the dialog box looks the same for both VMPlayer and VMWare Workstation).

In the "Select an Existing Disk" dialog, browse to the newly created .vmdk file (in our example, "system.vmdk") and click "Finish." At this point, if you get a message from VMPlayer (or Workstation) about converting the virtual disk format to a newer format, simply choose to keep the existing format. After you've added the new hard disk to the VM, boot it, log in, and open Windows Explorer to see the file system for the added disk. From here, you can view and access the VSCs using the same process we discussed earlier in the chapter.

FIGURE 3.11

VMWare Workstation "Select a Disk" dialog.

FIGURE 3.12

Adding an independent, nonpersistent disk.

If you're using VMWare Workstation, when you get to the "Select an Existing Disk" dialog, you will be presented with some additional options, as illustrated in Figure 3.12.

When adding the new .vmdk file as a hard disk to your VM, go to the Mode section of the dialog and select "Independent" and then "Nonpersistent." This will help ensure that any changes made to the image file as a result of your analysis (or by the operating system) are not written to the image. This is simply an additional step you should take as part of sound analysis practices; you should already be working with a copy of your image, not the original image.

TIP

VMDKs and SIFT

I mentioned in Chapter 1 that I had used the SANS SIFT v2.0 Workstation VM that Rob Lee put together. I was working out the kinks in some ideas that I had and was going to try to access a raw/dd image of a Windows XP system, but this specific experiment required that I access the image as a .vmdk file. In short, I found that LiveView did a much better job of creating the necessary VMWare files for use with the SIFT Workstation than did ProDiscover BE. When I added the .vmdk file created via ProDiscover BE as an additional hard drive to the SIFT VM and ran the *fdisk* command, I got some very odd output. However, when I did the same thing using the same image file, but using the VMWare files created through LiveView, everything worked just fine.

Automating VSC Access

As we've discussed, once you've attached an image to your analysis system using either the VHD or VMWare method, you'll be able to access the available VSCs.

One way to collect information from available VSCs is to image the entire VSC. So, you have an image attached to your analysis workstation, and you can image an available VSC from the attached volume, using George M. Garner, Jr.'s Forensic Acquisition Utilities (*http://gmgsystemsinc.com/fau/*). Download the archive and be sure to the use the appropriate version (32- or 64-bit) for your platform. You can then use the appropriate version of "dd.exe" to create a logical image of a VSC using the following command (substituting for the appropriate VSC number, of course):

```
C:\tools>dd.exe if=\\.\HarddiskVolumeShadowCopy20 of=D:\vsc20.img
  -localwrt
```

One thing to consider about this method is that you will likely need a considerable amount of storage space. For a 70-GB volume, if there are nine VSCs, you will need a total of 700-GB space: 70 GB for the original volume, and another 70 GB for each of the VSCs. This method for acquiring data from VSCs is resource-intensive, but there may be times when it is absolutely necessary.

When it comes to accessing and collecting information from the VSCs, you can also use the Windows native batch file functionality to automate a great deal of your data collection. Automation in this manner not only increases efficiency and reduces the chance of errors (e.g., typing the wrong command, or commands in the wrong sequence), but it's self-documenting, as well; simply keep a copy of the batch file (and any output) as your documentation. While we're discussing accessing VSCs within acquired images, you will see you can also use these same automation techniques to access VSCs on live remote systems, as discussed earlier in this chapter. Doing so will help you mitigate issues with the oldest VSCs being deleted through the normal function of the system while you're accessing it, as a batch file will run much quicker than typing all of the commands manually.

As we've discussed, once you've run the *vssadmin* command, you should see a list of the available VSCs in the output. You will see the list in the command prompt, or you can redirect the output of the command to a file and view the list that way. So let's say that you have four VSCs, listed as HarddiskVolumeShadowCopy20 through 23, and you'd like to run the same series of commands on each of these VSCs, in succession. You can do this using batch files, which is a capability native to Windows systems. For example, we can use the following command in a batch file (call it "vsc_sweep.bat" or something that you'd find meaningful) as the initial command that handles creating a symbolic link to each VSC:

```
for /l %i in (20,1,23) do mklink /d C:\vsc\vsc%i \\?\GLOBALROOT\
    Device\HarddiskVolumeShadowCopy%i\
```

Once this command has completed, you should have four symbolic links created, C:\vsc\vsc20 through vsc23. At this point you can run through the directories, running whichever commands you choose.

On April 13, 2010, a post to the Forensics from the Sausage Factory blog (*http://forensicsfromthesausagefactory.blogspot.com*) illustrated a command for using "robocopy.exe" to retrieve copies of specific files from the VSCs. That command, modified to work along with the previous command, looks as follows:

```
for %i in (20,1,23) do robocopyC:\vsc\vsc%i\Users C:\vsc_output\
    vsc%i *.jpg *.txt /S /COPY:DAT /XJ /w:0 /r:0 /LOG: C:\vsc_output\
    Robocopy_log_SC%i.txt
```

This command copies (via "robocopy.exe") all of the files that end with .jpg and .txt extensions from the user profiles within the VSCs to a specific directory on the analysis computer, and logs the activity. As such, a copy of "robocopy.exe" must be located in the same directory as the batch file, and you should make sure that the "C:\vsc_output" directory exists before running the commands.

After you're done accessing the VSCs, you can remove the symbolic links using the following command:

```
for /l %i in (20,1,23) do rmdir C:\vsc\vsc%i
```

In April 2011, Corey Harrell (author of the Journey into IR blog at *http://journeyintoir.blogspot.com*) contacted me with the interesting idea of running RegRipper (more specifically, "rip.exe") against successive VSCs to collect specific information. Using "&&" to append commands together in a single line in a batch file, Corey's idea was to collect information (Corey's original submission made use of the "recentdocs.pl" RegRipper plugin) from a specific user's NTUSER.DAT hive file. The specific command (modified for use in this example) that Corey had put together was as follows:

```
for /l %i in (20,1,23) do (echo ----------------------
--------------- >> output-file.txt && echo Processing
HarddiskVolumeShadowCopy%i>> output-file.txt && C:\tools\
rip.exe -r c:\vsc\vsc%i\Users\user-profile\NTUSER.dat -p
userassist2>>userassist.txt)
```

The batch file and various commands that we've discussed here are just a few simple examples of what you can do using batch file functionality that is native to Windows systems.

TIP

Batch Files

There are a number of very useful resources available online that provide references for batch file commands, such as *http://www.computerhope.com/batch.htm* and *http://ss64 .com/nt/*. You can also find tutorials, such as *http://commandwindows.com/batch.htm*, that will assist you in writing batch files.

Corey also created a more comprehensive and functional batch file, which he graciously consented to allow me to include in the additional materials associated with this book. The batch file is named "rip-vsc.txt" and can be found in the "ch3" directory in the associated materials (found at *http://code.google.com/p/winforensicaanalysis/ downloads/list*). Corey spent some time in documenting and explaining the use of the batch file, by adding comments (lines that begin with "REM") to the file.

Internet Evidence Finder version 4 (IEF4; *http://www.jadsoftware.com/go/?page_ id=141*) is a software application that can search files or hard drives for indications of a wide range of Internet-related artifacts, including Facebook, MySpace, mIRC, and Google chat, web-based emails, etc. The web page for IEF4 states that the application can also be used to search mounted VSCs.

ProDiscover

On March 3, 2011, Christopher Brown released version 6.9.0.0 of ProDiscover (all versions, including the Basic Edition). I've had a license for ProDiscover Incident Response Edition (IR) since version 3, for which I'm very grateful to Chris. Over the years, I've had the privilege of watching the evolution of this product, and used it to analyze a number of images. The latest update (as of this writing) provides access to VSCs, which (as we've discussed) can be extremely valuable to the examiner. I should note that in September 2011, Christopher released version 7.0.0.3 of ProDiscover.

FIGURE 3.13

ProDiscover "Mount Shadow Volume..." functionality.

FIGURE 3.14

ProDiscover "Mount Shadow Volume..." dialog.

To demonstrate accessing VSCs via ProDiscover IR, I have the application installed on a Windows XP SP3 system, and I have an image of a hard drive from a Dell laptop running Vista. First, I opened ProDiscover and created a new project, and then added the image of the hard drive to the project. Once the image was added (and I saved the project file), I clicked on the image file listing in the Content View to see the context menu, illustrated in Figure 3.13.

Then, I clicked on "Mount Shadow Volume..." in the context menu and saw the "Mount Shadow Volume..." dialog box illustrated in Figure 3.14.

As you can see in Figure 3.14, the mounted image has four partitions available, which, for those familiar with systems from Dell, is fairly common for default installations (when I purchase Dell systems for myself, the first thing I do is completely reinstall the operating system), as they include, at the minimum, a Dell maintenance partition. Once the "Mount Shadow Volume..." functionality was selected, ProDiscover located the volume where the VSCs reside (in this case, E:\) and populated a dropdown list with the available VSCs. There are a total of seven VSCs available, and as we progress through the VSCs in the dropdown list, the "Created date & time" will change to reflect the correct date and time for the selected VSC. Finally,

FIGURE 3.15

VSC mounted in ProDiscover.

whichever VSC was selected will be added to the Content View display as the G:\ volume (note that C:\ through F:\ are already populated).

When I clicked "OK," the selected VSC was mounted as the G:\ volume within the ProDiscover Content View interface. I then clicked on the volume letter, and the files were populated within the volume, as illustrated in Figure 3.15.

At this point, there's a great deal I can do with the available data in the VSCs. For example, I can navigate to the Users folder and select files to be copied out of the project for deeper examination, run ProScripts, etc. It all happened within the blink of an eye, right there while I was sitting in front of my analysis system. Along with the other functionalities inherent to ProDiscover (e.g., parsing Vista and Windows 7 Recycle Bin files, locating and parsing email archives, etc.), being able to mount and access the VSCs puts a whole new level of capabilities in the hands of the analyst.

TIP

Other Image File Formats

Throughout this chapter so far we've discussed accessing VSCs with raw/dd image files. As such, I'm sure that at some point someone's going to ask, "But I have an EnCase .EOx image file, and it's compressed—what do I do?" or "I have a snapshot of a VMWare virtual machine/.vmdk file—how can I use the VHD method?" Those questions are easy to answer. For the expert witness format (EWF) images (such as acquired via EnCase), you can open the image in FTK Imager and reacquire it to raw/dd format, making yourself a working copy of the image file. You can do the same thing with the .vmdk file and then use "vhdtool.exe" to prepare the image for mounting, or search for tools to convert the .vmdk file to .vhd file format.

SUMMARY

While VSCs may initially be somewhat mysterious to many analysts, they do provide a very valuable resource with respect to historical data. VSCs can be accessed via a number of methods, depending on how you're accessing them (i.e., on a live system or within an acquired image).

Keep in mind, however, that accessing VSCs on live systems can be a bit tricky, in that you have to move quickly and decisively, as VSCs are subject to the FIFO cycle—you may be attempting to gather information from a VSC that gets deleted during that process.

Finally, remember to be extremely careful with respect to how you access files within VSCs, both on live systems and within acquired images, as double-clicking the wrong file can lead to your analysis system being infected or compromised.

Reference

Carvey, H. (2011). *Windows registry forensics*. Burlington, MA: Syngress Publishing, Inc.

File Analysis

INFORMATION IN THIS CHAPTER

- MFT
- Event Logs
- Recycle Bin
- Prefetch Files
- Scheduled Tasks
- Jump Lists
- Hibernation Files
- Application Files

INTRODUCTION

As with any computer system, Windows systems contain a great number of files, many of which are not simply a standard ASCII text format. Many of these files may not have any relevance to the analysis at all, and only a few may provide critical information to the analyst. There also may be a number of files that are unknown to the analyst, and due to their format, may not provide keyword search hits. These files can often provide an analyst with a great deal of insight into their examination, if they know that the files exist and how to analyze them.

The purpose of this chapter is not to reiterate analysis techniques that have been discussed in detail in other resources. Instead, I'd like to discuss the existence of several files, as well as analysis techniques that may be of value with respect to these files, that haven't been widely discussed in other venues.

As I mentioned, Windows systems contain a number of files of various formats. These files can also contain data consisting of or embedded in various structures, some of which are well documented, while others have been discovered through analysis. Many analysts start their examinations by running keyword searches to identify likely sources of information, but there are a number of files that may provide critical information related to these keywords even though they don't return any search hits.

Many times, the structure where the data exist within a file adds relevance or provides context to that data. For example, during a data breach investigation, I got several hits for potential credit card numbers within a Registry hive file (Registry analysis is discussed in detail in Chapter 5). Further analysis indicated that the numbers were not key names, nor were they value names or data. Instead, they were located within unallocated space within the hive file. It turned out that the numbers detected in the search had been in sectors on the disk that had previously been part of another file, which had been deleted. As such, the sectors had been marked as available for use, and several of those sectors had been incorporated into the hive file as it grew in size.

What this demonstrates is that analysis must (and can) go beyond simply running a search, and it's critical that it actually does, to answer some very important questions. For example, consider the finding I just discussed: Would "I found credit card numbers in the Registry" really provide any value to the customer? Or would it be more important to develop an understanding of where those credit card numbers were found and how they got there? Understanding the structures of various files, and the value that understanding can provide, will be the focus of this chapter.

MFT

Within the NTFS file system, the master file table (MFT) serves as the master list of files and contains metadata regarding every file object on the system, including files, directories, and metafiles. These metadata can be extremely valuable during an examination, particularly if you suspect that file metadata have been manipulated in an effort to hide or mask activities (commonly referred to as "anti-forensics").

This chapter will not be a comprehensive treatise covering the complete structure of the MFT. Rather, we will focus on specific data structures (or "attributes") that can be extracted from MFT entries, and limit our discussion to a brief description of MFT entries and two specific attributes. Further, while we will be discussing various tools that you can use to parse the MFT, we won't be doing so to the depth that you would expect to be able to write your own such tools from scratch. Perhaps the best source for additional, detailed information regarding the MFT, the structure of MFT entry attributes, and the forensic analysis of file systems in general is Brian Carrier's book, *File System Forensic Analysis* (Carrier, 2005).

Each file and directory (folder) on a Windows system has a record in the MFT. Each record is 1024 bytes in length. As NTFS views each file as a set of attributes, the file's MFT record contains some number of attributes that hold metadata about the file or, in some cases, the file data (content) themselves. The first 42 bytes of each record comprise the File Record Header, which provides information such as the link count (how many directories have entries for this file, which helps determine the number of hard links for the file); whether the record is for a file or directory; whether the file or directory is in use or deleted; and the allocated and used size of the file.

All file and directory records will have a $STANDARD_INFORMATION attribute ($SIA), which is 72 bytes in length (for Windows 2000 and later systems) and contains (among other things) a set of time stamps. These time stamps are 64-bit FILETIME objects, as defined by Microsoft, which represent the number of 100-nanosecond intervals since January 1, 1601. These time stamps are what we most often "see" when interacting with the system (via the command prompt when using the *dir* command, or via the Windows Explorer shell), and are written into the MFT record in UTC format on NTFS systems. This means that when we see these time stamps through Windows Explorer (or via the *dir* command at the command prompt), they are translated for display to the user in accordance with the time zone information stored in the Registry for that system.

NOTE

Displaying Time Stamps in Forensic Analysis Applications

Most commercial forensic analysis applications have the ability to display file last modified, last accessed, and created (MAC) time stamps in accordance with the time zone settings on the analyst's system, although this functionality can be disabled. In the ProDiscover Incident Response Edition, that setting can be found by clicking the File menu option, and choosing the Preferences option, which opens the Preferences dialog, as illustrated in Figure 4.1.

FIGURE 4.1

ProDiscover time zone settings.

The time stamps that are stored within the $SIA attribute are the last modified time, the last accessed time, the MFT entry modified (changed) time, and the creation ("born") time, and are referred to collectively as "MACB" times, where each letter corresponds to each of the time stamps, respectively. Another way of referring to these times is "MACE" times" (for file *m*odified, file *a*ccessed, file *c*reated, and MFT *e*ntry modified); note that the last two times (MFT entry modified and file creation times) are transposed. For consistency, we will refer to these times as "MACB" times throughout the rest of this chapter. These time stamps are modified and updated during the course of normal operating system activity; for example, when a file is created, the time stamps are set to the current date and time. Whenever a change is made to the file itself (data are added, modified, or removed by the user or a service), the last modification time is updated. As we'll see in the "Last Access Time" box, modification to this time stamp is subject to a couple of conditions.

WARNING

Last Access Time

Most analysts think that when a file is opened or accessed in some other way, the last access time for that file (in the $SIA attribute in the MFT) is modified to reflect the appropriate time. However, the last accessed time for a file on the NTFS file system on the hard drive is not always current. NTFS delays writing the updated last accessed time to disk for performance reasons, although the correct time is maintained in memory. Windows will update the value on disk once the time differs from the value in memory by an hour or more (I am referencing *http://www.microsoft.com/resources/documentation/windows/xp/all/ proddocs/en-us/fsutil_behavior.mspx?mfr=true*).

In addition, there is a Registry value (*HKLM\SYSTEM\CurrentControlSet\Control\ FileSystem\NtfsDisableLastAccessUpdate*) that, when set to 1, disables updating of last access times. On Windows XP and 2003 systems, this Registry value does not normally exist in a default installation; however, the value can be added and set to 1, which is recommended to improve the performance of high-volume file servers. As of Vista (and continuing to Windows 7), this value exists and is set to 1. This does not mean, however, that the last access times on files on these systems are never updated; in fact, file creation, move, or copy can cause this time to be modified. What it affects is file accesses such as opening and viewing the file.

In addition, every file within the NTFS file system will have at least one $FILE_ NAME ($FNA) attribute in its MFT record. This attribute contains 66 bytes of file metadata, plus the filename itself. An MFT record for a file can have more than one $FNA attribute, as the file system may require that for files with long filenames, there is also a DOS 8.3 name (this can be disabled via a Registry value). This simply means that if you have a file named "This is a long file named 'file.doc,'" there will also be an $FNA attribute containing the name "this_i~1.doc," which consists of eight characters, the dot separator, and the three-character extension. As such, this file would have a $SIA and two $FNA attributes.

In addition to the filename, the metadata contained in the $FNA attribute include a reference to the parent directory (which allows tools to completely reconstruct the full path to the file), as well as four time stamps, similar to and in the same format as those within the $SIA attribute. The primary difference with the $FNA time stamps is that Windows systems do not typically update these values in the same way as those in the $SIA attribute; rather, the $FNA times correspond to the original date for when the file was created, moved, or renamed. As such, accessing the MFT, parsing the various attributes for the specific files, and noting any anomalies between the $SIA and $FNA values is a technique that analysts use to determine the likelihood of the $SIA time stamps being purposely modified in an attempt to disguise the file.

There are several free, open-source tools available that can be easily retrieved from the Internet that will allow us to extract the $SIA and $FNA attributes from the MFT. One such tool is David Kovar's Python script named "analyzeMFT.py" (*http://www.integriography.com/*). The Python script has some graphical components, so be sure to read the instructions and install the appropriate modules for your platform, or go into the script itself and change the line "noGUI = False" to "noGUI = True." If you're sticking to the Windows platform, David also provides an installer for a standalone Windows executable version of the tool. "AnalyzeMFT.py" has some useful options, one of which is that it provides for a modicum of "anomaly detection." This consists of checking for the upper 32 bits of the $SIA time stamps to see if they're all zeros, as well as checking to see if the creation date in the $FNA is after the $SIA creation date. Positive results to either of these two checks might indicate an attempt to modify time stamps to hide malicious activity. Something to keep in mind, too, is that when using anomaly detection, the comma-separated value (CSV) output of the tool consists of 53 columns (in MS Excel, A–BA).

I've also written my own "mft.pl" Perl script for parsing the time stamps (and other information) for files and directories listed in the MFT. This Perl script is included with the materials provided in association with this book, and provides a good framework from which I've been able to write other Perl scripts, with additional functionality. As you'll see later in this chapter, the script displays information from the MFT File Entry Header, as well as the $SIA and $FNA attributes in an easy-to-view format.

When analyzing the information derived from the MFT, it is important to keep in mind that other user actions (besides simply reading from or writing to a file) can have an effect on the file time stamps within the $SIA entry, as well, and several are described in Microsoft KnowledgeBase (KB) article 299648 (found at *http://support .microsoft.com/?kbid=299648*). For example, copying or moving a file between directories within an NTFS partition retains the last modification date on the file, but the copy operation will reset the creation date to the current date, whereas the move operation retains the original creation date of the file. Refer to the KB article for details, but keep in mind that when transferring files, whether or not time stamps are updated (and which time stamps are actually updated) depends on a number of factors, including whether the file is being copied or moved, and whether it is being transferred to a different location within the same drive partition, or from one partition to another.

NOTE

Testing

I have yet to find any clear, thorough documentation regarding how file time stamps are affected by all possible operations; as such, analysts should always test their hypotheses when faced with unusual conditions or situations. For example, if you suspect that a file was copied from a FAT32-formatted USB thumb drive to an NTFS partition, how would you expect the time stamps for both (the original and copied) files to appear? How about a file copied between NTFS shares? It is always a good idea to simulate the conditions of your hypothesis as best as possible and run your own tests for verification.

Not only do the aforementioned actions affect the time stamps in the $SIA attribute, but these values (within the $SIA) can be manipulated arbitrarily, as well. Essentially, if a user has write access to a file, he can modify the time stamps of that file to arbitrary values, and those modifications are written to the time stamps in the $SIA attribute (technically, per *http://msdn.microsoft.com/en-us/library/ cc781134*, these are also written to the directory entry). This is an anti-forensic technique that is often referred to as *time stomping*, named for a tool ("timestomp.exe") used to perform this function, which allowed the user of that tool to set the time stamps to arbitrary times (at the time of this writing, I was not able to find a copy of "timestomp.exe" online). Consider the effect on an investigation of finding illegal images on a system confiscated in 2011, only to find that the files had creation dates in 2014 and last access dates in 1984. Even one or two files with time stamps similar to this would be enough to cast doubt on other files. One of the drawbacks of using "timestomp.exe," however, was that the application reportedly had a resolution of 32 bits for the times, leaving the upper 32 bits of the 64-bit FILETIME object all zeros.

This would make the use of this technique relatively easy to detect; in fact, as mentioned previously in this chapter, checking for this is part of the "anomaly detection" performed by David Kovar's "analyzeMFT.py" Python script.

Another technique for modifying time stamps on files is copying the time values from another file, particularly one that was part of the original Windows installation, such as "kernel32.dll" (found in the "C:\Windows\system32" directory). This technique avoids the resolution issue faced by "timestomp.exe," does a better job of hiding the file from analysis techniques (see Chapter 7), and is easily accessible via native application programming interface (API) functions.

NOTE

Time Stomping

As I mentioned, while I was writing this chapter, I was not able to find a copy of "timestomp.exe"; however, using Perl, I can easily modify file time stamps by copying time stamps from another file on the system. After installing ActiveState's ActivePerl, I then installed the Win32API::File::Time Perl module using the following command:

```
C:\Perl>ppm install win32api-file-time
```

Once the module was installed, I could use this module to access two specific native Windows API functions, using the following lines of code (excerpted from the Perl script):

```
my ($atime, $mtime, $ctime) = GetFileTime ($file);
SetFileTime ($file2, $atime, $mtime, $ctime);
```

To demonstrate this functionality, I added a couple of checks for file time stamps using the Perl *stat()* function to the script, ran it against file ("C:\temp\test.txt"), copying the time stamps from "kernel32.dll." The output of the script appeared as follows:

```
C:\Windows\system32\kernel32.dll
Creation Time: Tue Feb 28 08:00:00 2006
Last Access : Mon May 30 21:14:22 2011
Last Write : Sat Mar 21 10:06:58 2009

C:\Temp\test.txt
Creation Time: Mon May 30 17:36:12 2011
Last Access : Mon May 30 17:36:12 2011
Last Write : Mon May 30 17:36:12 2011

C:\Temp\test.txt
Creation Time: Tue Feb 28 08:00:00 2006
Last Access : Mon May 30 21:14:22 2011
Last Write : Sat Mar 21 10:06:58 2009
```

The script first displays the output of the Perl *stat()* function for the file "kernel32.dll" (all times are displayed in local system time, and my system is set to Eastern Standard Time with daylight savings), as well as the current settings for the target file, "test.txt." After changing the time stamps on the target file, it then displays the new time values. As you can see, the last accessed time for "kernel32.dll" was modified when the script was run (the Perl script was run on a Windows XP SP3 system), and the time stamps on the "test.txt" file were modified in accordance with the time stamps copied from "kernel32.dll."

To verify this information, I extracted the MFT from the system (using FTK Imager) and extracted the information using "mft.pl"; the information for the "test.txt" file appears as follows (times are displayed in UTC or "Zulu" format):

```
70319 FILE Seq: 15 Link: 1 0x38 3 Flags: 1
0x0010 96 0 0x0000 0x0000
M: Sat Mar 21 14:06:57 2009 Z
A: Tue May 31 01:14:22 2011 Z
C: Tue May 31 01:14:23 2011 Z
B: Tue Feb 28 11:59:59 2006 Z
0x0030 112 0 0x0000 0x0000
FN: test.txt Parent Ref: 67947 Parent Seq: 49
M: Mon May 30 21:36:12 2011 Z
A: Mon May 30 21:36:12 2011 Z
C: Mon May 30 21:36:12 2011 Z
B: Mon May 30 21:36:12 2011 Z
0x0080 48 0 0x0000 0x0018
```

The first set of MACB time stamps were extracted from the $SIA attribute, and the second set were extracted from the $FNA attribute. As you can see, the time stamps extracted from the $SIA attribute reflect what was seen using the Perl *stat()* function (taking the time zone settings into account), while the time stamps from the $FNA attribute reflect the original times.

Extracting the $SIA and $FNA time stamps for comparison and analysis is only one example of how understanding the MFT can be beneficial to an analyst. Understanding additional elements of the MFT, as well as the structure of each individual MFT record, can provide additional details with respect to the status of various files.

File System Tunneling

Another aspect of Windows file systems that can affect the time stamps that you observe during your analysis (and isn't often discussed) is *file system tunneling*. This process applies to both file allocation table (FAT) and new technology file system (NTFS) file systems and is described in Microsoft KB article 172190 (found at *http://support.microsoft.com/kb/172190*). File system tunneling refers to the fact that within a specific time period (the default is 15 seconds) after a file is deleted, file table records (FAT or MFT) will be reused for files of the same name. In short, if you have a file named "myfile.txt" that is deleted or renamed, and a new file of the same name is created shortly after the deletion or rename operation, then the file table record is reused, and the original file's creation date is retained. According to KB article 172190, this "tunneling" functionality is meant to maintain backward compatibility with older 16-bit Windows applications that perform "safe save" operations.

To demonstrate file system tunneling, I created a text file named "test3.txt" on my Windows XP SP3 system that is 31 bytes in size, and waited a few days. Using the Perl *stat( )* function, the $SIA time stamps appear as follows, in UTC format:

```
c:\temp\test3.txt 31 bytes
Creation Time: Mon May 30 21:41:48 2011 UTC
Last Access : Mon May 30 21:41:48 2011 UTC
Last Write : Mon May 30 21:41:48 2011 UTC
```

I then deleted "test3.txt," and immediately (within 15 seconds) recreated the file using the *echo* command (i.e., *echo "A tunnel test" > test3.txt*) at the command prompt. The new version of "test3.txt" is 18 bytes in size, and the time stamps appear as follows (again, in UTC format):

```
c:\temp\test3.txt 18 bytes
Creation Time: Mon May 30 21:41:48 2011 UTC
Last Access : Fri Jun 3 20:39:18 2011 UTC
Last Write : Fri Jun 3 20:39:18 2011 UTC
```

As you can see, the creation date of the new file remains the same as the original "test3.txt," even though the new file was "created" on June 3, 2011. Using FTK Imager, I then exported the MFT and parsed it with the "mft.pl" Perl script; the $SIA and $FNA information for the "test3.txt" file appears as follows:

```
39630 FILE Seq: 60 Link: 1 0x38 3 Flags: 1
0x0010 96 0 0x0000 0x0000
 M: Fri Jun 3 20:39:18 2011 Z
 A: Fri Jun 3 20:39:18 2011 Z
 C: Fri Jun 3 20:39:18 2011 Z
 B: Mon May 30 21:41:48 2011 Z
0x0030 112 0 0x0000 0x0000
 FN: test3.txt Parent Ref: 67947 Parent Seq: 49
 M: Fri Jun 3 20:39:18 2011 Z
 A: Fri Jun 3 20:39:18 2011 Z
 C: Fri Jun 3 20:39:18 2011 Z
 B: Mon May 30 21:41:48 2011 Z
```

As you can see from the previous excerpt from the MFT, the "born" or creation dates in both the $SIA and $FNA attributes remain the same as the original file, but all other time stamps are updated to the current date and time, with respect to the file creation. Remember, all I did was create the file (from the command line); I didn't access (open) or modify the file in any way after creating it.

More than anything else, I've found the information discussed thus far to be very useful in establishing when files were really created on a compromised system. By comparing the creation dates from the $SIA and $FNA attributes for suspicious files, I've often found clear indications of attempts to hide the existence of those files from detection and closer inspection. This will become a bit clearer when we discuss timeline analysis in Chapter 7.

> **NOTE**
>
> **NTFS $130 Index Attributes**
>
> On September 26, 2011, Chad Tilbury, a SANS instructor, posted an entry to his blog titled "NTFS $130 Index Attributes" (found at *http://forensicmethods.com/ntfs-index-attribute*, and had originally been posted to the SANS Forensic blog). Chad does an excellent job of describing the index attributes, how they can be used to identify the names of deleted files, and how they can be parsed. Many times during incidents malware files may be deleted, often through actions taken by an intruder or inadvertently by an administrator or responder. Index attributes may provide indications of the deleted files, including time stamps associated with those files; as Chad points out, the time stamps are similar to those found in the $FILE_NAME attribute of an MFT record. Chad also demonstrates the use of Willi Ballenthin's "indxparse.py" Python script for parsing index attributes. Willi's discussion of the "indxparse.py" script can be found at *http://www.williballenthin.com/forensics/indx/index.html*.

EVENT LOGS

Windows systems are capable of recording a number of different events in the Event Log, depending on the audit configuration (we will discuss in Chapter 5 how to determine the audit configuration). The Event Log files on Windows 2000, XP, and 2003 systems are made up of event records that are stored in a well-documented binary format (found at *http://msdn.microsoft.com/en-us/library/aa363646(v=VS.85).aspx*). Part of this format includes a "magic number" that is unique to individual event records (including the header record, which contains information about the Event Log file itself), as illustrated in Figure 4.2.

As illustrated in Figure 4.2, the "LfLe" "magic number" can be used to identify event records within the Event Log file. The 4 bytes immediately prior to the event record (0xE0 in Figure 4.2) tell us the size of the event record in bytes. This information is not only useful in parsing through the Event Log file on a binary level,

FIGURE 4.2

Partial Windows XP event record format.

extracting each record in turn (and writing tools to help us do this), but it can also be used to extract event records from relatively unstructured data, such as unallocated space (or the page file), which will be described later in this section.

Many analysts have discovered that when extracting Event Log files from an acquired image and opening them in the Event Viewer on the their analysis system, they will often encounter a message stating that the Event Log is "corrupt." This is usually not due to the Event Log files actually being corrupted, but instead is often due to the fact that some message dynamic linked library (DLL) files may not be available on the analysis system. As such, I've written several tools to assist me with collecting information pertinent to my analysis from Event Log files. The first is the Perl script "evtrpt.pl," which collects information about the event records, such as the frequency of events based on event sources and identifiers (IDs), an excerpt of which, from an Application Event Log, appears as follows:

```
Source                  Event ID     Count
-------                 ----------   ------
SecurityCenter          1800         2
SecurityCenter          1807         192
Symantec AntiVirus      12           17
Symantec AntiVirus      14           17
Symantec AntiVirus      16           12
Symantec AntiVirus      53           3
```

This information is a quick way to determine the type and number of the various event records within the Event Log, based on event sources and IDs. This is a great way of providing an overview of the Event Log content, and whether or not I can expect to find any records of value to my analysis. Having this information available has let me see some things very quickly. For example, if I'm working a malware issue and see that there are several event records with the source "Symantec AntiVirus," I know that the system had the application installed at one point, and that can help guide my analysis. In particular, if I opt (as part of my malware detection process, something we will discuss in Chapter 6) to mount the image as a volume and scan it with an AV product, I know not to use the product that was installed on the system. Similarly, while I most often start my analysis of the Event Logs by looking at what is actually being audited via the audit policy, there have been times when, although logins are being audited, the system has been running for so long that no one has needed to log into it. As such, I have found Security Event Logs with no login events available in the visible event records.

"Evtrpt.pl" also provides the date range of all of the event records within the file, as follows:

```
Date Range (UTC)
Thu Jan 18 12:41:04 2007 to Thu Feb 7 13:39:25 2008
```

The date range information can be very useful, as well. There have been times when I've been asked to provide information regarding which user was logged into the system on a certain date or within a specific timeframe. Evtrpt.pl provides me with a quick view into whether or not digging deeper into the Event Logs is of value, or perhaps I should decrease the priority of the logs as a source of information and focus my analysis on more profitable targets.

NOTE

AV Logs

Most antivirus (AV) products produce some sort of logs; many produce text-based logs that are easy to view and parse, particularly if you load them into Excel. Many AV products will also write their logs to the Application Event Log, but for some, this can also be a configurable option. I have analyzed systems on which I have easily located the AV application logs, but have not seen any corresponding entries in the Application Event Log.

Another tool that I like to use for parsing Event Log records is the Perl script "evtparse.pl." This Perl script reads through the Event Log files on a binary level, locating and parsing the records without using any of the native Windows API functions. This has a couple of benefits; one is that you don't have to worry about the Event Log file being deemed "corrupted," as will sometimes occur when using tools (such as the Windows Event Viewer) that rely on native Windows application programming interface (API) functions. The other is that the Perl script is platform-independent; it can be used on Windows, Linux, and even Mac OS X. The script is capable of parsing event records into either CSV format, suitable for opening Excel, or into a format suitable for timeline analysis (which will be discussed in greater detail in Chapter 7).

Parsing the values is only half the battle, though. There are a number of resources available that provide information and details regarding what the various event records, either individually or correlated together, can mean. One of my favorite resources is the EventID web site (*http://www.eventid.net*). The $24 annual registration fee is well worth the expense, as I can log into the site and run searches to not only get additional information about Microsoft-specific events, but also see information with respect to issues that others (mostly system administrators) have observed or encountered, as well as links to pertinent Microsoft KB articles. All of this can be very revealing, even if it only provides me with additional leads or places to look. Application-specific event records are usually best researched at the vendor's web site, as blogs and forum posts can provide a great deal of information about various events generated by these applications.

Another resource for finding information about Security Event Log entries is the Ultimate Windows Security Event Log site (*http://www.ultimatewindowssecurity .com/securitylog/encyclopedia/default.aspx*). This site provides an easily searched list of Security Event Log entries, with some explanations to provide context. The site provides information regarding Security Event Log entries for Windows XP and 2003 systems, as well as corresponding entries for Vista and Windows 2008 systems.

> **TIP**
>
> Event Log Analysis
>
> When conducting analysis on a Windows system, I don't have specific event records that I search for every time; rather, what I look for depends heavily on the goals of the examination and the system's audit configuration. While many of the systems I've analyzed have had fairly default configurations (minimal changes, if at all, beyond the default, out-of-the-box settings), I have found great value in those systems where settings had been modified, to include the Event Log size being increased. I once had the opportunity to analyze a Windows XP system on which not only were both successful and failed logon events being recorded, but Process Tracking was also enabled. When analyzing this system, I created a timeline (discussed in detail in Chapter 7) of system activity, and the additional detail provided by the Event Log configuration was invaluable.

The Event Logs themselves are not always the sole source of event records on a system. Event Log records, like other data, may be found within the pagefile or within unallocated space. I was once asked to analyze a system from which very few event records were found in the Event Logs and the Security Event Log had an event ID 517 record, indicating that the Event Log had been cleared. As such, one of the steps in my analysis was to attempt to recover deleted event records. My first step was to use the Sleuthkit (*http://www.sleuthkit.org/*) tool "blkls.exe" to extract all of the unallocated space from the acquired image into a separate file. I then loaded that file into BinText (*http://www.mcafee.com/us/downloads/free-tools/bintext.aspx*) and saved the list of strings located within the file. I then wrote a Perl script to go through the list of strings and locate all those that contained the event record "magic number" (i.e., "LfLe"); when BinText reports the strings that it locates, it also provides the offset within the file where that string is located ("strings.exe," available from Microsoft, will do the same thing if you add the "-o" switch to the command line—the utility can be downloaded from *http://technet.microsoft.com/en-us/sysinternals/bb897439*).

For every string that BinText located that began with "LfLe," the Perl script would go to the offset within the file containing the unallocated space, "back up" 4 bytes (a "DWORD"), and read the size value. As the event record structure begins and ends with this 4-byte size value, the script would then read the total number of bytes, and if the first and last DWORDs in the sequence were the same, the event record was assumed to be valid, extracted, and parsed. Using this technique, I was able to recover over 330 deleted event records. Another way to do this would be to simply have a slightly modified version of either the "evtrpt.pl" or "evtparse.pl" script parse through unallocated space 4 bytes at a time, looking for the event record "magic number," and then processing each event found to be a valid record. However you go about doing this, it can be a very valuable technique, particularly if you're trying to construct a timeline, as discussed in Chapter 7. The point of this is to illustrate how understanding the various data structures on Windows systems can lead to the recovery of additional data that may significantly affect your overall analysis.

> **TIP**
>
> Interesting Artifacts
>
> While I do not have a list of specific event IDs that I look for during every analysis engagement, there are some records of interest that I do look out for when required by the goals of the engagement. As mentioned previously in the chapter, a Security Event Log entry with event ID 517 indicates that the Event Log was cleared. Further, on most systems, some Windows services being started will result in an event with the "Service Control Manager" source and an ID of 7035 being generated by the system shortly after the system is booted. As such, services started by a user hours or days after the system was last started may indicate normal system administration activity, or provide indications of a compromise, such as an intrusion or malware being installed. Further, a number of organizations may use tools such as "psexec.exe" (*http://technet.microsoft.com/en-us/sysinternals/bb897553*) to access and remotely manage systems; however, intruders will sometimes use "psexec.exe" or similar tools (such as "rcmd.exe," the remote command utility available from Microsoft) to remotely access systems. The use of such tools usually results in a service being started in the context of the user account used to launch the tool, and is preceded by a network logon (security event ID 540, type 3).

Windows Event Log

With Vista, Microsoft modified a great deal about how events are recorded, as well as the types of events recorded, the location where the events are recorded, and the structure of those recorded events. This new mechanism is referred to as the "Windows Event Log," rather than just "Event Log" as seen on Windows XP and 2003 systems. On Vista through Windows 7 systems, the Windows Event Logs are stored in the "C:\Windows\system32\winevt\Logs" folder (by default), and are stored in a binary extensible markup language (XML) format.

On a system with a default installation of Windows 7 and only MS Office 2007 installed, I found 134 different .evtx files in the "winevt\Logs" directory. There are two types of Windows Event Logs: Windows logs and Application and Services logs. Figure 4.3 illustrates these logs, visible via the Event Viewer.

You can see a number of the Event Logs that you'd expect to see on a Windows system in Figure 4.3. For example, there are the Application, System, and Security Event Logs, which correspond to "appevent.evt," "sysevent.evt," and "secevent.evt," respectively, on Windows XP/2003 systems. The Security Event Log records many of the same events as you may be used to seeing on Windows XP systems, including logons and logoffs (depending on the audit configuration, of course). However, there is a difference—many of the event IDs you would be interested in are different for the same event. For example, on Windows XP, an event ID of 528 would indicate a logon; for Windows 7, that same event would have an event ID of 4624. The difference between these two event IDs is 4096; this holds true for a number of Security events. The Ultimate Windows Security site has a fairly exhaustive listing of both Windows XP and Windows 7 Security Event Log records that you might expect to see, which can be found at *http://www.ultimatewindowssecurity.com/securitylog/encyclopedia/default.aspx*.

You will also see the Setup and Forwarded Event Logs in Figure 4.3. According to Microsoft, the Setup log contains events related to application setup; however,

FIGURE 4.3

Windows 7 Event Logs (via Event Viewer).

reviewing the various entries on a live system reveals that the statuses of Windows Updates are also recorded in this log. The Forwarded Event Log is intended to store events forwarded from other systems.

The remaining logs are Applications and Services logs and store events for a single application or component, rather than events that would affect the entire system. These logs have four subtypes: Operational, Admin, Analytic, and Debug. By default, on a normal Windows 7 system, you're likely to see Operational and Admin logs, although now and again you'll see Analytic logs. Admin events are targeted at end users and system administrators, and provide information that an administrator may use to fix an issue or take some other action. Operational logs are generally used to diagnose an issue. For example, the Microsoft-Windows-WLAN-AutoConfig/ Operational log provides information about wireless networks that the system has associated with, and through which network adapter, as illustrated in Figure 4.4. Events such as this can be instrumental not just in diagnosing problems, but can also provide clues to examiners during an investigation.

The Debug and Analytic logs are intended for developers and used to diagnose problems that cannot be handled through user intervention.

TIP

VHDs and VMs

I've done a bit of testing of virtual hard drives (VHDs) while writing this book (see Chapter 3), mounting and removing them from my Windows 7 system. As such, the Microsoft-Windows-VHDMP/Operational.evtx log has a number of events visible that are associated with the "surfacing" (mounting) of VHD files (event ID 1) and "unsurfacing" (removing) of those files (event ID 2). However, this log applies only to the mounting and removal of VHD files. The Microsoft-Windows-Virtual PC/Admin log maintains records of the use of Virtual PC to create and start virtual systems or machines (VMs), including "XP Mode," a version of Windows XP available to maintain compatibility with applications that may not run well (or at all) on Windows 7. This log also maintains information about applications installed in XP mode, but launched from Windows 7. Both of these may provide valuable information during exams, particularly when you're looking for files that may not be in the Windows 7 file system, but may have been accessed from a VHD or VM.

FIGURE 4.4

Event from the WLAN-AutoConfig/Operational log.

All this aside, what are some of the ways to get at the data within the Windows Event Logs? One means for parsing Windows Event Logs that I've found to be very effective is to install Microsoft's free Logparser tool (*http://www.microsoft.com/download/en/details.aspx?displaylang=en&id=24659*) on a Windows 7 analysis system, and then either extract the Windows Event Log files from the acquired image, or mount the acquired image as a volume. From there, I then use the following command to extract all of the event records from each log:

```
logparser -i:evt -o:csv "SELECT * FROM D:\Case\System.evtx" >
   output.csv
```

When using this command, it's important to remember that Logparser relies on the APIs (available via DLLs) on the analysis system. As such, you won't be able to use it to parse Vista or Windows 7 Event Logs if you're running Windows XP on your analysis system, as the Event Log APIs on Windows XP aren't compatible with the Vista/Windows 7 Windows Event Log format. Similarly, you can't use Logparser to parse Windows XP or 2003 logs on a Vista/7 analysis system. Sending the output of the Logparser command to CSV format allows for easy viewing and analysis via Excel, in addition to providing additional columns for you to add references or your own notes. The format also allows for easy parsing, as we will see in Chapter 7.

TIP

Converting Event Logs

While attempting to use Logparser running on a Windows 7 system to parse Windows XP Event Logs won't result in anything useful, you can use "wevtutil.exe" (native to Windows 7) to convert the XP Event Logs to Windows 7 Event Log format, using a command line similar to the following:

```
D:\tools>wevtutil epl appevent.evt appevent.evtx /lf:true
```

Andreas Schuster, whose blog can be found at *http://computer.forensikblog.de/en/*, has put a good deal of effort into deciphering and decoding the Windows Event Log format, and creating a Perl-based library and tools collection for parsing the events from a log. As of this writing, the version of his library is 1.08. You can download and install Andreas' library, or you can use tools that have the library and tools already installed, such as the SANS Investigative Forensic Toolkit (SIFT) Workstation that Rob Lee developed. SIFT version 2.1 was available at *http://computer-forensics.sans.org/community/downloads* when this chapter was being written.

RECYCLE BIN

Windows systems have a great deal of event recovery built into them. Microsoft understands that users make mistakes, or may delete a file that they later wish they hadn't. As such, the Windows Recycle Bin acts as a repository for files deleted by the user through normal means, such as hitting the Delete key or right-clicking the file and selecting "Delete" from the context menu (files deleted from remote shares or from the command line are not sent to the Recycle Bin).

TIP

Bypassing the Recycle Bin

According to *http://support.microsoft.com/kb/320031*, the Recycle Bin can be bypassed by right-clicking on the Recycle Bin, choosing "Properties," and checking the "Do not move files to the Recycle Bin" checkbox, as illustrated in Figure 4.5.

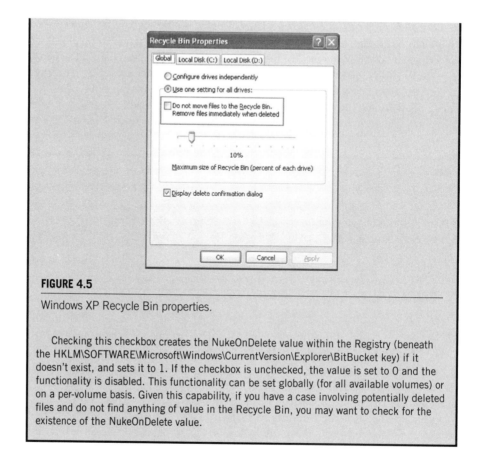

FIGURE 4.5

Windows XP Recycle Bin properties.

Checking this checkbox creates the NukeOnDelete value within the Registry (beneath the HKLM\SOFTWARE\Microsoft\Windows\CurrentVersion\Explorer\BitBucket key) if it doesn't exist, and sets it to 1. If the checkbox is unchecked, the value is set to 0 and the functionality is disabled. This functionality can be set globally (for all available volumes) or on a per-volume basis. Given this capability, if you have a case involving potentially deleted files and do not find anything of value in the Recycle Bin, you may want to check for the existence of the NukeOnDelete value.

On Windows XP systems, deleted files are moved to the Recycler directory, within a subdirectory based on the security identifier (SID) for the user. Figure 4.6 illustrates the subdirectory for the Administrator user on a Windows XP system.

When a file is deleted on a Windows XP system and moved to the Recycle Bin, the file is renamed in accordance with a standard format, which is outlined in the "How the Recycle Bin Stores Files" Microsoft KB article (found at *http://support .microsoft.com/kb/136517*). The name is changed so that the first letter is "D" (for "deleted"), the second letter is the drive letter from which the file originated, which is followed by the number of the deleted file, and the name ends with the original file extension. Figure 4.7 illustrates a deleted executable file that originated from the Z:\ drive.

As illustrated in Figure 4.7, the Recycle Bin also maintains an index file (named "INFO2") that keeps track of the original filename and location of deleted files,

FIGURE 4.6

Windows XP Recycle Bin in FTK Imager.

FIGURE 4.7

Deleted file in the Windows XP Recycler directory.

as well as when the files were deleted. The Perl script "recbin.pl" can be used to extract specific data from the "INFO2" file, as illustrated here:

```
C:\tools>recbin.pl -i d:\cases\info2
1 Mon Sep 26 23:03:27 2005 C:\Documents and Settings\jdoe\Desktop\
  lads.zip
2 Mon Sep 26 23:05:28 2005 C:\Documents and Settings\jdoe\LADS_
  ReadMe.txt
3 Mon Sep 26 23:05:28 2005 C:\Documents and Settings\jdoe\lads.exe
4 Mon Sep 26 23:23:58 2005 C:\Documents and Settings\jdoe\My
  Documents\Morpheus Shared\Downloads\Toby Keith - Stays In Mexico.
  mp3
```

As you can see, "recbin.pl" parses through the "INFO2" file and returns the index of the deleted file, the date and time the file was deleted, and the original filename of the deleted file.

Beginning with Vista, Microsoft changed the format of the files within the Recycle Bin. When files are deleted through the Windows Explorer shell, by default they will be moved to the Recycle Bin ("$Recycle.Bin" on disk) into a subfolder named for the user's SID. The file itself will be given a new filename, which starts with "$R," and is followed by six characters and ends in the original file's extension. A corresponding index file will be created, which starts with "$I," and contains the same remaining characters and extension as the "$R" file. Several deleted files and their index files are illustrated in Figure 4.8.

Figure 4.8 illustrates several deleted files and their corresponding index files. Figure 4.9 illustrates the binary contents of an index file. Each index file is 544 bytes in size. As you can see in Figure 4.9, the first eight bytes of the file appear to be a header, and the second eight bytes are the size of the original file, in little-endian

$IBE1KBP.vmcx	1 KB
$IDXQ3ZM.lnk	1 KB
$IIDSW0L	1 KB
$IPUCG07.exe	1 KB
$IRBIUU8	1 KB
$ITP40SN.zip	1 KB
$IZ5WDET.exe	1 KB
$IZKVKGL	1 KB
$IZYUOKM.vmcx	1 KB
$R38EAUM.url	1 KB
$RBE1KBP.vmcx	2 KB
$RDXQ3ZM.lnk	3 KB
$RDXQ3ZM.lnk.FileSlack	2 KB
$RPUCG07.exe	53,438 KB

FIGURE 4.8

Files populating the Windows 7 Recycle Bin, via FTK Imager.

```
000 01 00 00 00 00 00 00 00-32 04 00 00 00 00 00 00   ........2.......
010 10 70 B0 E8 1C AC CB 01-43 00 3A 00 5C 00 55 00   ·p°è-Ë·C·:·\·U·
020 73 00 65 00 72 00 73 00-5C 00 68 00 61 00 72 00   s·e·r·s·\·h·a·r·
030 6C 00 61 00 6E 00 5C 00-56 00 69 00 72 00 74 00   l·a·n·\·V·i·r·t·
040 75 00 61 00 6C 00 20 00-4D 00 61 00 63 00 68 00   u·a·l· ·M·a·c·h·
050 69 00 6E 00 65 00 73 00-5C 00 56 00 69 00 73 00   i·n·e·s·\·V·i·s·
060 74 00 61 00 33 00 32 00-2E 00 76 00 6D 00 63 00   t·a·3·2·.·v·m·c·
070 78 00 00 00 00 00 00 00-00 00 00 00 00 00 00 00   x···············
080 00 00 00 00 00 00 00 00-00 00 00 00 00 00 00 00   ················
090 00 00 00 00 00 00 00 00-00 00 00 00 00 00 00 00   ················
0a0 00 00 00 00 00 00 00 00-00 00 00 00 00 00 00 00   ················
0b0 00 00 00 00 00 00 00 00-00 00 00 00 00 00 00 00   ················
```

FIGURE 4.9

Partial contents of Recycle Bin index file, via FTK Imager.

hexadecimal format. Bytes 16–23 comprise the 64-bit FILETIME object for when the file was deleted, and the remaining bytes of the file are the name and path of the original file, in Unicode format. This structure makes the file relatively easy to parse and provide similar information as what is provided via the "recbin.pl" Perl script; once the index file (the one that begins with "$I") is parsed, you can then recover the actual file contents from the corresponding file that begins with "$R."

PREFETCH FILES

By now, most analysts recognize the forensic value of application prefetching, or just *prefetch files*. As with other artifacts, prefetch files can provide some interesting indicators, even if a user or intruder takes steps to hide her activity.

Since Windows XP, Windows systems have been capable of prefetching. All Windows systems perform boot prefetching, but only Windows XP, Vista, and Windows 7 perform application prefetching by default (Windows 2003 and 2008 can perform application prefetching following a Registry modification).

> **TIP**
>
> Enable Application Prefetching
>
> To enable application prefetching, navigate to the CurrentControlSet\Control\Session Manager\Memory Management\PrefetchParameters key in the System hive, and locate the "EnablePrefetcher" value. If this value is set to 1 ("prefetch only application launch files") or 3 ("prefetch both application and boot files"), application prefetching is enabled.

Application prefetching is intended to enable a better user experience within Windows systems by monitoring an application as it's launched, and then "prefetching" the necessary code to a single location so that the next time the application is launched, it launches faster. This way, the system doesn't have to seek across the file system for DLLs and other data that it needs to start the application—it knows exactly where to find it. These prefetch files are created in the "C:\Windows\Prefetch" directory, and end with the .pf extension. Each prefetch filename also includes the name of the application, a dash, followed by a one-way hash constructed using, among other things, the path to the application and any arguments used.

> **TIP**
>
> SSD Drives
>
> According to the Engineering Windows 7 blog (*http://blogs.msdn.com/b/e7/archive/ 2009/05/05/support-and-q-a-for-solid-state-drives-and.aspx*), if Windows 7 detects that it is running on a solid-state drive (SSD), certain functionality such as SuperFetch (which is responsible for producing application prefetch files) is automatically disabled. See the linked blog entry for a more detailed explanation, as well as a list of additional functionalities that may be disabled or modified if Windows 7 detects that it is running from an SSD drive.

To see an example of the creation of application prefetch files, particularly if you're running Windows XP, open a command prompt and change to the "C:\ Windows" directory, and type "Notepad." Close the Notepad window that appears and then return to the command prompt and change to the "C:\Windows\system32" directory. Then type "Notepad" again, and close the Notepad window that appears. Now, if you go to your Prefetch directory, you should see two different prefetch files that start with "Notepad.exe" and include two different hashes, as illustrated in Figure 4.10. This is also why you will sometimes see multiple prefetch files for "rundll32.exe."

Prefetch files contain metadata that can be useful to an analyst during an examination. For example, they contain the date that the application was last launched, as well as a "run count," or how many times that application has been launched. The prefetch file also contains information about the volume from which the application

Name ▲	Size	Type	Date Modified
NOTEPAD.EXE-189578DA.pf	14 KB	PF File	5/30/2011 9:38 AM
NOTEPAD.EXE-336351A9.pf	14 KB	PF File	5/30/2011 9:38 AM

FIGURE 4.10

Two prefetch files for "Notepad.exe."

was launched, as well as a list of DLLs and other files accessed by the application (in Unicode). There are a number of tools available that will allow you to parse this information from the files; due to the usefulness of this information, I wrote a Perl script called "pref.pl" to parse and display this information (this script is included in the ancillary materials available online). I found an odd prefetch file on a system and ran the "pref.pl" Perl script against the file; an excerpt of the metadata information available in the prefetch file is shown here:

```
C:\tools>pref.pl -f c:\windows\prefetch\0.8937919959151474.EXE-
  12EB1013.pf -p -i
c:\windows\prefetch\0.8937919959151474.EXE-12EB1013.pf Thu May 26
  16:46:19 2011
(1)
EXE Name : 0.8937919959151474.EXE
Volume Path : \DEVICE\HARDDISKVOLUME1
Volume Creation Date: Fri Jan 1 22:24:09 2010 Z
Volume Serial Number: A424-CE42
\DEVICE\HARDDISKVOLUME1\WINDOWS\SYSTEM32\NTDLL.DLL
\DEVICE\HARDDISKVOLUME1\WINDOWS\SYSTEM32\KERNEL32.DLL
\DEVICE\HARDDISKVOLUME1\WINDOWS\SYSTEM32\UNICODE.NLS
\DEVICE\HARDDISKVOLUME1\WINDOWS\SYSTEM32\LOCALE.NLS
\DEVICE\HARDDISKVOLUME1\WINDOWS\SYSTEM32\SORTTBLS.NLS
\DEVICE\HARDDISKVOLUME1\DOCUME~1\User\LOCALS~1\
  TEMP\0.8937919959151474.EXE
\DEVICE\HARDDISKVOLUME1\WINDOWS\SYSTEM32\USER32.DLL
\DEVICE\HARDDISKVOLUME1\WINDOWS\SYSTEM32\GDI32.DLL
```

As you can see in the previous output, there is a considerable amount of metadata available. For example, we can see the last time that the application was launched and the run count (respectively, *Thu May 26 16:46:19 2011* and *(1)*), as well as information about the volume where the application .exe file was found, and the actual path to the executable file (i.e., *\DEVICE\HARDDISKVOLUME1\ DOCUME~1\User\LOCALS~1\TEMP\0.893791995915174.EXE*).

I've also found other interesting information in the output from "pref.pl." In one instance, I found another very odd prefetch file, named "KARTCICYYIR .EXE-2CC557AD.pf"; using "pref.pl," an excerpt of the output I saw appeared as follows:

```
\DEVICE\HARDDISKVOLUME1\DOCUME~1\ABC\LOCALS~1\TEMP\KARCICYYIR.EXE
\DEVICE\HARDDISKVOLUME1\PROGRAM FILES\SOPHOS\SOPHOS ANTI-VIRUS\
  SOPHOS_DETOURED.DLL
```

```
\DEVICE\HARDDISKVOLUME1\WINDOWS\SYSTEM32\BDYAWUIS.DAT
\DEVICE\HARDDISKVOLUME1\WINDOWS\SYSTEM32\CONFIG\SOFTWARE
\DEVICE\HARDDISKVOLUME1\WINDOWS\SYSTEM32\MRYDUTAG.DAT
\DEVICE\HARDDISKVOLUME1\WINDOWS\SYSTEM32\MBQTAEPO.DAT
\DEVICE\HARDDISKVOLUME1\WINDOWS\SYSTEM32\CMD.EXE
```

Again, as with the first example, this is only an excerpt of the output, but it shows the artifacts that were most interesting and immediately caught my attention. You can see in the previous output excerpt not just the path of the actual executable file, but also that it appeared to be accessing three .dat files, as well as the Software Registry hive. This is an excellent example of how prefetch files can be valuable to an analyst, as it illustrates the concept of secondary artifacts that we discussed in Chapter 1.

The prefetch file parsed in the previous example was a secondary artifact created during a malware infection; that is, it was created by the operating system as the malware executed and interacted with its "ecosystem," or environment. As it turns out, the Application Event Logs from the system from which the prefetch file was retrieved included an event record that indicated that the malware file itself ("KARTCICYYIR .exe") had been detected by the installed antivirus application and deleted. However, the benefit of secondary artifacts is that they often are not deleted when an intruder "cleans up" after herself, or when malware is deleted; Registry keys and values, prefetch files, etc. often remain. The metadata in this prefetch file not only give us a clear indication of when the executable was launched, but also from where (via the volume path and serial number in the previous example output). The metadata also give us an indication of other files that may be associated with the malware, providing us with some context (we'll discuss the concept of context with respect to digital forensic analysis at greater length in Chapter 7) as to the creation of those files.

The "pref.pl" Perl script isn't the only tool available for parsing valuable metadata from prefetch files. Michael Spohn wrote "PFDump.exe," (*http://malware-hunters .net/all-downloads/*) as part of the "malware-hunters forensic toolkit." "PFDump.exe" extracts a considerable amount of metadata from prefetch files, and provides for output in tab-delimited format (for opening in MS Excel), HTML format, and XML format. If you prefer a graphical user interface (GUI) to your tools, Mark McKinnon has made several tools, including Prefetch Parser version 1.04, available at his web site (*http://redwolfcomputerforensics.com*). The GUI for Prefetch Parser is illustrated in Figure 4.11.

In Figure 4.11, you'll notice a "Windows Version" dropdown menu; this is due to the fact that from Windows XP and 2003 to Vista, the mechanism for how prefetching is performed and the format of the prefetch files changed (a brief description can be found at *http://technet.microsoft.com/en-us/magazine/2007.03 .vistakernel.aspx*). However, the only real change that is significant to forensic analysts is that the offset locations within the binary file for the time stamp and the run count changed between Windows versions. If you're using "pref.pl" (described earlier in this chapter) when you're extracting metadata from Vista or Windows 7 prefetch files, you will want to use the "-v" switch, as the script defaults to using the offsets applicable to Windows XP systems. If you're interested in these offset

FIGURE 4.11

Mark McKinnon's Prefetch Parser GUI.

values, simply open "pref.pl" in an editor (such as Notepad) and read through the code until you find the appropriate settings.

TIP

NTOSBOOT

When examining prefetch files, do not overlook the NTOSBOOT-B00DFAAD.pf file. This file can be parsed just like any other prefetch file, and some analysts have reported finding references to malware within the file path strings embedded within this prefetch file.

SCHEDULED TASKS

Windows systems are capable of a great deal of functionality, including being able to execute tasks on a user-determined schedule. These are referred to as scheduled tasks, and are accessible via several means, including the "at.exe" tool and the Scheduled Task Wizard, as illustrated in Figure 4.12.

Scheduled tasks allow various programs to be executed once, or on a regularly scheduled basis. This can be very useful; for example, regular housekeeping

FIGURE 4.12

Windows XP Scheduled Task Wizard.

Name ▲	Schedule	Next Run Time
Add Scheduled Task		
AppleSoftwareUpdate	At 10:13 PM every Tue of every week, starting 12/27/2...	10:13:00 PM ...

FIGURE 4.13

AppleSoftwareUpdate task.

functions can be scheduled to occur at regular, specific intervals. One example of this is if you install iTunes or another Apple product, you will likely see the file "AppleSoftwareUpdate.job" in the "C:\Windows\Tasks" directory on your system, as illustrated in Figure 4.13.

That being said, the existence of a scheduled task does not always correlate directly to a user creating the task, as these tasks can be created programmatically, through the appropriate API calls (which, with the appropriate credentials, can be accessed remotely). As such, the existence of a scheduled task may be associated with a software installation, or in some cases, a malware infection or compromise. Windows systems require that, to create a scheduled task, the user context have Administrator-level credentials. When the task executes, the running task itself has System-level privileges.

This can be very useful to administrators, particularly when System-level privileges are needed temporarily; an administrator can create a scheduled task to launch the command prompt (i.e., "cmd.exe") and have it run immediately. Once the command prompt appears, it will be running with System-level privileges, allowing the administrator access to areas of the system restricted to that privilege level. Microsoft KB article 313565 (found at *http://support.microsoft.com/kb/313565*) provides instructions for how to use "at.exe" to create scheduled tasks; while this article was written for Windows 2000, the commands work on later Windows versions.

On Windows 2000, XP, and 2003, the scheduled tasks themselves are found within the "C:\Windows\Tasks" folder, and have the .job file extension. These files have a binary format, a description of which is available at *http://msdn.microsoft .com/en-us/library/cc248285%28v=PROT.13%29.aspx.* The information available via this site allows for tools to be written to parse the .job file format to extract information that may be of particular value. For example, the fixed-length portion of the format contains an 8-byte SYSTEMTIME time stamp that indicates when the task was most recently run, and the variable-length data section includes a Unicode string that indicates the name of the author of the task. This can be valuable to an analyst, as anything useful to an administrator can also be useful to an intruder; scheduled tasks have been used as a persistence mechanism (see Chapter 6) for malware, as well as a means for activating Trojans, backdoors, or legitimate remote-access services to allow an intruder access to a system.

On Windows 7, .job files are stored in the "\Windows\System32\Tasks" folder, as well as subfolders beneath it, in XML format (i.e., those created via the Windows 7 API), which means that you can open them and read them in a text editor such as Notepad. An example of a portion of a Windows 7 .job file (opened in ProDiscover) is illustrated in Figure 4.14.

Windows 7 ships with a number of scheduled tasks already installed; for example, the RegIdleBackup task backs up the Registry (to the "\Windows\System32\ config\RegBack" folder) every 10 days, and limited defragmentation is scheduled for once a week. These tasks can be viewed on a live Windows 7 system via the Task Scheduler Control Panel applet (available within Administrative Tools), as illustrated in Figure 4.15.

Again, on Windows 7, these tasks (described within XML .job files) are stored in subdirectories beneath the "\Windows\System32\Tasks" folder.

Another means for creating scheduled tasks, aside from "at.exe" or using a wizard, is to use "schtasks.exe." This tool was introduced with Windows XP (Microsoft KB article 814596, found at *http://support.microsoft.com/kb/814596*, describes how to use "schtasks.exe" to create scheduled tasks on Windows 2003) and is available on all systems up through Windows 7. While "at.exe" produces tasks or "jobs" that are named "AT#.job," much like the wizard, "schtasks.exe" allows tasks to be created with more descriptive names.

```
ÿþ<Task xmlns="http://schemas.microsoft.com/windows/2004/02/mit/task">
  <RegistrationInfo>
    <Source>$(@%systemroot%\system32\defragsvc.dll,-800)</Source>
    <Author>$(@%systemroot%\system32\defragsvc.dll,-801)</Author>
    <Description>$(@%systemroot%\system32\defragsvc.dll,-802)</Description>
    <URI>Microsoft\Windows\Defrag\ScheduledDefrag</URI>
  </RegistrationInfo>
```

FIGURE 4.14

Portion of Windows 7 .job file (via ProDiscover).

FIGURE 4.15

Portion of the Windows 7 Task Scheduler applet.

WARNING

"at.exe" Versus "schtasks.exe"

When performing live response and using a batch file to collect volatile information from Windows systems, be sure to use both "at.exe" and "schtasks.exe" within the batch file to list the available tasks. It turns out that tasks created by one tool will not be "seen" by the other, when used to list the tasks.

Another useful bit of information available to the analyst is the scheduled tasks log file, named "SchedLgU.txt. This file is 32 kilobytes (KB) in size, by default, and is located in the "\Windows\Tasks" directory on Windows 2003 and later (it's in the "\Windows" directory on Windows XP). Many times, this file will simply contain entries that state that the Task Scheduler service started (or exited) at a specific date and time; this can be useful to establish a record (albeit short term, as the file isn't very large and older entries get overwritten) of when the system was running.

This log may also hold a record of various tasks that have executed, along with their exit code. In some instances, I have found indications of tasks having completed that were associated with an intrusion, and corroborated with an external data source (e.g., network traffic, etc.). In such cases, the task was created from a remote system using compromised domain administrator credentials, and once the task completed, it was deleted; however, the entry still remained in the "SchedLgU .txt" file, and we were able to correlate that information to other events. A complete discussion of timeline creation and analysis is covered in Chapter 7.

JUMP LISTS

Jump lists are something new to Windows 7. In short, jump lists are lists of files that the user has recently opened, organized according to the application used to open them, so in this way they are similar to the RecentDocs Registry key (Registry analysis will be discussed in Chapter 5). Users can view their recently accessed documents and files by right-clicking on the program icon in the Task Bar. Figure 4.16 illustrates a jump list for VMWare's VMPlayer application.

What the user sees depends on the program; for example, the jump list of Internet Explorer will show URLs, whereas the jump list for MS Word will show documents that the user has opened. Users can also choose to keep specific items persistent in the jump list by "pinning" them; that is, clicking on the push pin to the right of the item, as illustrated in Figure 4.16. While the items under the Recent list may change over time, items that the user chooses to "pin" will persist in the jump list. These jump lists may also appear alongside programs listed in the Start menu, as well.

From an analyst's perspective, the user's jump lists are maintained in the "AppData\Roaming\Microsoft\Windows\Recent\AutomaticDestinations" folder within the user profile, as illustrated in Figure 4.17.

As you can see in Figure 4.17, the jump list files are named with 16 hexadecimal characters, followed by ".automaticDestinations-ms." The first 16 characters of the jump list filename pertain to the specific application used, and are fixed across systems. For example, "b3f13480c2785ae" corresponds to "Paint.exe," "adecfb853d77462a" corresponds to MS Word 2007, and "918e0ecb43d17e23" corresponds to "Notepad.exe." These characters comprise the "application identifier," or "AppID," and identify the specific application, including the path to the executable file. Mark McKinnon of RedWolf Computer Forensics, LLC, posted a list of the AppIDs to the ForensicsWiki at *http://www.forensicswiki.org/wiki/ List_of_Jump_List_IDs*.

Several analysts within the community have noted that the jump list files follow a specific file structure. In fact, at a Microsoft cybercrime conference in the fall of 2008, Troy Larson, the senior forensic investigator at Microsoft, stated that jump lists were based on the compound document "structured storage" binary file format

FIGURE 4.16

VMPlayer jump list.

```
Administrator: C:\Windows\system32\cmd.exe

  Directory of  C:\Users\harlan\AppData\Roaming\Microsoft\Windows\Recent\Automatic
Destinations

04/13/2011   03:25 PM    <DIR>          .
04/13/2011   03:25 PM    <DIR>          ..
06/08/2011   08:27 AM           10,752 i2dc1ea8e34b5a6.automaticDestinations-ms
06/08/2011   08:27 AM           46,080 1b4dd67f29cb1962.automaticDestinations-ms

04/14/2011   10:27 AM            3,584 500b8c1d5302fc9c.automaticDestinations-ms

04/21/2011   01:19 PM            8,192 50620fe75ee0093.automaticDestinations-ms
04/13/2011   03:25 PM            5,120 65009083bfa6a094.automaticDestinations-ms

01/01/2011   12:46 PM            4,608 74d7f43c1561fc1e.automaticDestinations-ms

01/01/2011   12:44 PM            3,584 7a8db574299c8568.automaticDestinations-ms

05/23/2011   06:31 PM           19,456 7e4dca80246863e3.automaticDestinations-ms

02/10/2011   01:55 PM            7,168 9b9cdc69c1c24e2b.automaticDestinations-ms

01/04/2011   10:38 AM            4,096 b0459de4674aab56.automaticDestinations-ms

              10 File(s)        112,640 bytes
               2 Dir(s)  161,957,060,608 bytes free
```

FIGURE 4.17

Contents of user's "AutomaticDestinations" folder.

FIGURE 4.18

Jump list file open in the MiTeC Structured Storage Viewer.

(the format specification can be found at *http://msdn.microsoft.com/en-us/library/dd942138(v=prot.13).aspx*) that was used in Microsoft Office prior to version 2007. This structured storage file format was also referred to as a "file system within a file," in that the format was used to create a mini-file system within the contents of a single file, complete with "directories" and "files." Given this, according to Rob Lee (of SANS), one way to view the contents of a jump list file is to open it in the MiTeC Structured Storage Viewer (available at *http://mitec.cz/ssv.html*), as illustrated in Figure 4.18.

Each of the numbered streams visible via the Structured Storage Viewer are, in turn, based on the file format associated with Windows shortcut files; shortcut files, when by themselves, usually end with the .lnk extension and have the nickname "LNK" files. Microsoft has made the binary format of these files, referred to as shell link files, available at *http://msdn.microsoft.com/en-us/library/dd871305(v=prot.13).aspx*.

As these streams follow the binary format of shortcut files, they contain a considerable amount of information that can be valuable to an analyst. For example, the format contains last modified, last accessed, and creation time stamps (in UTC format) for the target file; that is, when a jump list stream is created, the MAC time stamps of the target file are used to populate these values within the jump list stream. Analysts need to understand what these time stamps represent, and that the jump list streams do not contain time stamps that indicate when the streams themselves were created, last accessed, or last modified.

The format can also contain additional information, such as command line arguments used, if any, and possibly a description string. One example of a jump list stream that may contain command line options (and a description string) has been seen in the use the Terminal Service client on Windows 7 to access remote systems, as illustrated here (extracted using a custom Perl script):

```
Stream: 1
M: Tue Jul 14 00:01:53 2009
A: Tue Jul 14 01:14:27 2009
C: Tue Jul 14 00:01:53 2009
C:\Windows\System32\mstsc.exe /v:"192.168.1.24"
Connect to 192.168.1.24 with Remote Desktop Connection
```

Other streams extracted from within the jump list file contain the same time stamps as just shown, as they represent the last modified, last accessed, and creation dates for the file "C:\Windows\System32\mstsc.exe." Remember, starting with Vista, updating of last access times on files has been disabled, by default.

The streams identified within the jump list file can also be extracted and viewed with a shortcut/LNK file viewer. For example, using the Structured Storage Viewer, we can extract a stream, rename the extension to .lnk, and then point the MiTeC Windows File Analyzer (interestingly enough, named "WFA.exe") at the directory where we saved the stream. The .lnk files within the directory will be parsed and the extracted information displayed, as illustrated in Figure 4.19.

The information available from the LNK streams within the jump list file will depend on the shortcut viewer application you choose. For example, the MiTeC Windows File Analyzer application does not have a column for a description string or command line options when parsing shortcut files.

FIGURE 4.19

LNK file information visible in WFA.

So how would this information be valuable to an analyst? Well, for the jump list to be created and populated, the user has to take some action. In the previous example, the user accessed the Remote Desktop Connection selection via the Windows 7 Start menu. As such, the existence of this information within the jump list may provide clues (possibly when combined with other information) as to the user's intent. The "user" may be a local user with legitimate access to the system, or an intruder accessing the system via some remote, shell-based access such as Terminal Services. In addition, jump list artifacts may persist well after the user performs the indicated actions or even after the target file has been deleted.

NOTE

DestList Stream

Figure 4.18 illustrates several streams within an "automatic" jump list file, including two numbered streams and a third one named "DestList." There isn't much information available about the structure of the DestList stream; however, research indicates that following a 32-byte header, the elements of the DestList stream follow a consistent format. Each element is associated with one of the numbered streams within the jump list file, and is 114 bytes long, plus a Unicode string. Table 4.1 provides information regarding the identified items within each element, along with the offset, size, and description of each item.

Table 4.1 DestList Stream Header Elements

Offset (Dec/Hex)	Size	Description
72/0×48	16 bytes	NetBIOS name of the system; zero padded to 16 bytes
88/0×58	8 bytes	Stream number; corresponds to the appropriate numbered stream with the jump list
100/0×64	8 bytes	FILETIME object
112/0×70	2 bytes	Number of characters in the Unicode string that follows; the string is actually (size * 2) bytes long

Each offset listed within the first column of Table 4.1 is indexed from the beginning of the element within the stream. The first element is found immediately following the 32-byte header, and each subsequent element is adjacent to the last, with no separator. The 8-byte FILETIME object within the element is most likely used to sort the elements into a most recently used (MRU) or most frequently used (MFU) list; this is further supported by research, by accessing several files through several applications (e.g., MS Word, Adobe Reader, MS Paint, etc.), recording the times, and then parsing the entire jump list file, including the DestList stream. This research was initially conducted by Jimmy Weg, a law enforcement officer and forensic analyst in Montana, and further validated by other analysts, including some of my own analysis.

The jump lists that we've looked at thus far have been from the "AutomaticDestinations" folder. Users can create custom jump lists based on specific files and applications, which populate the "CustomDestinations" folder (in the "AppData\Roaming\Microsoft\Windows\Recent\" folder within the user profile), with jump list files that end in "customDestinations-ms." As with the previously discussed jump lists, the files begin with a 16-character "AppID" name that is associated with a specific application; limited testing indicates a correlation between the two types of jump lists, with the same 16 characters associated with the same application between them. According to Troy Larson, these jump lists consist of one or more streams in the shortcut/LNK file format, without the benefit of each stream separated into individual streams, as is the case with the automatic destination jump lists.

There are a number of tools available to assist in parsing jump lists for inclusion in your overall analysis. Mark Woan has made not only a shortcut file analyzer (lnkanalyzer) freely available at *http://www.woanware.co.uk/?page_id=121*, but he has also made a jump list viewer application (JumpLister) available at *http://www.woanware.co.uk/?page_id=266*. Both tools require that .Net version 4.0 be installed on your system. I also found a description of a tool called "Jump List Extractor," from Alex Barnett, but could not find any way to download a copy of the tool for evaluation.

Using the Microsoft specifications for the compound document binary and shortcut file formats, I wrote my own jump list parsing tool (in Perl, of course!). This code consists of two Perl modules, one for parsing just the Windows shortcut file format, and the other for parsing the "AutomaticDestinations" folder jump list files as well as the DestList stream. This allows me a great deal of flexibility in how I can implement the parsing functionality, as well as how I choose to display the output. For example, using the two modules (literally, via the Perl "use" pragma), I wrote a script that would read a single "AutomaticDestinations" folder jump list file, parse the DestList stream, parse the numbered streams, and then display the entries in MRU order, as illustrated here:

```
Fri Apr 15 11:41:56 2011
C:\Windows\System32\mstsc.exe /v:" 192.168.1.12"
Tue Apr 5 16:26:19 2011
C:\Windows\System32\mstsc.exe /v:"192.168.1.10"
Wed Mar 16 18:45:58 2011
C:\Windows\System32\mstsc.exe /v:"ender"
Mon Feb 7 14:09:40 2011
C:\Windows\System32\mstsc.exe /v:" 192.168.1.7"
```

This example output is from the jump list file for the Remote Desktop Client, and illustrates connections that I made from my Windows 7 system to various systems in my lab, several of them virtual systems. This information could very easily have been displayed in a format suitable for inclusion in a timeline (see Chapter 7).

> **WARNING**
>
> Jump List Parser
>
> The Perl modules and scripts that I wrote for parsing jump lists are somewhat rough—perhaps a better term would be *alpha*—and at the time of this writing, not suitable for release, and are therefore *not* provided with the materials associated with this book. Also, I am concerned that even though Windows 7 has been available for some time, jump lists are relatively new and not well understood for their forensic value; as such, releasing a tool that provides information from jump lists without the analyst really understanding the nature or context of that information would simply lead to confusion. I do hope to release the tool at some point in the future, after I've had a chance to clean up the code and make it more usable.

ProDiscover (all but the free Basic Edition) also includes a built-in full featured Jump List Viewer, as illustrated in Figure 4.20.

To populate the Jump List Viewer, open your ProDiscover project, right-click on the Users Profile directory, and choose "Find Jump List Files…" from the dropdown menu. ProDiscover will scan through the subdirectories, looking for, cataloging, and parsing the various automatic and custom jump list files (sans the DestList stream in the automatic jump list files, as of ProDiscover version 7.0.0.3).

HIBERNATION FILES

Laptop systems running Windows XP or Windows 7 may often be found to contain hibernation files. These files are basically the compressed contents of Windows memory from when the system (usually a laptop) "goes to sleep." As such, a hibernation file can contain a great deal of very valuable historic information, including

ProDiscover Jump List Viewer.

processes and network connections from some point in the past. This information can be used to address issues of malware that may have been installed on the system and then deleted, or demonstrate that a user was logged in or that an application had been running at some point in the past. As with some other artifacts, hibernation files are often not included in "clean up" processes, such as application uninstalls, or when an antivirus application deletes detected malware.

The Volatility Framework (*http://code.google.com/p/volatility/*) can provide you access to the contents of a Windows hibernation file and allow you to analyze it just as if it were a memory dump. To install the Volatility Framework on your system, consult the Volatility Framework wiki for the appropriate instructions (as of the time of this writing, Jamie Levy, a volunteer with the Volatility project, has graciously compiled detailed installation instructions for version 1.4 of the framework).

Detailed discussion of memory analysis is beyond the scope of this book, particularly when there are other, much better suited resources that cover the subject, such as the *Malware Analyst's Cookbook and DVD* (Ligh et al., 2011). However, information found through analysis of the hibernation file can prove to be extremely valuable; analysts have found pertinent information, including keys for encrypted volumes, within hibernation files.

APPLICATION FILES

There are a number of application-specific files that may be found on Windows systems that may be crucial to an analyst. Application logging and configuration information may be critical to an analyst, but the value of those sources of information will depend in large part on the nature and goals of the examination. In the rest of this chapter, we will discuss some of the files that you may run across during an examination, based on some of the various applications that may be installed on the system being examined. In each case, we will also look to applications or tools that may be used to parse and further analyze these files. However, do not consider the rest of this chapter to be a comprehensive and complete list of those files; something like this is just impossible to produce. Application developers develop new tools and storage mechanisms for log and configuration data; for example, some browsers have moved away from text or binary files for bookmark and history/cache storage and have moved to SQLite databases.

TIP

Accessing SQLite Databases

One of the best tools I've found for accessing SQLite databases is the SQLite database browser (*http://sqlitebrowser.sourceforge.net*). The browser is free, as well as easy to use and set up. While it does provide command line functionality for accessing SQLite databases, it also has a GUI that provides much easier access to the database for browsing, etc.

With new applications being developed all the time and current applications changing, including adding new features, it would be impossible to keep up on all of that information, even if only from a digital forensic analysis perspective. My goal here is to have you consider alternate sources of data to corroborate your findings or to fill in gaps. For example, application logs can be very useful, as in many cases, entries are only added when the system is running and a user is logged in and using the application. As such, this information can be correlated with Event Log entries, or used in the absence of such information. While there is really no way to thoroughly address all applications or even provide an overview, my hope is to provide information about some of the types of files that you might consider including in your analysis.

Antivirus Logs

Logs produced by AV applications will be discussed in greater detail in Chapter 6, but I wanted to present at least a cursory discussion of the topic in this chapter, for the sake of completeness. AV logs can be extremely valuable to a forensic analyst in a number of ways. During one particular intrusion incident, I examined the AV logs and found that on a specific date (shortly after the files were created), an AV scan had detected and deleted several files identified as malware. Several weeks later, files with the same names appeared on the system again; however, this time, the files were not detected as malware. This information was valuable, in that the logs provided me with names of files to look for, and also allowed me to more accurately determine the *window of compromise*, or how long the malware had actually been on the system. This information was critical to the customer, not only because it was required by the regulatory compliance organization, but also because it reduced their window of compromise, but did so with hard data (the creation dates for the second set of files were verified through MFT analysis).

Another use for the AV logs is to help the analyst narrow down what malware might be on the system. For example, Microsoft's Malicious Software Removal Tool (MRT) is installed by default on many systems, and updated through the regular Windows Update process. MRT is an application meant to protect the system from specific threats (again, discussed in greater detail in Chapter 6), rather than provide more general protection in the manner of AV products. As such, checking the "mrt.log" file (located in the "Windows\debug" directory) will let you know when the application was updated, and the results of any scans that had been run. An example log entry is illustrated here:

```
Microsoft Windows Malicious Software Removal Tool v3.20, June 2011
Started On Wed Jun 15 21:13:25 2011
Results Summary:
----------------
No infection found.
Microsoft Windows Malicious Software Removal Tool Finished On Wed
   Jun 15 21:14:4
5 2011
Return code: 0 (0x0)
```

As you can see, the "mrt.log" file includes the date of when the MRT was updated; this can be compared to the table in Microsoft KB article 891716 (found at *http://support.microsoft.com/kb/891716*) to determine what the system *should* be protected against. Note that KB article 891716 also provides example log excerpts that illustrate malware being detected.

Skype

Skype is a useful communications utility that has been around for some time, and in the spring of 2011, Microsoft purchased Skype (for a reported $8.5 billion). Skype is not only available on Windows, Linux, and Mac OS X computers, but it can be downloaded and run from Apple products (iPhone, iTouch, iPad), as well as from some smart phones and tablets running the Android operating system. As such, it is a pretty pervasive utility for not only making video calls, but also for something as simple as instant messaging, for sharing information outside what may be considered more "normal" channels (as opposed to AOL Instant Messenger, or Internet relay chat).

I've had Skype available on a Windows XP system for some time, in part to test the application and see what tools were available for parsing any log files produced by the application. The version (as of this writing) of Skype that I'm using is 5.3, and the communications logs are maintained in the "main.db" file located within my user profile, in the "\Application Data\Skype*username*" subdirectory. Two tools available for parsing information from the database file are Skype Log View (*http://nirsoft.net/utils/skype_log_view.html*) and Skype History Viewer (*http://skypehistory.sourceforge.net*). Figure 4.21 illustrates a portion of the user interface for Skype Log View (run on my live system) with the contents of the "main.db" file displayed.

This information can be very useful to an analyst, illustrating not just communications between parties, but also who initiated the call, when the call was initiated, etc. This can also show when the system was in use, and may support or refute a user's claims regarding when they were accessing the system.

Record Number	Action Type	Action Time
93	Outgoing Call	6/2/2010 7:56:02 PM
94	Outgoing Call	6/2/2010 7:56:02 PM
103	Outgoing Call	6/2/2010 7:56:02 PM
123	Incoming Call	6/10/2010 3:02:03 PM
149	Incoming Call	6/28/2010 9:48:46 AM
157	Outgoing Call	6/28/2010 9:50:39 AM
164	Outgoing Call	6/28/2010 9:53:34 AM
168	Chat Message	6/28/2010 12:13:03 PM
169	Chat Message	6/28/2010 12:13:49 PM
170	Chat Message	6/28/2010 12:13:51 PM
171	Chat Message	6/28/2010 12:13:54 PM

FIGURE 4.21

Portion of Skype Log View UI, accessing "main.db."

Apple Products

Many of us may have products from Apple, including an iPod or iTouch, an iPhone, or even an iPad. Many of us may also use iTunes to sync and make backups of our devices. In April 2011, two researchers (Alasdair Allan and Pete Warden, article located at *http://radar.oreilly.com/2011/04/apple-location-tracking.html*) found that as of the release of iOS 4, the iPhone and iPad would track approximate longitude and latitude information, along with time-stamped information. On the iPhone, this information is reportedly recorded in the file "consolidated.db."

When a user syncs their Apple device to a Windows system via iTunes, the backup information is placed in the user's profile, in the path "Application Data\Apple Computer\MobileSync\Backup" (on Windows XP; on Windows 7, the path is "\Users*user*\AppData\Roaming\Apple Computer\MobileSync\Backup"). When I sync my iTouch to my Windows XP system, I have a subdirectory in that path with a name that is a long string of characters, as illustrated in Figure 4.22.

The backup information is maintained in that subdirectory in multiple files, also with long strings of characters for names. Within that directory, the "Info.plist" file is an XML file (you can open it in a text editor) that contains information about the device being backed up, and the "Manifest.mbdb" and "Manifest.mdbx" files contain filename translations, between the long strings of characters and the original filenames.

The iPhoneBackupBrowser (authored by "reneD" and available at *http://code.google.com/p/iphonebackupbrowser/*) is a freely available tool that allows you to access the backup information, reportedly beginning with iTunes v9.1.1, and parse the "Manifest.mbdb" file to map the backup filenames to their original names. The wiki at the Google Code site includes information about the format of the "Manifest.mbdb" file, as well as the "Manifest.mdbx" index file (so you can write your own parser, if need be). The iPhoneBackupBrowser application itself reportedly runs better on Windows 7 than Windows XP, due to some of the APIs accessed.

Once you download the tools and place them into a directory, you can run "mbdbdump.exe" (works just fine on Windows XP) against the "Manifest.mbdb" file by passing the path to the directory where the file is located to the tool, as follows:

```
D:\tools\iphone>mbdbdump [path to directory]>output.txt
```

The resulting output file contains the parsed contents of the "Manifest.mbdb" file, allowing you to search for specific files, such as the "consolidated.db" file.

FIGURE 4.22

Path to "MobileSync\Backup" subdirectory.

Once you determine which of the files with the long filenames is the "consolidated .db" file, you can use free tools for accessing SQLite databases, such as the SQLite Browser (mentioned previously in this chapter) or the SQLite Manager add-on for Firefox (available at *https://addons.mozilla.org/en-US/firefox/addon/sqlite-manager/*), to peruse the contents of the database and extract the location information. The researchers stated in their article that the information recorded for each location may not be exact; however, from an overall perspective, it can show routes and that the phone or tablet was in a particularly proximity at a specific time.

TIP

iTouch Backup

Even though I ran my initial tests against the backup of an iTouch, rather than an iPhone, some of the available information was pretty telling. Parsing through the "mbdbdump .exe" output, I could clearly see installed applications, as well as files that likely contained configuration information, such as wireless networks I'd connected to via WiFi. All of this information may be valuable to an analyst or investigator.

An analyst can use information within these backup files to develop more detailed information regarding specific devices attached to the system, as well as possibly gain further insight into the user's movements, not just geographically but also around the Web.

NOTE

Android Devices

Apparently, Apple products may not be the only devices to record location information. In April 2011, Cory Altheide (of Google) pointed me to Packetlss' Android-locdump site (*https://github.com/packetlss/android-locdump*), in which the author of the site describes which files on some Android devices (no specific devices were named) apparently maintain location information for WiFi sites and cell phone towers. I checked my BackFlip (Motorola MB300 handset, running kernel version 2.6.29) and didn't find the files mentioned at the site (the site does mention that you will need to be "root" or superuser to see the files). The site also includes a Python script for parsing the information in the "cache.wifi" and "cache.cell" files into a more readable format. As with Apple products, the information in these files may be extremely valuable to an investigator, and they may exist on a Windows system if the user copied them or backed up the information on their handset or device.

Image Files

I own a work phone and a personal cell phone, both of which can be described as "smart" phones, and both of which contain cameras. I also own an iTouch, which contains a camera. I can connect all of these devices directly to my computer and copy pictures and videos directly to a folder. There are very few similar devices available these days that do not contain a camera of some type, and most of the ones available are capable of producing very high-quality digital images and videos. Not only that, many of the devices have global positioning system (GPS) capabilities; a friend of mine once took a picture with his Droid phone, swiped his hand across the screen, and pulled up a Google map with a push-pin on the location where the digital photo was taken. This simply illustrates that digital images can contain a significant amount of metadata; the question is then, how can you access that data?

One excellent tool for doing exactly that is Phil Harvey's EXIFTool (*http:// www.sno.phy.queensu.ca/~phil/exiftool/*). EXIF stands for "exchangeable image file," which is a standard that specifies the formats of various tags used by digital cameras (as well as smart phones and scanners), and Phil's tool is capable of extracting embedded EXIF (metadata) information from within a number of image file formats. The tool can be used from the command line, an example of which follows:

```
D:\tools>exiftool -a -u -g1 D:\pictures\img_3791_2165.jpg
---- ExifTool ----
ExifTool Version Number      : 8.60
---- System ----
File Name                    : img_3791_2165.jpg
Directory                    : D:/pictures
File Size                    : 4.0 MB
File Modification Date/Time  : 2010:07:18 15:32:06-04:00
File Permissions             : rw-rw-rw-
---- File ----
File Type                    : JPEG
…snip…
---- IFD0 ----
Make                         : Canon
Camera Model Name            : Canon EOS DIGITAL REBEL XTi
Orientation                  : Horizontal (normal)
```

I added "…snip…" to the previous output to indicate that I'd removed some information to make it easier to view; neither the tool nor the camera added that to the output. I am able to verify the relevant output because I have seen the camera, and know that it is, in fact, a Canon EOS Digital Rebel XTi.

Further along in the output of the tool, we see the following additional information:

```
Canon Image Type       : Canon EOS DIGITAL REBEL XTi
Canon Firmware Version : Firmware 1.1.1
Owner Name             : unknown
Serial Number          : 2271247134
Canon Model ID         : EOS Digital Rebel XTi / 400D / Kiss Digital X
…snip…
Internal Serial Number : H3624774
```

From this, we can see that we have two possible candidate serial numbers to uniquely identify the camera. So, if the user had copied the image from the camera and the camera was available to be analyzed, you could use this and other information (e.g., image file hashes, information from the computer system Registry indicating that the camera had been connected to the system, etc.) to definitively tie the image to the devices, and to the user.

What other information might be available within images? Well, many smart phones come with GPS capability enabled, and GPS information may be embedded within the images. Phil's tool is capable of extracting that information, as well as a great deal of additional information that may be embedded within a number of image file formats.

TIP

File Metadata

Phil Harvey's EXIFTool is reportedly capable of reading metadata from file formats other than just images. For example, the web site for the tool indicates that it can read metadata embedded in MS Office 2007 (and later) file formats (i.e., .docx, .pptx, and .xlsx file extensions), making it a very versatile and potentially valuable tool. Another tool capable of reading metadata from MS Office 2007 file formats is "read_open_xml.pl," available from *http://blog.kiddaland.net/downloads/*. Information derived from the use of either of these tools can be very useful, depending on your investigation.

A final thought on metadata such as we've discussed in this section of the chapter. While metadata can be very useful and even immensely valuable to an analyst, the simple fact is that not all files have metadata, and not all files that do have metadata necessarily have all metadata fields populated. If the metadata aren't there, they aren't there. For example, some images captured via cell phone cameras may not have GPS coordinates as part of the image EXIF data. This may be due to the fact that the cell phone is not a "smart" phone and did not have a GPS receiver, or that the software used to capture the image did not embed the data, or there could be other reasons.

SUMMARY

Windows systems contain a number of files in a variety of both open and proprietary formats. Depending on the type of case that you're working on or what you're looking for, these files will be of varying importance. However, my intention in this chapter has been to make you aware of some of the various files (and formats) available, and how their contents have been used to further examinations.

One particularly important aspect of this chapter has been to help you understand that in many cases, a file can be much more than just a binary data stream. For example, if you understand the structure of the data, and how the various elements of the structure are used by an application or even the operating system, you will then have some context associated with that data. I once worked with another analyst who had identified a particular string—a filename—within a Windows portable executable (PE) file (the structure of these files is discussed in *Windows Forensic Analysis*, Second Edition (Carvey, 2009)). Before reporting this finding to the customer, further analysis needed to be completed; for example, did this filename refer to a DLL within the import table of the PE file, or was it the name of a file used as a data repository? The answer to these questions, while relatively easy to determine, can have a significant impact on the overall examination.

References

Carrier, B. (2005). *File system forensic analysis*. Upper Saddle River, NJ: Pearson Education.

Carvey, H. A. (2009). *Windows forensic analysis* (2nd ed.). Burlington, MA: Syngress Publishing.

Ligh, M. H., Adair, S., Hartsteing, B., & Richard, M. (2011). *Malware analyst's cookbook and DVD*. New York: Wiley.

Registry Analysis

5

CHAPTER OUTLINE

INFORMATION IN THIS CHAPTER

- Registry Analysis

INTRODUCTION

The Registry is a key component of every Windows system, and as Windows systems have become more complex, progressing from Windows 2000 to XP and on to Windows 7, the value of the Registry as a source of forensic data has likewise increased. As such, what is available to an analyst through analysis of the Registry needs to be better understood. As the Windows versions have progressed, each new version has brought with it new data that can be critical to an investigation. As applications come to rely more on the Registry, and the "user experience" is monitored and optimized, even in part by the Registry, more useful data are available to be incorporated into an examination.

In this chapter, we will not be discussing the Registry in detail, as other resources have already laid the groundwork on this subject. Details of the Registry are covered in *Windows Forensic Analysis,* Second Edition (Carvey, 2009) and even more so in *Windows Registry Forensics* (Carvey, 2011). Much of what was covered in these two books (particularly the binary structure of the Registry, as well as Registry analysis techniques and tools) applies across all versions of Windows, including Windows 7. The *Malware Analyst's Cookbook and DVD* (Ligh et al., 2011) provides considerable information regarding how the Registry can be a valuable forensic resource when analyzed in conjunction with or as part of Windows physical memory and malware analysis. With this considerable treatment of the topic, there is really no significant value in repeating what's already been said. As such, in this chapter, we will assume that the reader (that's you) has a basic understanding of the Registry—for example, where the hives are located within the file system, or the difference between a "key" and a "value" that some of the tools use to collect information from the Registry (including but not limited to RegRipper)—and focus on information available in the Registry that is specific to Windows 7.

Also, I'd like to take something of a different approach in this chapter; rather than providing a list of keys or values of interest, I'd like to discuss the Registry in terms of addressing analysis questions through case studies or investigative processes. Many resources leave it up to the analyst to flip back and forth between the various pages, trying to track information among hives; instead, I think it may be useful to present all of the components of a case study together. Hopefully, this approach will be valuable to analysts.

REGISTRY ANALYSIS

All of the information presented and discussed in the first two chapters of the book *Windows Registry Forensics* applies across all versions of Windows, particularly analysis concepts, the binary structure of the Registry (including key and value cells), and the tools that can be used to extract and view information from the Registry, such as RegRipper (available at *http://code.google.com/p/winforensicaanalysis/downloads/list*). This book also covers the use of RegRipper in detail, including how to set it up, how to use it, and even how to create your own plugins for extracting and translating information of interest from the Registry. As such, there's really no need to repeat content and graphics of what the Registry "looks like" with respect to the native Registry Editor or files on the system, or when the hive file is opened in another, non-native viewer, such as the MiTeC Windows Registry Recovery (WRR) tool (*http://www.mitec.cz/wrr.html*). Other tools for extracting and viewing information from Registry keys and values, or monitoring accesses to the Registry on a live system (such as Process Monitor, found at *http://technet.microsoft.com/en-us/sysinternals/bb896645*) work equally well on Windows XP and Windows 7 systems.

As an example, the information from Chapter 3 of *Windows Registry Forensics* regarding using tools such as "pwdump7.exe" to extract and view the password hashes in the SAM hive applies equally as well to Vista, Windows 2008, and Windows 7. However, it is important to keep in mind that the LAN Manager password hash field will (in most cases) say "no password" or "blank" (depending on the tool used), as the "NoLMHash" value (discussed in Microsoft KB article 299656, found at *http://support.microsoft.com/kb/299656*) exists and is set to 1 by default on those versions of the Windows operating system.

Instead, the approach I'd like to take in this chapter is to address analysis questions through case studies, or investigative steps that you can take to answer some common questions when it comes to Registry analysis. In several instances (albeit not all), these case studies will correlate data from multiple hive files, so it makes sense to present the information all together in a single process flow, rather than spreading that information across multiple chapters.

TIP

Registry Structure

A key concept discussed in Chapter 4 is applicable in this chapter as well; that is, locating data in a Registry hive file using something like "strings.exe" or the BinText application tells us that the string is there. But understanding the structure of the data (e.g., Is the string a key name or value name? Is it embedded within value data or located in unallocated space within the hive file?), where the string exists within the "container," and how that data are used by an application provides us with *context* to that information. This can be extremely valuable, as the location of the string can have a significant impact on your examination. For example, if the string that you're interested in is a key name, that information will take your examination in a vastly different direction than if the string were a value name, or if the string was actually located within unallocated space within the hive file.

This is an important concept to keep in mind. As such, we also discuss the context of data with respect to surrounding data at other points in this book, including within Chapter 7, when we explore creating and analyzing timelines of system activity.

Registry Nomenclature

Before we begin our discussion of Registry analysis and dive into some case studies, one thing I think is important to reiterate is Registry nomenclature. Many analysts may not completely understand the names of various objects within the

FIGURE 5.1

Registry viewed via "RegEdit.exe."

Registry, or why they're important. Figure 5.1 illustrates a fairly standard view of the Registry on a live system via the native Registry Editor tool.

As you can see in Figure 5.1, the Registry is made up of keys, values, and value data. It is important for analysts to understand the differences between these various objects, as they have different properties associated with them. For example, Registry keys (the folders visible in the left pane in Figure 5.1) contain subkeys and values, and also have a property referred to as the LastWrite time. This is a 64-bit FILETIME (a description of the FILETIME object can be found at *http://support .microsoft.com/kb/188768*) time stamp that refers to the last time the key was modified in some way. This can include the key being created (creation or deletion being the extreme form of modification), or subkeys or values within the key being added, deleted, or modified. This is an important distinction, as Registry values do not have LastWrite times; however, some Registry values may contain time stamps within their data that refer to some other function or action having occurred. The value of the Registry key LastWrite times, as well as time stamps recorded within the data of various values, will be discussed through case studies in this chapter, and are also discussed in Chapter 7.

The Registry as a Log File

Microsoft refers to the "structured storage" file format (known as "COM structured storage" or "OLE structured storage," the format used for Word documents up to and including MS Office 2003, as well as jump list and Sticky Notes files on Windows 7; the binary format specification can be found at *http://msdn.microsoft .com/en-us/library/dd942138(v=prot.13).aspx*) as a "file system within a file." If you think about it, the same thing can be said about a Registry hive. Keys are often viewed as folders, as they contain other keys as well as values. As such, values can then be viewed as files, with the value data comprising the file contents. Taking this a step further, we can view a Registry hive file as a log file, as various system and user activity is recorded within the hive files, along with modifications to time stamps (e.g., Registry key LastWrite times). This is important to keep in mind, as some of the most valuable data can be derived from the Registry when combining value data with available time stamps, much like one would do when conducting log file analysis.

All that being said, I think we're ready to take a look at some of the analysis that can be done through the Registry.

USB Device Analysis

Tracking the use of USB devices—in particular, thumb drives or external drive enclosures (also referred to as "wallet" drives)—can be a very important aspect of an investigation. For example, determining that a specific removable device was connected to a system, along with information such as who was logged into the system at the time and what data were accessed during that time period, may provide indications that an employee copied sensitive corporate data onto that device. Alternately, combining information about external device connection with events relating to a malware infection may not only identify a thumb drive as the source of the infection, but also which specific device introduced the malware.

Windows 7 systems record a great deal of information with respect to USB devices that users connect to those systems, most of which is stored in the Registry (we'll discuss where information is stored in the Windows Event Log later in this section). Starting with the Registry, an analyst may discover some very interesting information with respect to devices that were connected to a Windows 7 system. For example, it may be possible to not only discover which types of devices were connected to the system, but also to uniquely identify those devices (via a unique instance identifier, or serial number) and determine *when* the devices were connected to the system. To do this, however, we need to not only extract information from multiple locations within a hive file, but we also need to look to information within multiple hive files (System, Software, and NTUSER.DAT). What we will do in this section is walk through a couple of examples of connecting devices to a Windows 7 system, and extracting the information and artifacts of those connections for analysis.

TIP

Analysis Checklists

For analyzing USB thumb drives and drive enclosures that have been connected to Windows systems, Rob Lee, faculty fellow at the SANS Institute, created checklists that can be used in your USB device analysis. The checklist for USB keys and thumb drives is available at *http://blogs.sans.org/computer-forensics/files/2009/09/USBKEY-Guide.pdf*, and the checklist for drive enclosures is available at *http://blogs.sans.org/computer-forensics/files/2009/09/USB_Drive_Enclosure-Guide.pdf*.

In our first example, we will start with a thumb drive. In this case, I used a 1-GB thumb drive that I purchased at Best Buy several years ago. The device has a "Geek Squad" logo on it, as well as a "U3 Smart" logo (I removed the U3 components from the device awhile back).

TIP

U3-Enabled Devices

To see artifacts left by U3-enabled devices, see Chapter 4 of *Windows Forensic Analysis, Second Edition*.

The Geek Squad thumb drive had never been connected to my target Windows 7 system before. I connected it to the system at approximately 8:13 am EDT (equates to 12:13 pm UTC), and disconnected approximately 40 minutes later. Then I reconnected the thumb drive to the same Windows 7 system at approximately 9:14 am EDT (approximately 1:14 pm UTC), and used FTK Imager version 3.0.0.1442 to extract the System and Software hive files, as well as the NTUSER.DAT from my user profile, from the system. I then shut down the system.

So the first place to start looking for information about the device is in the USBStor keys within the System hive. This has long been known as an initial location where information about USB removable storage devices (e.g., thumb drives, "wallet" drives, and as we'll see later in this chapter, other devices recognized as removable storage) is maintained. The full path to this key on a live system is:

```
HKLM\System\CurrentControlSet\Enum\USBStor
```

TIP

Locating the Current ControlSet

You will notice when viewing the System hive file (using the Registry Editor or another viewer such as WRR) extracted from an acquired image, you won't see a key named CurrentControlSet. Instead, you will see two (or possibly three) keys with names such as ControlSet001 and ControlSet003. To determine which of these was treated as the current ControlSet, go to the Select key and look at the value "Current." This will tell you which ControlSet you should look to as the CurrentControlSet.

In this case, we'll be looking at the subkey beneath the ControlSet001 key. Following the path and looking at the subkeys beneath the USBStor key, we see an entry for the Geek Squad device, which is illustrated in Figure 5.2.

As you can see in Figure 5.2, immediately beneath the USBStor key we see the device instance identifier (device class ID, or just device ID) for the device, and then immediately beneath that key we see the unique instance ID key for the device itself. This unique instance ID is, in fact, the serial number maintained in the device descriptor (*not* the storage section) of the Geek Squad thumb drive.

FIGURE 5.2

USBStor subkeys, seen via WRR.

```
Disk&Ven_Best_Buy&Prod_Geek_Squad_U3&Rev_6.15

Idx: 18922
Relative Offset: E70088
Number of Subkeys: 1
Security Key Offset: 2C8788
Date Modified: 7/17/2011 12:13:21 PM
```

FIGURE 5.3

USBStor device subkey properties seen via WRR.

> **WARNING**
>
> **Device Mapping**
>
> This unique instance ID is used on Windows 7 and Vista systems to map the device found beneath the USBStor key to other elements that are critical to our analysis, such as which drive letter was used to mount the removable device. On Windows XP systems, a value named *ParentIdPrefix* was created and used to perform this mapping. While this value is not created by Vista and Windows 7 systems, the unique instance ID (or serial number) is used instead.

If we view the relevant Registry keys with WRR, we can right-click on the device ID and, choosing "Properties," we can see the LastWrite time for the device ID key, as illustrated in Figure 5.3.

From Figure 5.3, we see that the LastWrite time of the device ID key correlates to the time that the device was first connected to the system since the last time the system was rebooted. What this means is that after the system is booted, a device can be (and in this case, was) connected to the system multiple times; the LastWrite time of the device ID key correlates to the **first** time that the device was connected to the system following the most recent reboot. Prior to the system being shut down, the device can be disconnected and reconnected multiple times, but the LastWrite time of this key will—in most cases—reflect when the device was first connected during that boot session. However, this may not always be the case; some analysts have reported finding cases where multiple devices had been connected to a Windows system, and all of the devices listed beneath the USBStor key had the same LastWrite time. There is speculation within the community that this anomaly may be the result of a Service Pack or patch having been installed, or of a Group Policy Object (GPO) that modifies the access control list (ACL) on the keys; further analysis of the system itself (perhaps using the timeline creation techniques discussed in Chapter 7) would be recommended.

TIP

Driver Events

When a USB device is connected to a Windows 7 system for the first time, an entry is written to the C:\Windows\inf\setupapi.dev.log file (per *http://support.microsoft.com/kb/927521*, this file contains information about Plug and Play devices and driver installation), and events with identifier (ID) 20003 and 20001 and source "UserPnp" are written to the System Event Log. There may also be event IDs 10000 and 10002 (source is "DriverFrameworks-UserMode"), indicating the installation or update of a device driver. These events will contain an identifier or name of the device that can be correlated to information extracted from the Registry. When drivers are loaded to support a USB device, several events are generated in the Microsoft-Windows-DriverFrameworks-UserMode/Operational Event Log, with IDs of 1003, 2003, 2010, 2004, 2105, etc., all containing a name or identifier for the device. When the device is removed from the system, a series of events (IDs 2100, 2102, 1006, 2900, etc.) are written to the DriverFrameworks-UserMode/Operational Event Log, as the driver host process for the device is shut down. As such, the System Event Log can be useful in correlating information about USB devices being connected to a Windows 7 system for the first time, and the Microsoft-Windows-DriverFrameworks-UserMode/Operational Event Logs, if available, can provide information regarding when devices were connected and removed from the system, allowing you to see how long the device had been connected.

At this point, we also have the unique instance ID (or serial number) of the device, which can uniquely identify the device. I say "can" simply because there is no guarantee that each and every USB thumb drive with a serial number has (or must have) a unique serial number. Some analysts have reported seeing several devices from the same manufacturer, all with the same serial number. Further, some devices do not have serial numbers within their device descriptors and are assigned a unique instance ID by the Windows system to which they're connected.

We can tell the difference between a serial number and a unique instance ID assigned by the operating system, as the one assigned by the operating system has an "&" as the second character. As you can see in Figure 5.2, our example serial number listed (0C90195032E36889&0) has an "&" as the *second to last character*, but a unique instance ID assigned by the operating system will have an "&" as the second character. This allows the device to be uniquely identified on that system. The algorithm used to create a unique instance ID for a device that does not have a serial number is not publicly available, but it is important for analysts to know and understand the distinction in unique instance IDs.

FIGURE 5.4

Enum\USB subkeys visible via WRR.

```
0C90195032E36889

Idx: 18527
Relative Offset: E06C98
Number of Subkeys: 3
Security Key Offset: 2C8788
Date Modified: 7/17/2011 1:14:52 PM
```

FIGURE 5.5

Enum\USB subkey properties visible via WRR.

Next, we navigate to the Enum\USB subkey within the same ControlSet, and locate the subkey of which the name is the serial number (or unique instance ID) of the device in question. The key for the device we're interested in, visible in WRR, is illustrated in Figure 5.4.

Right-clicking on the key named for the unique instance ID (in this example, the serial number for the device) and selecting "Properties," we can see the LastWrite time of the key, illustrated in Figure 5.5.

The LastWrite time of the unique instance ID/serial number key correlates to the last time that the device was connected to the system. This finding appears to be fairly consistent across Windows systems.

Next, we need to navigate to the MountedDevices key at the root of the System hive, and within the values, locate the volume globally unique identifier (volume GUID) that contains the device serial number within its data. In our example, the data for the volume GUID "\??\Volume{b7d8834c-b065-11e0-834c-005056c00008}" contains the device unique instance ID (i.e., serial number), as illustrated in Figure 5.6.

As you can see in Figure 5.6, the device serial number is selected within the value's binary data. Also within the data, we can also see the device ID ("Ven_Best_Buy&Pord_Geek_Squad_U3"). Now, as it turns out, the MountedDevices key also contains a value named "\DosDevices\F:," which contains the same data as the volume ID value seen in Figure 5.6. This tells us that the device had been mapped to the F:\ volume on the system; this information can be very useful during

```
5F00 3F00 3F00 5F00 5500 5300 4200 5300    _.?.?._.U.S.B.S.
5400 4F00 5200 2300 4400 6900 7300 6B00    T.O.R.#.D.i.s.k.
2600 5600 6500 6E00 5F00 4200 6500 7300    &.V.e.n._.B.e.s.
7400 5F00 4200 7500 7900 2600 5000 7200    t._.B.u.y.&.P.r.
6F00 6400 5F00 4700 6500 6500 6B00 5F00    o.d._.G.e.e.k._.
5300 7100 7500 6100 6400 5F00 5500 3300    S.q.u.a.d._.U.3.
2600 5200 6500 7600 5F00 3600 2E00 3100    &.R.e.v._.6...1.
3500 2300 3000 4300 3900 3000 3100 3900    5.#.0.C.9.0.1.9.
3500 3000 3300 3200 4500 3300 3600 3800    5.0.3.2.E.3.6.8.
3800 3900 2600 3000 2300 7B00 3500 3300    8.9.&.0.#.{.5.3.
6600 3500 3600 3300 3000 3700 2D00 6200    f.5.6.3.0.7.-.b.
3600 6200 6600 2D00 3100 3100 6400 3000    6.b.f.-.1.1.d.0.
2D00 3900 3400 6600 3200 2D00 3000 3000    -.9.4.f.2.-.0.0.
6100 3000 6300 3900 3100 6500 6600 6200    a.0.c.9.1.e.f.b.
3800 6200 7D00                             8.b.}.
```

FIGURE 5.6

Volume GUID data seen in WRR.

Value name:
#(97a89b9e-b3c7-11e0-88a1-0024e8a94181)

Value data:
```
0000   50 00 47 00 50 00 64 00    P.G.P.d.
0008   69 00 73 00 6B 00 56 00    i.s.k.V.
0010   6F 00 6C 00 75 00 6D 00    o.l.u.m.
0018   65 00 31 00                e.1.
```

Value name:
#(307dd434-9d94-11e0-8a7f-0024e8a94181)

Value data:
```
0000   54 72 75 65 43 72 79 70    TrueCryp
0008   74 56 6F 6C 75 6D 65 5A    tVolumeZ
0010
```

FIGURE 5.7

PGPDisk and TrueCrypt volumes listed within the MountedDevices key.

an examination (e.g., for mapping to file paths, volumes listed in Windows short-cuts/LNK files and jump lists, etc.). What this also indicates is that no other device had been mapped to the F:\ volume after the Geek Squad device was removed from the system; had another device been connected and mounted as the F:\ volume, we would likely see another device's information in the data, as opposed to that of the Geek Squad device.

This is a good time to mention that you may find indications of a variety of other types of volumes within the MountedDevices key. For example, TrueCrypt and PGPDisk volumes can also be seen listed here, as illustrated in Figure 5.7.

As you can see, the value names for these volumes appear listed a bit differently, beginning with "#" rather than "\??\Volume." The use of TrueCrypt and PGPDisk volumes may be part of legitimate business practices; forensic analysts will often use both of these methods to protect data being stored or shipped. However, it may also indicate specific attempts to hide data.

TIP

DeviceClasses

Within the System hive, the DeviceClasses subkeys maintain some very good information about USB devices. If you navigate to the ControlSet001\Control\DeviceClasses key (or whichever ControlSet is marked "current"), and then locate the {53f56307-b6bf-11d0-94f2-00a0c91efb8b} subkey (the GUID refers to devices identified as disks), then beneath this subkey you will find a subkey that starts with "##?#USBSTOR" and contains the device ID ("VEN_BEST_BUY&PROD_GEEK_SQUAD_U3") and unique instance ID ("0C90195032E36889") for the thumb drive in question. If you look for the {53f5630d-b6bf-11d0-94f2-00a0c91efb8b} subkey (refers to volumes) beneath the DevicesClasses key, you should find a subkey that starts with "##?#STORAGE#VOLUME#_??_USBSTOR," and also contains the device ID and serial number of the thumb drive. In both cases, the LastWrite time for the keys containing the device ID and unique instance ID of the device corresponds to the first time that the device was connected to the system during the most recent boot session.

This may not seem like very valuable information, but the fact that these keys are available provides additional, correlating information for an analyst. This information can be particularly helpful when someone has taken steps to cover his tracks, and has perhaps deleted the contents of the USBStor key mentioned earlier in this chapter in an attempt to hide the fact that he connected a device to the system, as remnants may still exist in other locations within the Registry.

Now we can navigate to the Software\Microsoft\Windows\CurrentVersion\Explorer\MountPoints2 key within the NTUSER.DAT hive file for a user, and locate the subkey with the same name as the volume GUID ({b7d8834c-b065-11e0-834c-005056c00008}). Right-clicking that key and choosing "Properties" we can see that the LastWrite time for that key corresponds to the last time that the device was connected to the system, as illustrated in Figure 5.8. The information illustrated in Figure 5.8 not only allows us to see when the device was last connected to the system, but also under which user context it was connected.

By now, you should be able to see that there is a great deal of information available within the Windows 7 Registry regarding USB thumb drives. Starting with the ControlSet00x\Enum\USBStor subkeys (where "x" refers to the ControlSet marked as "current" within the Select key) in the System hive, we can determine the device class and unique instance IDs of devices connected to the system. We can

FIGURE 5.8

MountPoints2 volume GUID subkey LastWrite time (via WRR).

use the unique instance ID to then map to the MountedDevices key (at the root of the System hive) and determine the volume GUID, and possibly the drive letter to which the device was mounted. Then using this information, we can determine both when the device was first connected during the most recent boot session (LastWrite times from USBStor and DeviceClasses subkeys), as well as when the device was last connected to the system (LastWrite time from USB subkey in the System hive, and MountPoints2 subkey in the NTUSER.DAT hive).

Interestingly enough, there's even more information available about USB-connected devices in the Windows 7 Registry. For instance, continuing with our previous example and navigating to the Microsoft\Windows Portable Devices\ Devices key in the Software hive, we see a subkey named as follows:

```
WPDBUSENUMROOT#UMB#2&37C186B&0&STORAGE#VOLUME#_??_
  USBSTOR#DISK&VEN_BEST_BUY&PROD_GEEK_SQUAD_U3&REV_6.15#0C901950
  32E36889&0#
```

The LastWrite time for this key (viewed via WRR) correlates to the first time that the device was connected to the system during the most recent boot session. Also, the key has a value named "FriendlyName," of which the data are "Test."

Next, if we navigate to the Microsoft\Windows NT\CurrentVersion\EMDMgmt key within the Software hive, we see a key named as follows:

```
_??_USBSTOR#Disk&Ven_Best_Buy&Prod_Geek_Squad_U3&Rev_6.15#0C9019503
  2E36889&0#{53f56307-b6bf-11d0-94f2-00a0c91efb8b}TEST_1677970716
```

Available information online indicates that the EMDMgmt key is associated with ReadyBoost, a technology available with Windows 7 that allows the system to use a USB-connected device as a source of RAM. Within the name of the key, we can see the device ID, the unique instance ID, and the word "TEST" are actually the name of the FAT16 volume on the device. As with the Devices key discussed previously, the LastWrite time on this key appears to correlate to the first time that the device was connected to the system during the most recent boot session. In addition, the key contains several values, as illustrated in Figure 5.9.

As you can see in Figure 5.9, the available values could potentially provide some valuable information, in particular the "LastTestedTime" value. If this value and the "CacheSizeInMB" value were populated with nonzero data, this might

Value	Type	Data
CacheSizeInMB	REG_DWORD	0x00000000
Attributes	REG_BINARY	03 00 00 00 BC 1A E6 7A C4 A1 6C 80 00
DeviceStatus	REG_DWORD	0x00000001
LastTestedTime	REG_QWORD	00 00 00 00 00 00 00 00

FIGURE 5.9

EMDMgmt subkey values, visible in WRR.

indicate that the device was used as a ReadyBoost drive, and provide information regarding when it was last tested. If nothing else, this key and its values provide an additional indication of certain devices that had been connected to the system, even if they hadn't been tested by ReadyBoost.

Another piece of information available from the EMDMgmt key, particularly for USB hard drive enclosures ("wallet drives"), is the volume serial number for the mounted volume. Now, this is not the drive or disk signature seen in the MountedDevices key. A volume serial number is used to identify a volume and is changed whenever the volume is formatted.

As an example, I have a SimpleTech 500-GB drive that I had attached to my Windows 7 system at one point; the EMDMgmt subkey for the device is RIG___ ST500_1354504530. The volume name is "ST500," and I can view the volume ID using the following command:

```
G:\>vol
Volume in drive G is ST500
Volume Serial Number is 50BC-1952
```

If I open the Windows calculator tool ("calc.exe") and switch to the scientific view, I can convert the value from the EMDMgmt subkey (i.e., 1354504530) from decimal to hexadecimal; when I do this, I get "50BC1952."

Remember, I said that the volume serial number is *not* the same thing as the drive signature; these are often confused, or considered to represent the same artifact. A drive signature is a 4-byte value stored at offset 0x1B8 within the master boot record (MBR). A volume serial number is a unique value assigned by Windows to a volume when the volume is formatted. The drive signature for the wallet drive in question, which is available via the MountedDevices key, is "23 48 3D D4." I verified this by plugging the device back into the system, and then viewing the physical disk via FTK Imager. I saw the drive signature within the 4 bytes starting at offset 0x1B8 (440 in decimal) within the drive MBR.

WARNING

USBStor Subkey LastWrite Times

There have been a number of posts to online forums asking about a specific observation regarding LastWrite times on the USBStor subkeys. Several analysts have reported seeing all of the subkeys with identical LastWrite times—not within seconds or minutes, but the same time stamps. Several analysts have asked how it would be possible for a user to connect all of the devices at the same time. It is important to remember that the LastWrite times on these keys do *not* indicate when the device was last connected to the system. Also, other analysts have reported creating timelines (see Chapter 7) of system activity and observing that the key LastWrite times appear to have been updated shortly after an update or Service Pack was installed on the system.

The process for tracking "wallet" or external drives (also referred to as "drive enclosures") on Windows 7 systems is just a bit different. As an example, I connected a Seagate FreeAgent GoFlex external USB drive to my Windows 7 system (the serial number written on the label was NA02VNHQ), and as you'd expect, an entry was created in both the USBStor key and the USB key within the System hive. The keys that were created are illustrated in Figure 5.10. As you can see in Figure 5.10, the unique instance ID subkey for the device is, in fact, the serial number of the device. Also, as with thumb drives, the LastWrite time of the unique instance ID key beneath the USB key correlates to the last time the device was connected to the system.

The biggest difference between drive enclosures and other USB removable storage devices is that we do not use the unique instance ID to determine the volume ID from the MountedDevices key. Remember, this should allow us to then determine which user may have had access to the device. Instead, we have to use the drive or disk signature, which is the 4 bytes located at offset 440 (0x1B8) within the MBR of the drive. As I have access to the drive, I can use a hex editor or forensic analysis software to view the disk signature, as illustrated in Figure 5.11.

USBStor subkey

    Disk&Ven_Seagate&Prod_FreeAgent_GoFlex&Rev_0148
       NA02VNHQ&0

USB subkey

    VID_0BC2&PID_5021
       NA02VNHQ

FIGURE 5.10

USBStor and USB subkeys for external hard drive enclosure.

```
00000001a0 00 00 00 00 00 00 00 00-00 00 00 00 00 00 00 00
00000001b0 00 00 00 00 00 00 00 00-B6 19 F4 04 00 00 00 01
00000001c0 01 00 07 FE FF FF 3F 00-00 00 02 4C 38 3A 00 00
```

FIGURE 5.11

Drive/disk signature.

With the disk signature (which is set by the operating system whenever the drive is formatted), we can then parse the contents of the MountedDevices key using the "mountdev.pl" RegRipper plugin and find the volume GUID for the drive enclosure, which appears as follows:

```
\??\Volume{5d3e617b-b2c7-11e0-8563-005056c00008}
  Drive Signature = b6 19 f4 04
```

Once we have this information, we can then parse the contents of the MountPoints2 key within the user's NTUSER.DAT hive using the "mp2.pl" RegRipper plugin, to determine when the device was last connected to the system. In this case, that information appears as follows:

```
Wed Jul 20 15:07:15 2011 (UTC)
  {5d3e617b-b2c7-11e0-8563-005056c00008}
```

As it turns out, this is not only the same LastWrite time for the unique instance ID key found beneath the USB key, it's also the last time I actually plugged the device into the system, although this time is displayed in UTC. As with other USB removable storage devices, the first time that the device was connected to the system can be found by examining the Windows Event Logs (as discussed earlier in this chapter) or the "setupapi.dev.log" file.

Thumb drives and external "wallet" drives (those in drive enclosures) are not the only devices that can be attached to Windows systems. Other devices may be connected, including smart phones and even devices capable of capturing video and still images, such as the Apple iTouch. This can be particularly important during an exam if images are found to contain EXIF metadata (see Chapter 4), and the analyst finds that a device (e.g., smart phone, iTouch, digital camera) of the type identified in that data had also been connected to the system. To demonstrate what these devices might "look like" to an analyst examining the Registry from an acquired image from a Windows system, I connected an Android smart phone (Motorola Backflip) and an Apple iTouch to a Windows 7 system, disconnected them, repeated the connection–disconnection process later, and then finally rebooted the system. To view artifacts from this activity, I extracted the Registry hive files from the system and parsed them using RegRipper, or more specifically, the command line tool, rip (RegRipper is available at *http://code.google.com/p/winforensicaanalysis/downloads/list*). Using the "usbstor.pl" plugin, we see the following:

```
C:\tools>rip.pl -r f:\system -p usbstor
Launching usbstor v.20080418
ControlSet001\Enum\USBStor

...
Disk&Ven_Motorola&Prod__MB300&Rev__001 [Wed Jul 20 13:24:27 2011]
  S/N: TA538029DP&0 [Wed Jul 20 13:24:27 2011]
   FriendlyName : Motorola MB300 USB Device
```

Now, this device was first plugged into the Windows 7 system at 9:24 am, July 20, 2011 EST. This can be verified by examining the "setupapi.dev.log" file, as well as the Windows Event Log, as mentioned previously in this chapter. We also know that the LastWrite time on the device ID and unique instance ID keys do not specifically correlate to when the device was last connected to the system; in this case, the LastWrite times correlate to the first time the device was connected to the system during the most recent boot session, but only because this was the first time that the device had been connected to the system.

Something else interesting is that I don't see any indication of the Apple iTouch in the output from the "usbstor.pl" plugin. However, using the "usbdevices.pl" plugin, we see the following:

```
C:\tools>rip.pl -r f:\system -p usbdevices
Launching usbdevices v.20100219
...

Apple iPod [VID_05AC&PID_129E\b9e69c2c948d76fd3f959be89193f30a500a0d50]
  Class               : WPD
  Service             : WUDFRd
  Location Information : Port_#0003.Hub_#0004
  Mfg                 : Apple Inc.
```

This shows us that the Apple iTouch is identified as an iPod, with unique instance ID (or serial number) "b9e69c2c948d76fd3f959be89193f30a500a0d50." During testing, the iTouch was last connected to the system at 11:02 am, July 11, 2011 EST, and the LastWrite time for the unique instance ID, when viewed via WRR, is "7/20/2011 3:02:37 PM," which correlates to the last time the device was connected to the Windows 7 system, expressed in UTC.

Using the "mountdev.pl" plugin to examine the MountedDevices key within the System hive, we see the following:

```
C:\tools>rip.pl -r f:\system -p mountdev
Launching mountdev v.20080324
Get MountedDevices key information from the System hive file.
...

Device:
  _??_USBSTOR#Disk&Ven_Motorola&Prod__MB300&Rev__001#TA538029DP&0#
  {53f5630 7-b6bf-11d0-94f2-00a0c91efb8b}
  \??\Volume{5d3e6180-b2c7-11e0-8563-005056c00008}
```

This indicates that the smart phone was mounted to the system with the volume GUID "{5d3e6180-b2c7-11e0-8563-005056c00008}." The iTouch, however, does not appear to have been recognized as a removable storage device, and does not appear to have been mounted as a volume. Using the "devclass.pl" plugin to look at the devices mounted as disks indicates the following:

```
C:\tools>rip.pl -r f:\system -p devclass
Launching devclass v.20100901
DevClasses - Disks
ControlSet001\Control\DeviceClasses\
  {53f56307-b6bf-11d0-94f2-00a0c91efb8b}
```

```
...
Wed Jul 20 13:24:27 2011 (UTC)
  Disk&Ven_Motorola&Prod__MB300&Rev__001,TA538029DP&0
```

As mentioned previously in this chapter, the smart phone was first connected to the system at 9:24 am, July 20, 2011 EST. We also know from previous discussions that the LastWrite time for the device key listed under the DevicesClasses disk device subkey will tell us when the device was first connected during the most recent boot session; in this case, "Wed Jul 20 13:24:27 2011 (UTC)."

With the volume GUID for the smart phone, we can now run the "mp2.pl" plugin against the NTUSER.DAT hive file extracted from the system, to parse the MountPoints2 key. Running the plugin, we see the following:

```
C:\tools>rip.pl -r f:\ntuser.dat -p mp2
Launching mp2 v.20090115
MountPoints2
Software\Microsoft\Windows\CurrentVersion\Explorer\MountPoints2
...
Volumes:
...
Wed Jul 20 15:11:34 2011 (UTC)
  {5d3e6180-b2c7-11e0-8563-005056c00008}
```

Again, as discussed previously in this chapter, the LastWrite time for the volume GUID key for the smart phone (i.e., "Wed Jul 20 15:11:34 2011 (UTC)") indicates (and does in fact correlate to) when the device was last connected to the system.

We can then use the "port_dev.pl" plugin to parse the contents to the Microsoft\Windows Portable Devices\Devices key from the Software hive, and when we do, we see the following:

```
C:\tools>rip.pl -r f:\software -p port_dev
Launching port_dev v.20090118
Microsoft\Windows Portable Devices\Devices
Device    :
LastWrite : Wed Jul 20 12:56:48 2011 (UTC)
SN        :
Drive     : Apple iPod
...
Device    : DISK&VEN_MOTOROLA&PROD__MB300&REV__001
LastWrite : Wed Jul 20 13:24:30 2011 (UTC)
SN        : TA538029DP&0
Drive     : F:\
```

The output of the "port_dev.pl" plugin indicates key LastWrite times that correlate to the first time that each device was connected to the system during the most recent boot session. It also indicates that the smart phone had been mapped to the F:\ volume, which is not something that we got from the contents of the MountedDevices key (from the System hive), as another device (not part of the testing) had been connected to the system and mounted as the F:\ drive *after* the smart phone had been disconnected from the system. This can be determined by comparing the two sets of output and their associated time stamps.

Finally, the EMDMgmt key (full path within the Software hive is Microsoft\ Windows NT\CurrentVersion\EMDMgmt) contains a subkey named_??_USBSTOR# Disk&Ven_Motorola&Prod__MB300&Rev__001#TA538029DP&0#{53f56307-b6bf-11d0-94f2-00a0c91efb8b}_946156644, which corresponds to the smart phone (including the device model and serial number). Again, the EMDMgmt key is specific to ReadyBoost, and this device was not tested for its suitability for ReadyBoost functionality. However, the EMDMgmt key does provide indications of devices that had been connected to the system, which can be particularly useful when a user deletes some of the other Registry keys in an attempt to hide her activities.

TIP

Deleted Registry Keys

When Registry keys are deleted, much like files, they aren't really gone. Instead, the space that they consume within the hive file is simply marked as being available, and can be overwritten. As discussed in Chapter 2 of *Windows Registry Forensics*, Jolanta Thomassen's "regslack.exe" (provided in the RR.zip archive at *http://code.google.com/p/ winforensicaanalysis/downloads/list*) utility does a great job of recovering deleted keys and values, in addition to illustrating free space within the hive file.

As we began this section on USB device analysis, I mentioned a couple of checklists for this type of analysis that Rob Lee had created. Hopefully you took the time to download those checklists and take a look at them. Regardless, I put together similar checklists based on the information provided in this section, including where within the Registry to look for specific pieces of information, and, where appropriate, which RegRipper plugin can be used to retrieve and display that information. These checklists are included with the materials associated with this book, and can be found at *http://code.google.com/p/winforensicaanalysis/ downloads/list*.

System Hive

Many times, Registry analysis may not involve multiple keys or hives, but will instead involve just a single hive, or even just a single key. As one would think, the System hive maintains a great deal of information regarding the system, including devices that have been attached, services and drivers that should (or should not) be running, etc. As such, analysts may find a good deal of very useful information within the System hive. So far in this chapter, we've already discussed some of the information available that can be used to determine when USB devices had been connected to the system, and we also included references to the MountedDevices key in that discussion.

Again, in this chapter, I do not want to provide a voluminous list of keys and values; instead, my goal is to present possible solutions to questions commonly posed as such, therefore we will not be going through each hive, a key at a time. Instead, we will focus on providing solutions.

Services

Analyzing available services can be an important part of investigations for a number of types of incidents, including compromises, data breaches, and even malware infections. Windows services serve as a great persistence mechanism for malware (something that will be discussed in more detail in Chapter 6), as many services start automatically when the system is started (no user login or other inter-action required), and services often run with elevated privileges. An attacker may compromise a system and leave a backdoor running as a Windows service, knowing that if the service is set to start when the system boots, that backdoor will be available as long as the system is running. As such, analyzing the available services may prove to be fruitful.

When you open the System hive in WRR, locate the "current" ControlSet, and expand the Services key, you'll likely see a great number of subkeys; not all of these are actually services. Many of the subkeys you'll see are for device drivers installed with the operating system or with applications. As you click your way down through the available services (I'll stop on BITS, or Background Intelligent Transfer Service), you'll see the values for each key, with information similar to what is illustrated in Figure 5.12.

From these values, you can see considerable information, including the Start value. In this case, a value of 3 indicates that the service is set to a Manual start—that is, on demand, usually via some user- or application-initiated action. Other services may have a Start value of 2, indicating that they are set to an Automatic start when Windows boots. We can also see the DisplayName (previous versions of Windows, particularly XP, actually had names and description fields in the Registry,

Value	Type	Data
DisplayName	REG_SZ	@%SystemRoot%\system32\qmgr.dll,-1000
ImagePath	REG_EXPA...	%SystemRoot%\System32\svchost.exe -k netsvcs
Description	REG_SZ	@%SystemRoot%\system32\qmgr.dll,-1001
ObjectName	REG_SZ	LocalSystem
ErrorControl	REG_DWORD	0x00000001
Start	REG_DWORD	0x00000003
DelayedAutoStart	REG_DWORD	0x00000001
Type	REG_DWORD	0x00000020
DependOnService	REG_MULTI...	RpcSs‖EventSystem‖
ServiceSidType	REG_DWORD	0x00000001
RequiredPrivileges	REG_MULTI...	SeCreateGlobalPrivilege‖SeImpersonatePrivilege‖Se1
FailureActions	REG_BINARY	80 51 01 00 00 00 00 00 00 00 00 00 03 00 00 00 14

FIGURE 5.12

Service key values, via WRR.

FIGURE 5.13

Enum\Root\LEGACY_IMDISK keys, via WRR.

rather than references to strings in DLLs) and the ImagePath, which can be used to help identify suspicious services.

> **NOTE**
>
> **ImagePath Value**
>
> Some malware may maintain persistence by referencing a malicious executable in the ImagePath value. However, malware may use a more subtle persistence method by loading a malicious DLL into a valid executable. In these cases, the ImagePath will reference a legitimate Windows file—frequently "%SystemRoot%\system32\svchost.exe"—while the malicious DLL will be referenced in the service's Parameters subkey under the ServiceDLL value.

More information about the various values and their meaning can be found in Microsoft KB article 1030000, found at *http://support.microsoft.com/kb/103000.*

There is also more information regarding Windows services available in the System hive. If we navigate to the Enum\Root key within the appropriate ControlSet, we'll see a number of subkeys of which the names all start with "LEGACY_." You should recognize the remaining portions of the names as being the same as some of the services and drivers we saw listed beneath the Services key. These keys are created automatically by the operating system as part of normal system function. Many of the LEGACY_* keys will also have a subkey named "0000," as illustrated in Figure 5.13.

In this case, the LEGACY_IMDISK (ImDisk is a virtual disk driver available at *http://www.ltr-data.se/opencode.html/#ImDisk*) key illustrated in Figure 5.13 refers to a legacy driver; we can see this listed in the Class value beneath the "0000" subkey. Now, the really interesting thing is that the LastWrite time for the LEGACY_IMDISK is "Tue Jan 4 11:35:45 2011 (UTC)" (extracted using the RegRipper "legacy.pl" plugin), which correlates to the *first* time that the device driver was launched, and the LastWrite time for the LEGACY_IMDISK\0000 key is "Wed Jan 5 16:50:32 2011 (UTC)," which refers to the *last* time the device driver was launched. Not only can this be very useful during malware and data breach investigations (particularly when you need to identify a "window of compromise," or how long the system has been compromised), but the *really* interesting thing is that the ImDisk driver is no longer installed on the system. After installing it and

FIGURE 5.14

Portion of keys at the Software hive root, via WRR.

using it briefly, I uninstalled the driver, yet the LEGACY_ key for that driver persisted on the system. This information can clearly be extremely useful during an investigation.

Software Hive

As the Software hive contains information regarding installed software, as well as the system-wide configuration of that software (the user's hive will contain user-specific settings), analysis of this hive can prove to be very valuable during an examination.

Application Analysis

Many times, analysts want to know what applications are installed on the system to begin the process of determining user activity, to see what applications the user may have had access to, to determine if there was a violation of corporate acceptable use policies, or to tie specific activities to an application. The simplest way to start going about this is to check the available keys at the root of the Software hive, as illustrated in Figure 5.14.

As you can see from Figure 5.14, the system in question has the 7-Zip archive utility installed, as well as some Broadcom, Dell, and Intel applications. This information can provide the analyst with some indications of installed applications.

Next, the Uninstall key (the key path is "\Microsoft\Windows\CurrentVersion\ Uninstall" within the Software hive) should also be examined. The subkeys beneath the Uninstall key may appear to be GUIDs or readable names, and many will contain values that provide information regarding installation date, install path and source, as well as the string used to uninstall the application. As with those keys at the root of the Software hive, the Uninstall keys are most often the result of applications that are installed via an installation package, such as the Microsoft installer. Applications that are simply executable files copied to a directory do not generally

FIGURE 5.15

Wow6432Node key, via WRR.

create Install or Uninstall keys, although some will leave traces in the Registry once they have actually been executed. One such example is the MS SysInternals utilities; these tools have an end user license agreement (EULA) that must be accepted before the tool will run, and running the tool will create an entry in the Registry for that tool.

Applications installed via a Microsoft installer package (a file that ends in "*.msi") are logged or recorded in the Software hive in the path "\Classes\Installer\ Products." Each subkey beneath the Products key has a name with a long sequence of hexadecimal characters, and the ProductName value will tell you the name of the product that was installed. The "msis.pl" RegRipper plugin will extract this information for you, and sort the various installed packages by their key LastWrite times (which correlates to the package installation date/time). An example of this information collected from one Windows 7 system appears as follows:

```
Thu Apr 21 16:51:24 2011 (UTC)
  VMware Player;C:\Users\harlan\AppData\Local\Temp\
  vmware_1303404464\vmware player.msi
Wed Apr 13 18:54:38 2011 (UTC)
  ActivePerl 5.8.9 Build 829;F:\tools\ActivePerl-5.8.9.829-
  MSWin32-x86-294280.msi
```

These are not the only places that an analyst should look for installed applications. On 64-bit Windows 7 systems, 32-bit applications may appear beneath the Wow6432Node key at the root of the Software hive, as illustrated in Figure 5.15.

In addition, the analyst should also check the root of the NTUSER.DAT hive for indications of installed applications, and the Uninstall key within the user hive (the key path is "\Software\Microsoft\Windows\CurrentVersion\Uninstall") should also be examined. These keys will contain information regarding application data specifically installed by and available to a particular user.

FIGURE 5.16

Classes subkeys from Software hive.

TIP

Browser Analysis

Many times when the subject of browser or web history analysis comes up in online forums, one of the first responses you'll usually see is "check the TypedURLs key in the user hive"; however, this key applies to Internet Explorer, and there are several other browsers that users can download and install. As such, the first step in browser analysis is to determine which browser the user was using during the timeframe in question (tips on determining the browser in use, from system or user file associations or other information found in the Registry, are discussed in greater detail later in the chapter). Do not assume that simply because the system is Windows, or because the TypedURLs key is populated with values, that at the time in question, the user was using Internet Explorer.

Yet another way for an analyst to gather information regarding applications on a system is through what I have referred to as "file extension analysis." This technique has proven itself to be useful for finding not only installed applications (in the sense that the application had an installer, such as an MSI file or a "setup.exe" file), but also for standalone applications (that do not necessarily appear in the Registry) that the user has associated with certain file types. We want to start by accessing the Software hive, navigating to the Classes key, and looking at each of the subkeys that starts with a "." (see Figure 5.16).

From each of these file extensions, we can determine considerable information. For example, if we open each of the keys (as illustrated in Figure 5.16) and look for the "Default" value, for most of them we'll see what type of file the extension refers to; for example, the "Default" value for the .3g2 key is "WMP11.AssocFile.3g2." If we then go to the Classes\ WMP11.AssocFile.3g2 key and then navigate to the shell\open\command subkey, we'll see that the command used to access or execute files that end in the .3g2 extension appears as follows:

```
"%ProgramFiles(x86)%\Windows Media Player\wmplayer.exe" /prefetch:6
/Open "%L"
```

What this tells us is that the files ending in the .3g2 extension are associated with the Windows Media Player, and when the user double-clicks one of these files, the Windows Media Player will open automatically to run the file.

The way you would find this information on a live system is by opening a command prompt and typing the command *assoc*. A lot of file extensions would go flying by, so let's say that you just wanted to see one ... say .jpeg. So you'd type the command *assoc | find ".jpeg"*, and you'd see *.jpeg = jpegfile* returned. Then you'd type the command *ftype jpegfile*, and you'd see something similar to the following:

```
%SystemRoot%\System32\rundll32.exe "%ProgramFiles%\Windows Photo
   Viewer\PhotoViewer.dll", ImageView_Fullscreen %1
```

This is great information, but it's for a live system. To determine similar information from an acquired image, you'd want to run the "assoc.pl" RegRipper plugin against the Software hive from the system, using the following command:

```
C:\tools>rip.pl-r f:\software -p assoc
```

The "assoc.pl" plugin processes information from the Software hive in a manner similar to running the *assoc* and *ftype* commands already mentioned. You will also want to check the keys at the root of the user's USRCLASS.DAT hive file. I had installed the Google Chrome browser in my Windows 7 system, and the "Default" value for the ".https\shell\open\command" appears as follows:

```
"C:\Users\harlan\AppData\Local\Google\Chrome\Application\chrome.
exe" -- "%1"
```

Also at the root of my USRCLASS.DAT hive file is a key named .shtml, and the "Default" value is "ChromeHTML"; mapping back to the Software hive, the value for the "Classes\ChromeHTML\shell\open\command" is the same as what appears above, indicating that if I double-click a file the ends in ".shtml" (or ".https"), the file will be opened via the Chrome browser.

From an analyst perspective, this is great information, as it provides indications of applications installed on the system. However, it also helps us answer another question. Many times I will see a question in lists and online forums similar to, "Does anyone know what application uses a file with this extension?" Many times, this question is a result of some analysis that has already been performed, and the analyst has apparently run across an unfamiliar file. In cases such as this, searching via Google may provide a number of possible solutions, but analysis of the Registry from the system that is being examined will likely provide the most accurate information.

Finally, another means for seeing what applications the user may have accessed involves examining the contents of the UserAssist subkeys, which is discussed in detail later in this chapter. This can be a valuable avenue of investigation, as the contents of these keys persist even though the application itself may have been uninstalled or deleted.

NetworkList

Windows systems have always maintained information regarding network connections, including wireless access points (WAPs) to which the system (usually a laptop)

Value	Type	Data
ProfileGuid	REG_SZ	{F9A38942-A362-4D6D-B9BB-A4AD8F11C28C}
Description	REG_SZ	linksys
Source	REG_DWORD	0x00000408
DnsSuffix	REG_SZ	<none>
FirstNetwork	REG_SZ	linksys
DefaultGatewayMac	REG_BINARY	00 0F 66 58 41 ED 00 00

FIGURE 5.17

Values from a NetworkList\Signatures\Unmanaged subkey.

has connected. Tools used to manage these connections maintain historical information regarding the connections, and we can often see these within the user interface for the application. As you might expect, this information is maintained in the Registry, and on Vista and Windows 7 there is considerable information available to the analyst.

To start examining these data, we first have to navigate to the following Registry key within the Software hive:

```
Microsoft\Windows NT\CurrentVersion\NetworkList\Signatures
```

Beneath this key, you will usually see two subkeys: Managed and Unmanaged. Managed refers to connections for which the system is managed by a domain controller; Unmanaged refers to connections for which the system is not managed by a domain controller. Beneath both of these keys you will find subkeys with names that are a long series of letters and numbers; what we're looking for is the values within each of these subkeys. An example of these values is illustrated in Figure 5.17.

From the available values, you can see how they can be valuable. For example, the "Description" and "FirstNetwork" values refer to the service set identifier (SSID) of a WAP. The "DefaultGatewayMac" value is the media access control (MAC) address of the WAP, which we can use in WiFi geolocation mapping.

TIP

WiFi Geolocation Mapping

Over the years, there have been a couple of databases compiled for use in WiFi geolocation; that is, providing a mapping between wireless router MAC addresses (usually compiled via "wardriving" or submissions) and the coordinates (latitude and longitude) of the physical location of the router. Some of these services focused primarily on mapping major metropolitan areas. One such service that was publicly available was the Skyhook Wireless database, and I had implemented access to the database to retrieve the latitude/longitude pair for wireless routers in their database in a Perl script called "maclookup.pl." (While the script worked very well for some time, at the time of this writing, it would appear that the Skyhook database may no longer be accessible; however, the script continues to serve as an example of what can be achieved.) As an example, I extracted the MAC address of a wireless router from the Registry of one of my systems and was able to obtain coordinates, which I then submitted to Google Maps. The map location for the wireless router in question is illustrated in Figure 5.18.

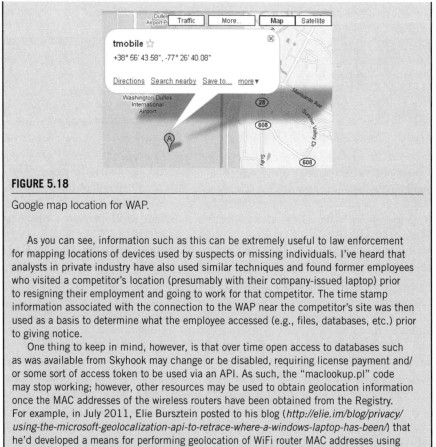

FIGURE 5.18

Google map location for WAP.

As you can see, information such as this can be extremely useful to law enforcement for mapping locations of devices used by suspects or missing individuals. I've heard that analysts in private industry have also used similar techniques and found former employees who visited a competitor's location (presumably with their company-issued laptop) prior to resigning their employment and going to work for that competitor. The time stamp information associated with the connection to the WAP near the competitor's site was then used as a basis to determine what the employee accessed (e.g., files, databases, etc.) prior to giving notice.

One thing to keep in mind, however, is that over time open access to databases such as was available from Skyhook may change or be disabled, requiring license payment and/ or some sort of access token to be used via an API. As such, the "maclookup.pl" code may stop working; however, other resources may be used to obtain geolocation information once the MAC addresses of the wireless routers have been obtained from the Registry. For example, in July 2011, Elie Bursztein posted to his blog (*http://elie.im/blog/privacy/ using-the-microsoft-geolocalization-api-to-retrace-where-a-windows-laptop-has-been/*) that he'd developed a means for performing geolocation of WiFi router MAC addresses using the Microsoft Live API, and that he would be giving a presentation on the topic at the upcoming BlackHat Briefings conference in Las Vegas, NV, in August 2011. The white paper and PDF of the presentation slides can be found at *https://www.blackhat.com/html/ bh-us-11/bh-us-11-archives.html#Bursztein*.

Finally, we can use the "ProfileGuid" value to map to the appropriate profile in the NetworkList\Profiles key. The data for the "ProfileGuid" value should correspond to one of the available profiles beneath the Profiles key. The values for the profile identified in Figure 5.17 are illustrated in Figure 5.19.

As we can see in Figure 5.19, the "ProfileName" and "Description" values should match the "Description" and "FirstNetwork" values that we saw in Figure 5.17. The "NameType" value refers to the type of connection of the profile, where 0x47 is a wireless network, 0x06 is a wired network, and 0x17 is a broadband (a.k.a., 3G) network (as indicated by the MS TechNet blog located at *http://blogs.technet.com/b /networking/archive/2010/09/08/network-location-awareness-nla-and-how-it-relates- to-windows-firewall-profiles.aspx*). The "DateCreated" and "DateLastConnected"

Value	Type	Data
ab ProfileName	REG_SZ	linksys
ab Description	REG_SZ	linksys
Managed	REG_DWORD	0x00000000
Category	REG_DWORD	0x00000000
DateCreated	REG_BINARY	D8 07 02 00 06 00 10 00 0C 00 02 00 0F 00 20 00
NameType	REG_DWORD	0x00000047
DateLastConnected	REG_BINARY	D8 07 02 00 01 00 12 00 0B 00 02 00 30 00 5A 00

FIGURE 5.19

Windows 7 NetworkList key profile values.

Value	Type	Data
ab ServiceName	REG_SZ	{D4DC0CE9-90F2-4DCE-9294-7091519EFE56}
ab Description	REG_SZ	DW1501 Wireless-N WLAN Half-Mini Card

FIGURE 5.20

Values for NetworkCards\12 key.

values are a 128-bit SYSTEMTIME structure, a description of which can be found at *http://msdn.microsoft.com/en-us/library/ms724950(v=vs.85).aspx*. These values refer to when the profile was created (the system first connected to the network) and when the system was last connected to the network; however, according to Microsoft, these time stamps can be "either in coordinated universal time (UTC) or local time, depending on the function that is being called."

NetworkCards

All versions of the Windows operating system also maintain information about network interface cards within the Registry. For example, a quick look in the Software hive ("HKLM\Software") at the \Microsoft\Windows NT\CurrentVersion\NetworkCards key shows two subkeys (named 12 and 8, respectively), one of which contains the values illustrated in Figure 5.20.

The ServiceName value illustrated in Figure 5.20 is the GUID for the network interface card (NIC) and the Description value is what is seen when you type "ipconfig/all" at the command prompt on a live system; in fact, it's actually listed after "Description" in the output of the command. We can then go to the System hive, and navigate to the ControlSet00*n*\services\Tcpip\Parameters\Interfaces key (where *n* is the number of the ControlSet identified as current) and locate the subkeys named for the ServiceName value we found beneath the NetworkCards key. This key will contain a great deal of pertinent network settings and information that refers to the interface, such as whether dynamic host configuration protocol (DHCP) was enabled (or the interface had a hard-coded IP address), the DHCP server, default gateway, etc. This information can be useful, particularly when attempting to identify the system being analyzed in association with other external sources, such as network packet captures, firewall/web server/network device logs, etc.

FIGURE 5.21

TaskCache\Tree subkeys, via WRR.

Scheduled Tasks

Vista, Windows 2008, and Windows 7 systems manage scheduled tasks a bit differently from previous versions of Windows. Starting with Windows Vista, Microsoft introduced Task Scheduler 2.0, which stored information regarding scheduled tasks in the Registry's Software hive beneath the following key (note that these Windows versions ship with a number of default tasks):

```
Microsoft\Windows NT\CurrentVersion\Schedule\TaskCache
```

The XML files that contain the scheduled task settings and instructions are located in the "C:\Windows\System32\Tasks" folder (and subfolders; refer to Chapter 4 for a detailed discussion of scheduled tasks information maintained within the file system). Most of the human-readable information regarding scheduled tasks within the Registry is found beneath the Tree subkey, as illustrated in Figure 5.21.

On a default installation of Windows 7, most of the scheduled tasks will have keys listed beneath the Tree\Microsoft\Windows subkey. For each scheduled task, there will be an "Id" value that contains a GUID, and an index value. The values for the Microsoft\Windows\Registry\RegIdleBackup task are illustrated in Figure 5.22.

We can then use the GUID value to navigate to the TaskCache\Tasks key, and locate the subkey with the ID GUID as its name. Beneath this key, you will find the values illustrated in Figure 5.23.

Most notable are the "Path" and "Hash" values. The Path value clearly provides the path to the scheduled task file. The Hash value is a bit more interesting, as the hash is of the XML task file itself and used to verify the integrity of that file. Bruce Dang (of Microsoft) gave a presentation at the 27th Chaos Communications Congress (the video of which is available online at *http://www .vimeo.com/18225315*), during which he discussed Microsoft's efforts in analyzing the Stuxnet malware. During that presentation, Bruce stated that the hash algorithm used at the time to identify changes in the scheduled task files was the

Value ▲	Type	Data
Id	REG_SZ	{CA4B8FF2-A4D2-4D88-A52E-3A5BDAF7F56E}
Index	REG_DWORD	0x00000003

FIGURE 5.22

Values in RegIdleBackup key, via WRR.

Value ▲	Type	Data
DynamicInfo	REG_BINARY	03 00 00 00 A8 1C 18 30 41 04 CA 01 00 00 00 00 00 00 00 00 0(
Hash	REG_BINARY	AE 0D B2 F3 1A 30 B2 08 E0 C5 0E F6 4C 29 94 8A 82 86 12 AC
Path	REG_SZ	\Microsoft\Windows\Registry\RegIdleBackup
Triggers	REG_BINARY	15 00 00 00 00 00 00 00 01 12 72 FB FE 07 00 00 00 C0 76 40 0$

FIGURE 5.23

Values beneath a TaskCache\Tasks*GUID* key.

CRC-32 algorithm, for which it is very easy to generate collisions. Analysis of the malware determined that one of the vulnerabilities it would exploit was to modify a scheduled task and pad the file so that when the Task Scheduler verified the task's hash prior to running it, the hash would match what was stored in the Registry. According to Bruce, Microsoft decided to replace the algorithm with the SHA-256 algorithm; this fix appears to have been provided in security update MS10-092, found online at *http://support.microsoft.com/kb/2305420*. Note that the KnowledgeBase article states that any scheduled tasks that have already been corrupted by malware may be validated following the installation of this security update; as such, the article recommends that the actions associated with the tasks be verified, which is excellent advice.

TIP

Wow6432Node

As long as you're examining a Software hive, don't forget to take a look in the Wow6432 Node key. This key is used for Registry redirection of calls from 32-bit applications on 64-bit systems, and can contain some very useful information. For example, I've found values within the \Wow6432Node\Microsoft\Windows\CurrentVersion\Run key in the Software hive from a 64-bit Windows 7 system, and these values were not also included in the \Microsoft\ Windows\CurrentVersion\Run key. I've also found a significant number of subkeys beneath the \Wow6432Node\Microsoft\Windows\CurrentVersion\Uninstall key, indicating applications and updates that had been installed on the system.

User Hives

As with other Registry hives, there are some similarities between keys and values found in the user profile hives on the more familiar (to analysts) Windows XP systems and newer Windows 7 systems. Some keys and their values remain relatively unchanged; one such key is the ubiquitous Run key, as the path and use

FIGURE 5.24

ComDlg32 subkeys, via WRR.

Value	Type	Data
MRUListEx	REG_BINARY	01 00 00 00 00 00 00 00 FF FF FF FF
0	REG_BINARY	63 00 63 00 74 00 75 00 6E 00 65 00 00 00
1	REG_BINARY	70 00 72 00 6F 00 67 00 72 00 61 00 6D 00 00 00

FIGURE 5.25

WordWheelQuery values.

(in both the Software and NTUSER.DAT hives) has remained essentially the same. Some keys have changed slightly; for example, beneath the Software\Microsoft\Windows\CurrentVersion\Explorer\ComDlg32 key we no longer find the familiar LastVisitedMRU and OpenSaveMRU keys we were used to from Windows XP. Instead, we find other keys, as illustrated in Figure 5.24.

As you can see from Figure 5.24, there are some new keys, as well as some keys with different names. However, the LastVisitedPidMRU, LastVisitedPidMRULegacy, and OpenSavePidMRU keys are very similar to their Windows XP brethren.

What I hope to do in the rest of the chapter is discuss some of the keys that are new to Windows 7, and different from Windows XP. Have no illusions, I will not be able to address every new key and every change, as something like that is beyond the scope of this book. Instead, I will try to address some of the significant changes that are important to analysts and investigators. I will focus primarily on those keys and values associated with the operating system itself, as it is impossible to address every possible application. So, please consider this a start, but I hope one in which you find significant value.

WordWheelQuery

With Windows XP, searches that the user ran via the Search functionality accessed via the Start menu appeared in the ACMru key within the user's hive. When Vista was deployed, analysts found that searches performed by the user were no longer maintained in the Registry, but were instead stored in a file. Shortly after the release of Windows 7, analysts found that user searches were again stored in the Registry, this time in the following key:

```
Software\Microsoft\Windows\CurrentVersion\Explorer\WordWheelQuery
```

The values within this key are stored in Unicode format, and maintained in a most recently used (MRU) list, as illustrated in Figure 5.25.

As with other MRU list keys, the LastWrite time for the key in questions corresponds to when the most recent search was conducted. As illustrated in Figure 5.25, the search terms are stored as binary values, with the actual terms listed in Unicode. As such, item 1 (the byte sequence "70 00 72 00 6F 00 67 00 72 00 61 00 6D 00 00 00") indicates that the user searched for the term "program." When viewing the Properties for the WordWheelQuery key via WRR, we see that the LastWrite time for the key is "3/13/2010 1:34:03 PM," which indicates the date and time (in UTC format) that the user searched for item 1. We know this because the first 4 bytes (or DWORD) in the MRUListEx value ("01 00 00 00") indicate that the value named "1" was the most recent search term. The RegRipper "wordwheelquery.pl" plugin will assist in enumerating this information.

TIP

Historical Registry Data

This is as good a place as any to point out how historical Registry data can be accessed and used. Windows 7 maintains Volume Shadow Copies (VSCs), which can provide access to previous versions of files, to include Registry hives. Accessing VSCs from an analyst's perspective (e.g., from within an acquired image) is discussed in detail in Chapter 3. What this means is that while Registry keys that maintain MRU lists (e.g., the WordWheelQuery key, RecentDocs, etc.) only provide information about the most recent activity, historical information can be retrieved by mounting the appropriate VSCs and running queries for the same Registry keys and values. For example, the value named "0" in Figure 5.25 is "cctune," but the MRUListEx value indicates that the most recently used value is "1," and as such the LastWrite time for the key indicates when the user searched for the term in value "1." The date and time for which the user ran the search for "cctune" may be determined by mounting the appropriate VSC from the acquired image and querying the WordWheelQuery key. This can be a very useful analysis technique, and can be used to provide greater detail and context to timelines (discussed in detail in Chapter 7).

Shellbags

When conducting research on Windows forensic analysis, you may see mention of shellbags and wonder exactly what this refers to. *Shellbags* are a set of Registry keys and values that store user-specific preferences for Windows Explorer display options. One of the nice things about Windows systems is that when you open Windows Explorer to a particular file path and position and size the window that you have open, Windows "remembers" these settings, so that the next time you go to that directory or folder, you are presented with the same settings. This information is maintained in the Registry hives within the user profile. This way, if you log into a system as "userA," you would likely have different settings than if you logged in using another account. An example of how this Registry information can affect a system from a user perspective is available in Microsoft KB article 813711 (found at *http://support.microsoft.com/kb/813711*); this article describes a situation in which changes in size, view, icon, and position of folders are not remembered on

Windows systems. As such, these settings can be said to contain user preferences for displaying certain information—settings the user would have had to configure.

The shellbags Registry keys that we're interested in are named "Shell" and exist within the two hive files located in the user profile on Windows 7 systems: the NTUSER.DAT hive in the root of the profile, and the USRCLASS.DAT hive located in the "AppData\Local\Microsoft\Windows" folder in the profile. Within the NTUSER.DAT hive, the path to the Shell key is "Software\Microsoft\Windows\Shell," and the subkeys that we're interested in are Bags and BagMRU. Within the USRCLASS.DAT hive, the path to the Shell key is "Local Settings\Software\Microsoft\Windows\Shell," and the subkeys we're interested in are also Bags and BagMRU. (By now, you can see why this section is called "Shellbags.")

Further research indicates that there may also be shellbags data in the USRCLASS.DAT hive (on Vista and Windows 7 systems, found in the "Users*username*\AppData\Local\Microsoft\Windows" folder, and merged with the NTUSER.DAT file to create the HKEY_CURRENT_USER hive when the user logs in), beneath the Wow6432Node key on 64-bit systems. While a review of a limited number of systems failed to identify a "Local Settings\Software\Microsoft\Windows\Shell\Bags" key path beneath this key, it is worth keeping an eye out for during an exam.

TIP

Tracking User Activity

User actions that result in a persistent change to the system can be useful to an investigator. The key is for analysts to understand what actions may lead to the creation or modification of an artifact (or specific set of artifacts), and developing supporting, corroborating information through the inclusion and analysis of additional data sources. For example, the existence of a prefetch file (discussed in Chapter 4) indicating that the Windows defragmentation utility had been launched doesn't implicitly indicate that the user launched the utility; in fact, Windows systems run a limited "defrag" on a regular basis. However, the existence of artifacts related to the user launching the utility, preceded by file deletions and/or applications being removed from the system, would provide indications of user intent.

Apparently, the data beneath the Bags and BagMRU keys can be used to reconstruct some potentially valuable information regarding access to folder paths. For example, much like Windows shortcut (LNK) files, the binary data within certain values beneath the keys contain embedded creation, modification, and access time stamps for the accessed folder. The keys themselves also contain LastWrite times, indicating when the folder was first accessed, or when the configuration was most recently updated. Analysts can access this information through the use of the Windows shellbag parsers "sbag.exe" tool, available at *http://tzworks.net/prototype_page.php?proto_id=14.*

71	01/07/11 00:05:50.383	Win2008			01/05/2011	17:07:00	01/05/2011	17:13:40	01/05/2011
77	06/21/11 21:20:51.048	New folder			01/18/2011	01:24:50	01/18/2011	01:24:50	01/18/2011
78	06/21/11 21:20:51.048	user			01/18/2011	01:24:50	01/18/2011	01:24:50	01/18/2011
79	06/21/11 21:20:51.048	user23			01/18/2011	01:25:00	01/18/2011	01:25:00	01/18/2011
83	06/21/11 21:20:51.048	ProDiscoverRelease6800Basic.zip			01/21/2011	15:18:54	01/20/2011	23:25:48	01/21/2011
104	06/21/11 21:20:51.048	Shadow_Analyser_Beta_U52.zip			02/09/2011	18:41:04	02/10/2011	01:24:04	02/09/2011
20	07/20/11 16:16:41.134	D:							
34	04/21/11 17:19:03.427	fau-1.3.0.2390a.zip			01/04/2011	11:43:10	01/04/2011	11:43:26	01/04/2011

FIGURE 5.26

Extract of output from "sbag.exe."

Using the "sbag.exe" tool is quite simple; it's a command line interface (CLI) tool and requires only the path to the hive file of interest. For example, you can easily dump the shellbags information from a hive file extracted from an acquired image using the following command:

```
C:\tools> sbag f:\usrclass.dat
```

With the amount of information that can be available, it's a good idea to redirect the output to a file. The output of the tool produces 10 pipe-separated columns that include the bag number (i.e., "NodeSlot"), LastWrite time of the key being parsed, the path, embedded creation, modification and access times, and the full path for the folder accessed. The pipe-separated output can be opened in Excel for analysis; a portion of output from "sbag.exe," open in Excel, is illustrated in Figure 5.26.

This information can be very valuable to an analyst, illustrating access to specific resources, along with the date and time that those resources had been accessed. For example, the parsed shellbag information can illustrate access to zipped archives and folders that no longer exist on the system, removable storage devices, and even network shares. As with other artifacts located in the Registry, the shellbags provide indications of access to resources that persist after the resource (i.e., folder) is no longer available.

Some interesting artifacts I've found in USRCLASS.DAT hives from Windows 7 systems are filenames, as you can see illustrated in Figure 5.26—specifically, "fau-1.3.0.2390a.zip," "ProDiscoverRelease6800Basic.zip," and "Shadow_analyser_beta_U52.zip." This is interesting because the available information regarding the BagMRU keys is that the data within the values refers to folders. However, keep in mind that when a user "sees" a zipped archive in Windows Explorer and double-clicks it, by default a folder window opens, which accounts for the existence of these files listed in the BagMRU information.

Also, if you run "sbag.exe" against an NTUSER.DAT hive file from a Windows 7 system, you may see files listed beneath a key with a name that appears as follows:

```
\Software\Microsoft\Windows\Shell\Bags\1\Desktop\
ItemPos1920x1080x96(1)
```

This key (and ones like it) appears to contain information (via the key's values) about icons available on the desktop, which can include ... well, any file.

C:\Program Files\AIM6\aim6.exe	REG_SZ	AIM
C:\Program Files\AIM6\anotify.exe	REG_SZ	AOL
C:\Program Files\Apple Software Update\SoftwareUpdate.exe	REG_SZ	Apple Software Update
C:\Program Files\Dell\QuickSet\quickset.exe	REG_SZ	QuickSet
C:\Program Files\Google\Picasa3\Picasa3.exe	REG_SZ	Picasa
C:\Program Files\Google\Picasa3\PicasaPhotoViewer.exe	REG_SZ	Picasa Photo Viewer
C:\Program Files\HP\Digital Imaging\bin\hpqdirec.exe	REG_SZ	hpqdirec.exe
C:\Program Files\Internet Explorer\iexplore.exe	REG_SZ	Internet Explorer
C:\Program Files\iTunes\iTunes.exe	REG_SZ	iTunes

FIGURE 5.27

Partial contents of MUICache key.

From the NTUSER.DAT from a Windows 7 system, I found references to "{CLSID_RecycleBin}," "Crimson Editor SVN286.lnk," and "Google Chrome .lnk." On a Windows XP system, I found references to a considerable number of PDF files. Information such as this can be correlated with the contents of the user's RecentDocs key, and perhaps application (image viewer) MRU lists to determine where particular files that the user accessed were located.

MUICache

The MUICache key first came to my attention several years ago when I was looking into some interesting malware artifacts; specifically, one antivirus vendor indicated in several write-ups that malware was creating entries beneath these keys. This was not, in fact, the case; instead what was happening was that the entry was being created by the operating system as a result of how the malware was being executed for testing.

On Windows 7 systems, the MUICache key is located in the USRCLASS.DAT hive within the user profile, in the path "Local Settings\Software\Microsoft\Windows\ Shell\MuiCache." The values beneath this key, specifically ones that do not begin with "@," appear to provide indications of applications that had been run on the system. An example of the partial contents of an MUICache key is illustrated in Figure 5.27.

As you can see in Figure 5.27, the MUICache key contains a list of applications that have, at some point, been run on the system by the user. However, since each program entry is a value, there is no time stamp information associated with when the program may have been executed. The value of this key during an investigation is that the running of the program can be associated with a particular user, even after the program itself has been removed (deleted or uninstalled) from the system. Further, comparing visible values beneath the MUICache key from USRCLASS .DAT hives in VSCs can provide a timeframe during which the user ran the program. Finally, on more than one occasion, I've found indications of oddly named programs beneath this key that, when the program file was found and examined, turned out to be malware.

UserAssist

The purpose and use of the UserAssist subkeys have been discussed at length in a number of resources; suffice to say at this point that the contents of this key provide some very valuable insight into user activity, as the key appears to be used to track certain user activities that occur via the shell (Windows Explorer). When users double-click icons to launch programs, or launch programs via the Start menu, this activity is documented in the UserAssist subkeys, along with a date and time of the most recent occurrence of the activity, and the number of times the user has performed that activity. Each subsequent time the user performs the activity, the time stamp and counter are updated accordingly. The value names beneath the subkeys are "encrypted" using a Rot-13 (rotation 13) translation cipher, which can be easily decrypted. The RegRipper "userassist2.pl" plugin decrypts the value names beneath the subkeys and parses the time stamps and count (number of times the activity has occurred) from the binary data. Didier Stevens' UserAssist tool (*http://blog.didierstevens.com/programs/ userassist/*) does this, as well.

To run the RegRipper plugin on an NTUSER.DAT file within an image mounted as a volume, simply use the following command line:

```
C:\tools>rip -r F:\users\jdoe\NTUSER.DAT -p userassist2
```

The output from this command would appear at the command prompt (you would need to redirect the output from STDOUT to a file to save it), and an excerpt of a sample output appears as follows:

```
Wed Apr 13 19:06:47 2011 Z
  D:\Tools\RFV.exe (3)
Wed Apr 13 19:06:39 2011 Z
  D:\Tools\bintext.exe (1)
Wed Apr 13 19:06:29 2011 Z
  D:\Tools\PEview.exe (1)
Wed Apr 13 18:59:08 2011 Z
  F:\tools\PEview.exe (1)
  F:\tools\RFV.exe (1)
  F:\tools\bintext.exe (1)
  F:\tools\PEDUMP.exe (1)
```

As you can see, the information is presented sorted in order of occurrence with the time stamps listed in UTC format. The applications launched are followed by their run count in parentheses.

TIP

Adding UserAssist Data to Timelines

We discuss timeline creation and analysis in Chapter 7, but this is a good point to mention that you can output the information from the UserAssist keys to timeline (TLN) format using the "userassist_tln.pl" plugin, via the following command line:

```
C:\tools>rip-r F:\users\jdoe\NTUSER.DAT-p userassist_tln>
    events.txt
```

The information from the UserAssist keys can be used to demonstrate access to the Date Time Control Panel applet, installing or launching applications, etc. Most often, it's a good idea to include what you find in the UserAssist subkeys with other data, such as information from the RecentDocs key, to corroborate and validate your findings. In this way, you may find that a user launched MS Word and created a document, and metadata (file metadata was discussed in Chapter 4) from within the document may correlate back to the user.

NOTE

XPMode

To provide compatibility with older applications that ran under Windows XP and may not run within the Windows 7 environment, Microsoft provides a free download of a custom virtual environment called Windows XP Mode, or just XPMode. XPMode can be installed and run on Windows 7 Professional, Ultimate, and Enterprise systems using Microsoft's VirtualPC (*http://windows.microsoft.com/en-US/windows7/products/features/windows-xp-mode*). Applications installed in XPMode can be run from the Windows 7 host environment through a Windows shortcut or LNK file. As this interaction occurs via the shell, it appears in the user's UserAssist subkeys within the Windows 7 environment. Using the RegRipper plugin "userassist2.pl" to extract and translate the values and their data, indications of the use of applications launched via XPMode appear as follows:

```
Wed Apr 13 19:25:57 2011 Z
    {A77F5D77-2E2B-44C3-A6A2-ABA601054A51}\Windows Virtual PC\
    Windows XP Mode Applications\RFV (Windows XP Mode).lnk (1)
```

Information from the UserAssist subkeys may also correlate to other activity that the analyst has available that is separate from the system being examined. For example, information from the UserAssist subkeys may indicate that the user launched the Terminal Server Client, and the Terminal Server Client key, as well as the jump lists for the application (discussed in Chapter 4), would provide indications of which system the user had attempted to connect to. The Windows Event Logs on the remote system might indicate that the user successfully logged in, and network device logs might provide additional information regarding the connection, such as correlating information regarding the date and time of the connection, total number of bytes transferred, etc.

Another great thing about the contents of the UserAssist subkey information is that it persists beyond activity associated directly with applications. Let's say that a user downloads and installs an application, runs it a couple of times, then deletes the application and any data files created. Weeks or even months after the deleted files are overwritten and unrecoverable, the information within the UserAssist subkeys is still available. I once performed an examination in which this was precisely the case. We were able to determine that the user had installed Cain & Abel, a password recovery tool available at *http://www.oxid.it/cain.html*. The user had installed

FIGURE 5.28

"Software\Microsoft\Virtual PC" key path, via WRR.

Value	Type	Data
PublishedName	REG_SZ	RFV
Alias	REG_SZ	c6d3bf33
AppPath	REG_SZ	C:\Documents and Settings\All Users\Start Menu\Programs\RFV.exe
VAppPath	REG_SZ	%SYSTEMDRIVE%\Documents and Settings\All Users\Start Menu\Programs\RFV.exe
SMFolder	REG_SZ	\
Arguments	REG_SZ	
Extensions	REG_SZ	

FIGURE 5.29

Partial contents of c6d3bf33.Windows.XP.Mode key.

and run the tool to collect password information, viewed several of the output files, and then deleted the application files themselves.

TIP

Historical UserAssist Data

Information within the UserAssist subkeys provides us with indications of user activity, but only the most recent occurrence of that activity. For example, if we see that a user launched a particular application 14 times, we can see the date and time that he did so, but we have no information regarding the previous 13 times that he launched that application. By mounting available VSCs within the acquired image (see Chapter 3 for techniques for mounting VSCs) to access previous versions of the Registry hives, we may be able to determine the dates and times when the user previously launched the application.

Virtual PC

When a Windows 7 system (Professional, Ultimate, or Enterprise) has Virtual PC and XPMode installed, a user may be using it to run legacy applications from the special Windows XP environment. On a Windows 7 system with XPMode installed, I wanted to run an application that I could not run in Windows 7, so I ran it from the Windows XP environment. Once installed in the XPMode environment, the application appeared on the Windows 7 Start menu under "Windows XP Mode Applications." A reference to the application also appeared in "Software\Microsoft\ Virtual PC" key path within the NTUSER.DAT hive, as illustrated in Figure 5.28. Beneath the final key in the path (c6d3bf33.Windows.XP.Mode), several values were added, as illustrated in Figure 5.29.

FIGURE 5.30

TypedPaths key in Explorer Address Bar.

The AppPath value visible in Figure 5.29 illustrates where the application executable file is located within the XPMode environment. This information can be very useful, as it can also be correlated with information found beneath the UserAssist subkeys to determine how many times the user accessed the application, and the most recent time and date that he did so.

TypedPaths

A Registry key that is new to Windows 7 is the TypedPaths key, found in the user's hive file, in the path "Software\Microsoft\Windows\CurrentVersion\Explorer\ TypedPaths." Values within this key are populated when the user types a path into the Windows (not Internet) Explorer Address Bar, as illustrated in Figure 5.30.

The first value added is named "url1," and as each new value is added, that value appears to be named "url1" and previous values are "pushed down." As such, the LastWrite time of the TypedPaths key would correlate to when the "url1" value was added to the list.

Additional Sources

As you can see from this chapter so far, a great deal of potentially valuable information can be retrieved from the Registry on a Windows 7 system. However, while we've focused on information that can be derived by analyzing an image acquired from a system, most of what we've discussed so far has involved what would correlate to the Registry visible via the Registry Editor on a live system. As it turns out, Windows 7 has much more Registry data available, if you know where to find them and how to access them. Knowing the structure of Registry keys and values, we can search the pagefile, unallocated space, and even the unallocated space within hive files for additional information.

RegIdleBackup

Earlier in this chapter, we discussed Registry keys associated with scheduled tasks. Figure 5.23 illustrates a task named "RegIdleBackup," which is a default task that ships with Windows 7. If we locate the file for that scheduled task and open it in

Notepad, we'll see that the task backs up the SAM, Security, Software, and System hives to the "C:\Windows\System32\config\RegBack" folder every 10 days. So whenever you acquire an image from a Windows 7 system, you should expect to find backups of the Registry hives, and on an active system, those backups should be no more than 10 days old. The information may be very helpful to the analyst, possibly showing historical Registry information, or showing keys that were deleted from the hive file after the last backup was made.

TIP

Diff

If you install ActiveState Perl and then install the Parse::Win32Registry module (via "C:\perl>ppm install parse-win32registry"), a script called "regdiff.pl" will be installed in the "Perl\site\bin" folder. You can use this script, or the "regdiff.bat" batch file that is also installed, to "diff" the current active hives against the backed-up hive files, to see what changed since the last backup was made.

Volume Shadow Copies

In Chapter 3, we discussed how to access VSCs within images acquired from Vista and Windows 7 systems. Using these mounting techniques, multiple previous versions of the Registry hives (including the NTUSER.DAT and USRCLASS.DAT hives) can be accessed and parsed using tools such as RegRipper (and the associated "rip.pl/.exe" command line tool) to retrieve historical data from those hives. This technique can be added to analysis to search previous versions of hive files for earlier versions of data, or for keys and values that were subsequently deleted from the Registry. Information such as this may prove to be extremely valuable to the analyst or the investigator.

TIP

Evidence Eliminators

Users may sometimes elect to run "evidence eliminator" tools to hide their illicit activities. Depending on which tool is used (I've seen a tool called "Window Washer" run on systems), the Registry keys or values that get deleted may vary. Besides searching the unallocated space within hive files for deleted keys, another method for recovering this information would be to compare the current version of the hive files to previous versions of those files.

Virtualization

As discussed in Chapter 1, virtualization is available to a much greater degree on Windows 7 systems than in previous versions of the operating system. For example, not only is Virtual PC (VPC) freely available for download and installation on several versions of Windows 7, but a special virtual environment called XPMode can also be installed on those versions. This special version of Windows XP not only allows the user to more easily run legacy applications that may not run on Windows 7, but users can also access and interact with the Windows XP environment. For example, a user can access the XPMode virtual machine as "XPMUser" and install applications, surf the Web, etc., and none of that activity will appear within the host Windows 7 environment.

In addition to XPMode, users can create and use other virtual guest systems within VPC. Users may do this to hide their illicit activities within the virtual guest system; if the virtual system is run via VPC, then analyzing that virtual hard drive (.vhd) file would be essentially no different from analyzing an image acquired from a physical system; these systems would have their own Registry files. The same is true for VMWare .vmdk files, as well. Virtual systems can prove to be extremely valuable sources of information.

Memory

Beyond these sources, and beyond the scope of this chapter (memory analysis is a chapter, or perhaps even a book unto itself), Registry information may be available in Windows memory, either in a dump of physical memory or in a hibernation file (which is essentially a frozen-in-time snapshot of memory) and is accessible using the open-source Volatility framework (*http://code.google.com/p/volatility/*). Brendan Dolan-Gavitt (a.k.a, "moyix"; his blog is located at *http://moyix.blogspot.com/*) has done considerable work in locating and extracting Registry data from memory and his work is incorporated in the Volatility framework. One of the key aspects of accessing Registry data within memory is that there are several volatile keys, which are keys that exist only in memory and not on disk. In fact, the structures that identify volatile keys themselves only exist in memory. While this is not usually an issue, as many volatile keys are created and used for legitimate purposes by the operating system (such as the CurrentControlSet key within the System hive), it is possible that a volatile key could be created and used for malicious purposes (e.g., Registry-based mutex indicating that the system was infected with a particular bit of malware, temporary staging area for stolen data, etc.). As such, looking for available Registry information should be part of an analyst's investigative process whenever she has a memory dump or hibernation file available. If you are interested in information regarding memory analysis specifically for malware analysis, be sure to consult the *Malware Analyst's Cookbook and DVD* (Ligh et al., 2011).

Tools

Before we close out this chapter, I wanted to make a couple of comments regarding tools. Throughout this chapter, I've mentioned a number of RegRipper plugins, and specific information regarding RegRipper and how to go about creating plugins can be found in *Windows Registry Forensics* (Carvey, 2011). However, it's worth mentioning again here that there are two ways to go about listing the available plugins, which hive each is intended to be run against, and a brief description of what each plugin does.

FIGURE 5.31

Plugin Browser interface.

The first way to do this is to use "rip.pl" (or the "compiled" Windows execut-able, "rip.exe") with the appropriate switches. For example, typing "rip.pl –l" at the command prompt will list all of the available plugins in order, in a table format. An example of this format is illustrated as follows:

```
180. winzip v.20080325 [NTUSER.DAT]
 -Get WinZip extract and filemenu values
181. win_cv v.20090312 [Software]
 -Get & display the contents of the Windows\CurrentVersion key
182. wordwheelquery v.20100330 [NTUSER.DAT]
 -Gets contents of user's WordWheelQuery key
183. xpedition v.20090727 [System]
 -Queries System hive for XP Edition info
```

Adding the "-c" switch to the previous command tells "rip.pl" to format the out-put in a comma-separated value format, suitable for opening in Excel, as illustrated in the following command:

```
C:\tools>rip.pl -l -c>plugins.csv
```

The other way to view the available plugins is to use the GUI-based Plugin Browser, illustrated in Figure 5.31.

After selecting the directory where the plugins are located, you will see each plugin listed beneath the "Browse" tab, and as each plugin is selected (by clicking

FIGURE 5.32

Partial Registry Decoder UI.

on the plugin name), the plugin information (i.e., name, version, hive, and the short description are all included in the code for each plugin) will appear to the right. The Plugin Browser is part of the "RR.zip" archive that contains the tools that are part of the *Windows Registry Forensics* (Carvey, 2011) book, and can be found at *http://code.google.com/p/winforensicaanalysis/downloads/list*.

Another tool that definitely deserves attention is the Registry Decoder. In September 2011, Andrew Case released the Registry Decoder (the announcement for the release of the tool can be found at *http://dfsforensics.blogspot.com/2011/09/announcnig-registry-decoder.html*), which is an open-source (Python) project that was initially funded by the National Institutes of Justice, and was released to the public.

The Registry Decoder consists of two components; the online acquisition component safely acquires copies of Registry hives from live systems by using the System Restore Point functionality on Windows XP, or the Volume Shadow Service on Vista and Windows 7. Creating the Restore Point or VSC ensures that there is a current, read-only copy of the hives that are not in use by the operating system. The second component provides a GUI for offline analysis of Registry hives. Figure 5.32 illustrates the results of a plugin run across a Windows 7 Software hive file loaded into the Registry Decoder.

The Registry Decoder allows an analyst to create a case and load multiple hive files (including those extracted from VSCs) and process those hives (e.g., run searches, "diff" hives, run plugins across all of the "mounted" hives, generate reports, etc.). Registry Decoder can process acquired images, Registry hives, and even acquired databases. Once the information is loaded, the tool performs a one-time preprocessing of all of the information, and generates databases and metadata files that contain all of the information needed for analysis. Andrew was interviewed by Ovie Carroll regarding the Registry Decoder, and you can listen to the interview, which contains a great deal more information regarding the tool, in the

September 26, 2011 CyberSpeak podcast (found at *http://cyberspeak.libsyn.com/ cyber-speak-sep-26-2011-registry-browser*). Both components of the Registry Decoder can be downloaded from *http://code.google.com/p/registrydecoder/*.

SUMMARY

The Registry contains a great deal of forensically valuable data, and understanding what is available, as well as how to access and interpret the data, can provide a great deal of context and additional (perhaps even critical) investigative detail to an analyst. While the Registry does contain a great deal of information, it cannot be used to answer every question; for example, analysts have asked in online forums where records of file copy operations are maintained in the Registry, and the simple answer is that they aren't. However, the good news is that there are a number of questions that can be answered through Registry analysis, but there is so much information that no one resource can be written to contain it all. As further research and analysis are conducted, new artifacts are discovered and cataloged, and often the best approach, beyond referencing resources such as this book (as well as the other books and resources mentioned in this chapter), is to collaborate with other analysts and conduct some of your own research.

References

Carvey, H. A. (2009). *Windows forensic analysis* (2nd ed.). Burlington, MA: Syngress Publishing.

Carvey, H. A. (2011). *Windows registry forensics*. Burlington, MA: Syngress Publishing.

Ligh, M. H., Adair, S., Hartstein, B., & Richard, M. (2011). *Malware analyst's cookbook and DVD*. New York: Wiley.

Malware Detection

6

CHAPTER OUTLINE

INFORMATION IN THIS CHAPTER

- Malware Characteristics
- Detecting Malware

INTRODUCTION

If you own or use a computer, at some point malware is just going to be a part of your life. This is especially true for system and network administrators, who are often responsible for managing and maintaining hundreds of systems. However, this is also true for small businesses, which are often without the benefit of a dedicated system administrator, and even home users. We all know of friends and family who have suffered the frustration of having systems infected with malware; in most cases, the complaints are about how the system has slowed down, or about annoying pop-ups and messages that appear on the screen. What most folks don't realize is that the truly insidious malware is what we *aren't* seeing on the screen: the key loggers; the malware that grabs the contents of web browser form fields whenever we log into our online banking account; or the Trojan that captures your keystrokes when you order something online, before the data are encrypted and sent to the server on the other end of the web browser session.

The presence of malware on a system can have a significant impact on an organization. For example, the presence of malware may indicate a violation of acceptable use policies within that organization, in addition to potentially exposing the organization to risk in the eyes of compliance and regulatory bodies. Further, understanding the nature of the malware (based on the identification of the malware through the analysis of associated artifacts) can help an organization address business issues, such as reporting and notification.

This chapter is not about malware reverse engineering; there are extremely high-quality books available that address that topic far better than I ever could, such as *Malware Analyst's Cookbook and DVD* (Ligh et al., 2011). The purpose of this chapter is to provide analysts and responders with an understanding of malware characteristics to aid in detecting suspicious and malicious files within an acquired image; if not the malware itself, then indications of malware having executed on the system. We will discuss various techniques for performing a thorough examination for malware and malware artifacts, as well as provide a checklist of these techniques.

MALWARE CHARACTERISTICS

While I was a member of an emergency computer incident response services team, I began to notice that, as a team, we were receiving calls regarding as well as responding to a good number of malware infection incidents. As such, I felt that it would be valuable, and indeed important, to develop a framework for not only better understanding malware in general, but also to come up with a way for all of the consultants on our team to respond intelligently and speak authoritatively about malware, and be able to explain what they were seeing to our customers. After all, as consultants we were approaching the problem from a technical perspective: which systems were infected, what network traffic was being observed, etc.

However, the customer was coming at the problem and concerned about the issue from a business perspective: How does this affect me from a legal or compliance perspective, what data were stolen (if any), and where did the data go? During some examinations, this will be the primary target of your analysis; during others, the malware will be a secondary artifact, installed on a system following a compromise. As such, I wanted to develop a framework that allowed our consultants (and others) to easily address the situation and bridge the technology–business gap. Customers very often aren't so much concerned with the technical aspects of the malware as they are with what data may have been exposed as a direct (or indirect) result of the infection, what risk they may be exposed to, and what issues they may have with respect to compliance and regulatory bodies.

What I came up with (and blogged about several times at *http://windowsir .blogspot.com*) were four simple malware characteristics that could be used to understand, respond to, and eradicate malware, as well as answer the customer's questions. These characteristics are:

1. The initial infection vector (how the malware got on the system).
2. The propagation mechanism (how the malware moves between systems, if it does that).
3. The persistence mechanism (how the malware remains on the system, and survives reboots and when the user logs out).
4. Artifacts (what traces the malware leaves on a system as a result of its execution) that you can look for during an examination.

I've found that when understood and used by responders (either consultants who fly in or onsite IT staff) these characteristics also provide a framework for locating malware on a system, as well as collecting information about a malware sample found on a system.

For the types of cases where malware is likely to play a role (e.g., intrusion incidents), most customers want to know things like what data, if any, were exposed, as well as if the malware was specifically targeted to their organization. Developing a more complete picture of malware and the effects on its ecosystem (not just the system it's installed on, but the entire infrastructure) can guide us in answering those questions. Understanding how the malware behaves allows us to understand its capabilities. For example, some malware behaves differently if it finds that it's in a virtual environment, or depending on the version of Windows it's running on. There is also malware that will install itself differently on systems depending on the level of privileges available. Knowing things like how malware gets on a system or how it communicates off of the system (if it does) helps us understand where else we should be looking for artifacts; subsequently, we learn more about the malware when these artifacts are found (or when they're not found!—think back to Chapter 1 . . .) and ultimately provide better answers to our customers.

It's important for everyone to understand the characteristics of malware. If you think back to Chapter 1, we talked about convergence—the fact that no one area of computer/digital forensic analysis is really as separate from others as we might think.

When law enforcement officers (LEOs) have to deal with an issue of contraband (often called "illicit") images or fraud, it's very likely that someone will ask about or make the claim that malware (a Trojan) was responsible for the observed activity, or at least contributed to it. As such, LEOs are no longer simply dealing with cataloging contraband images, as they now have a malware investigation to complete. As such, turning to those who address malware detection and user activity analysis issues on a regular basis would likely provide a great deal of assistance and expertise.

WARNING

The "Trojan Defense"

The claim by defendants that "a virus did it" is nothing new. In 2003, Aaron Caffrey was accused in the United Kingdom of hacking into computer systems in the United States. He claimed that someone had hacked into his system and run an attack script; essentially, "a Trojan did it." Even though no indication of a Trojan (although the attack tools were found) was found, Caffrey was acquitted.

That being said, let's go ahead and take a look at the four malware characteristics in greater detail.

Initial Infection Vector

Not to be circular, but the initial infection vector is how the malware initially infected or made its way onto a system or infrastructure. There are a number of ways that systems can be infected; the user opens or double-clicks on an email attachment that is really a malicious document, the user clicks on a link to a malicious or infected web site, other browser "drive-bys," etc. Systems can also be infected when removable storage devices (e.g., thumb drives, iPods, etc.) that are infected are connected to the system. Peer-to-peer (P2P) file sharing infrastructures are other popular means by which systems can get infected. The more interconnected we become, and the more devices that we have that can be updated and synchronized by connecting them to our computer systems, the more we are open to infection from malware.

Another prevalent infection mechanism is social networking sites, such as MySpace and Facebook. In their book *Cybercrime and Espionage*, Will Gragido and John Pirc mentioned a quote reportedly attributed to the infamous bank robber, Willy Sutton; when asked why he robbed banks, Mr. Sutton reportedly replied, "because that's where the money is." Well, this provides us a glimpse as to why those who spread malware use email and target social media/networking sites—if they're looking to infect a large number of systems, then they have to go where the users are, and in particular where they can find massive numbers of users. If the goal is to create masses of infected systems (for botnet activity, collecting user's personal data, etc.), then casting as wide a net as possible would likely be the best way to achieve that goal. The motivations of the malware authors are often predicated by the predilections of their target prey or "user community," in that the vast majority of users like to browse the Web, click links, use email and open email attachments, etc.

Speaking of email and attachments, the February 2011 Symantec.cloud MessageLabs Intelligence report (*http://www.symanteccloud.com/globalthreats/ overview/r_mli_reports*) indicated that "malicious PDF files outpace the distribution of related malicious attachments used in targeted attacks, and currently represent the attack vector of choice for malicious attackers." Didier Stevens (whose blog can be found at *http://blog.didierstevens.com/*) has spent considerable effort writing tools to detect malicious contents in PDF files, and his tools have even been included in online malware analysis sites such as VirusTotal (*http://www.virustotal .com*). These demonstrate not only that those who proliferate malware gravitate to using infection vectors that tend to be "popular" (i.e., applications may be targeted not so much because they are vulnerable to exploit, but because they are so widely used), but also that the security community will often follow suit in providing appropriate and novel detection mechanisms.

Targeting users isn't the only way to gain access to systems. Vulnerable Internet-facing applications and servers are generally found through network scanning. For example, vulnerable web servers (as well as applications running on those servers) can provide access to systems, through such means as SQL injection attacks. Systems can also be exploited via functionality inherent to the operating system, such as automatically executing the commands in an "autorun.inf" file on a USB thumb drive that is inserted into or connected to the system. In short, there are more vectors that allow malware to infect a system than simply getting a user to click a link or open a file.

The initial infection vector of malware is important to understand, as it is very often one of the questions that the customer wants answered: "How did this malware originally get on my system or into our infrastructure?" For some, this information is needed to clearly establish a "window of compromise"; that is, what was the initial infection vector, when did the initial infection occur, and therefore how long have we been infected? Identifying the initial infection vector can also be used to find gaps in protection or detection mechanisms or user awareness training.

TIP

Phishing Training

Aaron Higbee is the CTO and a cofounder of the Intrepidus Group, and responsible for the PhishMe.com site, which allows someone to send phishing emails into their own infrastructure to baseline or test their user awareness training with respect to clicking on links and attachments offered through email. The idea is that following (or even prior to) user awareness training with respect to the dangers and risks of phishing attacks, an organization can use the PhishMe.com site to validate and reinforce their training.

The initial infection vector can also help determine if the malware infection is a targeted attack. In some instances, a malware infection is simply opportunistic, such as when a user (coincidentally) visits a compromised web site infected with a downloader; the downloader gets on the user's system through a vulnerability or misconfiguration in their browser, and then downloads additional malware. For example, about two years ago, a friend of mine contacted me for advice because his work laptop was infected with malware. It seemed that his son (a fourth grader) was doing homework, which required that students go to the National Geographic web site and complete a task. As it turned out, the site had been compromised and every visit to the web site using a Windows system (apparently, regardless of the actual web browser used) resulted in an infection. The intent of such attacks is to infect any and all visitors to the site.

However, some infections occur when a user is sent an email with an attachment or link that is designed to be interesting to them, and appears to come from a known, trusted source. These types of attacks are often preceded by considerable open-source intelligence collection, and target victims are selected based on their employer and projects that they may be working on or know something about. These attacks are referred to as *spear phishing*, during which specific individuals are sought to launch an attack against. As such, the answer to the question of "Was this a targeted attack?" would be yes.

Propagation Mechanism

Once malware has infected an infrastructure, there is generally some means by which that malware moves to other systems. This may be via network-based vulnerability exploitation (such as with Conficker), making use of operational business functionality by writing to available network shares, or by parsing the user's address book or contact list and sending out copies of itself or other malware to everyone listed with an email address.

Malware's propagation mechanism can be particularly insidious when it takes advantage of the day-to-day operational business infrastructure within the organization to spread, such as writing to existing network shares. Many organizations have home directories for users as well as file shares that users will access or be automatically connected to when they log in, and if the malware writes to these shares, the user systems may end up being infected. When the malware propagates using the infrastructure in this manner, it makes incident response and malware eradication efforts difficult. The affected functionality is most often required and critical to business operations, and taking that infrastructure offline for an indeterminate amount of time is simply not an acceptable response measure. Additionally, taking some systems offline for "cleaning" without understanding how they were infected in the first place may result in the systems becoming reinfected shortly after connecting them back to the network, making effective eradication and clean-up procedures impossible. Without understanding the infection or propagation method used, it is impossible to take appropriate measures, such as installing patches, making configuration changes, or modifying permissions, to prevent reinfection.

Depending on which system(s) you're looking at within an infrastructure, the propagation mechanism (how the malware moves between systems) may appear to be the initial infection vector. In some instances, malware may initially make its way into an infrastructure as a result of a browser "drive-by" or as an email attachment. This initial infection may then be described as a "Trojan downloader," which in turn downloads a worm that infects systems within the infrastructure through some vulnerability or other mechanism. If you're looking at the fifth or tenth system infected by the worm within the infrastructure, the initial infection vector for that system would appear to be the worm. However, if you missed "patient 0" (the originally infected system), you would not be able to "see" how the infrastructure was originally infected.

In other instances, the propagation mechanism may, in fact, be the same as the initial infection vector, in that the means by which the malware infected the first system was also used to infect subsequent systems. An example of this may be when an employee takes her laptop home, and it becomes infected with a network worm while attached to the home wireless network. When the employee then brings the laptop back to the office and connects it to the network, the worm propagates using the same method as the initial infection vector.

The propagation mechanism needs to be identified and understood, not simply because it impacts the infrastructure, but also because the manner in which the malware spreads to other systems may impact and lead to the infection of other, external organizations, such as vendors and business partners, or even customers. In the case of malware that spreads through email attachments, customers may also be impacted. At the very least, this can bring undue attention to an organization, negatively impacting the brand image of that organization, and possibly even exposing vulnerabilities within that infrastructure to public scrutiny.

Another reason the propagation mechanism needs to be understood is that this mechanism will very likely play an important role in the response to the incident. Depending on the situation, patches may need to be applied or configuration modifications may need to be made to devices, or to the infrastructure itself. As such, correctly understanding the propagation mechanism so that it can be addressed as part of an overall security response plan will ensure that resources are correctly applied to the issue.

NOTE

Least Frequency of Occurrence (LFO)

In Chapter 1, we discussed the concept of least frequency of occurrence (LFO). The malware propagation mechanism is closely related to LFO, and tied directly into the malware artifacts (discussed later in this chapter). "Back in the day" (I love to say that …) malware would infect an infrastructure and then start spreading out of control. Patient 0 (the first system to be infected) would infect other systems, but as other systems became infected, patient 0 would become reinfected, and so on. Malware had no means to identify already-infected systems, and pretty soon individual systems would become so massively infected that they would be completely unusable.

As cybercrime and the bad guy's motives have evolved, there has been a need to not have that happen anymore, as denying the user from using the system has the side effect of preventing the attacker from using it, as well. As such, malware authors have used techniques such as unique Registry keys or files, or mutexes (memory objects), to identify already-infected systems. The malware can check for and recognize these "flags," ensuring that only a single infection or single instance of the malware is present on any given computer. As such, the malware becomes the least frequently occurring process on the system.

Persistence Mechanism

Jesse Kornblum pointed out in his paper, "Exploiting the Rootkit Paradox" (*http:// jessekornblum.com/publications/ijde06.html*), that malware most often wants to remain persistent on the infected system. (In his paper, he was specifically referring to rootkits, but the concept applies to malware in general.) What use is a Trojan or backdoor that disappears and is no longer accessible after the system is rebooted, particularly if this happens regularly? As such, most malware has some mechanism that allows it to be automatically restarted when the system is rebooted, when a user logs in, or via some other trigger. Again, this is a general statement, as some malware has been identified that takes advantage of the fact that the system itself must remain online and is unlikely to be rebooted; therefore, the malware doesn't employ what would be defined as a "traditional" persistence mechanism. Instead, an attacker uses some vulnerability or identified technique to inject the malware into the server's memory; should the system be taken offline or rebooted for some reason, the attacker hopes that he can reinfect the system using the same or a similar method. In this case, the malware remains persistent in memory as long as the server remains online and functioning. However, our discussion in this chapter focuses on detecting malware within an acquired image, so some form of persistence mechanism is assumed.

Perhaps one of the most popular malware persistence mechanisms employed by malware authors is to make some use of the Registry, using what's commonly become known as an *autostart* mechanism. While the Registry contains a great deal of configuration and user tracking information, it also contains a considerable number of locations from which applications can be automatically started, without any interaction from the user beyond booting the system or possibly logging in. For example, when a Windows system is booted, Windows services are started, and entries within the Run key in the Software hive are parsed and launched, and a number of other Registry keys and values are also parsed. When a user logs in, the Run key within the user's hive is parsed, as are other entries. There are even autostart mechanisms that can be engaged when a user takes a specific action, such as running a program or launching a GUI-based application. The Registry can also be modified to ensure that the malware is launched even if the system is started in Safe Mode.

WARNING

Memory Scraper

I once encountered an interesting piece of malware found on back-office point of sale (POS) servers. This malware used a Windows service as its persistence mechanism, but rather than launching immediately when the system booted, the service started a timer to wait or "sleep" for a random amount of time. When the timer had expired the service would "wake up" and run a series of other tools, the first of which would extract the virtual memory used by any of eight named processes (all of which were associated with processing credit card information). The malware then launched a Perl script (that had been compiled into a standalone executable file with the "Perl2.exe" application) to parse the virtual memory dump, looking for track 1 and 2 data (the data found in the magnetic stripe on the back of your credit card). This was an interesting approach to data theft. First, it targeted the only location within the credit card processing system at the local site where the data were not encrypted (i.e., in memory). Second, it waited for a random period after the system was booted, because when the system was booted, there was no credit card data in memory. By waiting for a random amount of time (in one instance, 41 days), the malware author ensured that there were data in memory to collect and parse.

Not all persistence mechanisms reside within the Registry, however. In fact, once analysts become aware of the Registry as a source for malware persistence, it's just their luck that the very next case involves malware that uses a persistence mechanism that does *not* reside within the Registry. Some malware may be identified as a file infector, for example, and therefore doesn't need to use the Registry to maintain persistence on an infected system. Instead, such malware would infect executable files or data files, so that the malware would be run whenever the executable was launched or the data file accessed.

An example of malware of which the persistence mechanism does not require the Registry was originally identified as "W32/Crimea" (the write up can be found at *http://home.mcafee.com/VirusInfo/VirusProfile.aspx?key = 142626*) in July 2007. This malware was placed on a system as a DLL, and persistence was achieved by modifying the import table (within the header of the portable executable, or PE, file) of the file "imm32.dll" (a legitimate Windows PE file) to point to a function in the malicious DLL. As such, any process that loaded "imm32.dll" became infected.

One means for malware to remain persistent on a system that really came to light in the summer of 2010 had originally been documented by Microsoft as normal system behavior in 2000. Nick Harbour, a malware reverse engineer for the consulting firm Mandiant, was the first to publicly describe this specific issue in an M-union blog post titled "Malware Persistence Without the Windows Registry" (the blog post can be found at *http://blog.mandiant.com/archives/1207*). In particular, a malicious DLL was added to the "C:\Windows" directory and named "ntshrui .dll," which also happens to be the name of a legitimate DLL and shell extension that is found in the "C:\Windows\system32" directory. However, unlike other shell extensions listed in the Registry, this shell extension does not have an explicit path listed for its location, and when "Explorer.exe" launches to provide the user shell, it uses the established and documented DLL search order to locate the DLL by name only (no other checks, such as for MD5 hash or digital signature verification, are performed), rather than following an explicit path. As such, the "Explorer.exe" process starts looking in its own directory first, and finds and loads the malicious DLL. In this way, the malware relies on how the system operates, rather than adding a key or value to the Registry as its persistence mechanism.

Yet another persistence mechanism to consider is the Windows scheduled tasks functionality. Scheduled tasks allow administrators to run tasks or "jobs" at designated times, rather than every time the system is booted or when a user logs in. For example, if you use Apple products such as iTunes, Safari, or QuickTime on your Windows system, you can expect to see a scheduled task that launches the software update application on a weekly basis. As such, it's relatively easy to get malware on a system and schedule it to run at specifically designated times.

Yet another example of a persistence mechanism that does not rely on the Registry is to use other startup locations within the file system. For example, the Carberp Trojan, which is reportedly replacing Zeus/ZBot as the preeminent malware for stealing a user's online banking information, does not appear to use the Registry for persistence. The Symantec write-up for this Trojan (found at *http://www.syman-tec.com/security_response/writeup.jsp?docid = 2010-101313-5632-99&tabid = 2*) indicates that the malware remains persistent by placing an executable file in the "\Start Menu\Programs\Startup" folder within a user's profile, which causes the file to be launched when the user logs onto the system. Further, on September 23, 2011, Martin Pillion wrote a post titled "Malware Using the Local Group Policy to Gain Persistence" to the HBGary blog (the blog is found at *http://www.hbgary.com/hbgary-blog*; there is no direct link available to the post) that described the use of the Windows Local Group Policy (the article specifically addresses Windows 7) functionality for running scripts during specific events (e.g., logon, logoff) as a persistence mechanism. In the article, Martin stated that this was a particular due to the fact that the Microsoft AutoRuns tool (updated to version 11 on September 20, 2011 and found at *http://technet.microsoft.com/en-us/sysinternals/bb963902*) reportedly does not check these locations.

Additionally, malware doesn't have to *be* or reside on a system to remain persistent on that system. In networked environments, "nearby" systems can monitor infected systems and ensure that the malware that spread to those systems is running. This is a particularly insidious approach to use, as many organizations only perform detailed monitoring at their network perimeter and egress points. Unusual or suspicious traffic seen at the perimeter will lead back to the systems that are communicating out of the infrastructure; however, the systems that are ensuring that malware is running on those systems will likely not be seen by the monitoring. Therefore, IT staff will respond to the systems identified via egress monitoring and "clean" or even reprovision those systems, which (depending on the method used) may become reinfected shortly after being placed back on the network. This sort of approach ensures that the malware remains persistent on the infrastructure as a whole, rather than focusing on persistence on a specific host.

> **WARNING**
>
> Multiple Persistence Mechanisms
>
> One has to be careful when determining what the persistence mechanism is for a particular bit of malware. I once responded to a malware infection incident that wasn't particularly widespread, but did seem to be particularly persistent. The local IT staff had determined that the persistence mechanism for the malware was apparently a Windows service. However, when they deleted the service and corresponding file on disk and then rebooted the system, the malware was back. Close examination of one of the systems indicated that there was a second Windows service involved that monitored the first service. If this service did not detect the other malware service when the system started, it would reinfect the system.

Yet another mechanism for remaining persistent doesn't even involve *being* on the system in question. What happens is that the intruder is able to gain access to another system, adjacent or logically "nearby" on the network, and is then able to execute commands on the apparently infected system. This may be through the use of a vulnerability to repeatedly compromise the system, or simply using remote command mechanisms (via tools similar to Microsoft's own "psexec.exe") in conjunction with the appropriate credentials (usually those for a domain administrator). As such, the observed activity (e.g., network traffic or device logs) that appear to indicate an issue with the system is not the result of a malware being persistent on that system, but instead that system being accessed again and again from another "nearby" system.

The purpose of this section has not been to list all possible persistence mechanisms; instead, my goal has been to open your eyes to the possibilities for persistence on Windows systems. One aspect of this has been obvious over time—that is that responders will continue to learn from intruders and malware authors as they identify and use new persistence mechanisms. As Windows systems provide more functionality to users and become more complex, new persistence mechanisms are invariably discovered and employed; as such, the goal for responders and analysts is to recognize this and keep malware's need for persistence in mind, as understanding that there *is* a persistence mechanism is the first step to identifying that mechanism.

Artifacts

Artifacts are those traces left by the presence and execution of malware, but are not themselves specifically used by the malware to maintain persistence. Malware persistence mechanisms appear to be similar to artifacts, and based on this definition, can be considered to be a subset of the more general "artifacts" description. However, the best way to look at this is that persistence mechanisms are artifacts used for a specific purpose, while the more general use of the term applies to other artifacts not specifically used for persistence. For example, some malware creates or modifies Registry keys or values to remain persistent on an infected system, whereas that same malware may also create Registry values to maintain configuration information, such as servers to contact or encryption keys.

FIGURE 6.1

Enum\Root\Legacy_* keys.

That being said, not all artifacts are directly created by the malware itself; some artifacts are created as a result of the ecosystem in which the malware exists. (Remember when we talked about indirect artifacts in Chapter 1?) I know, you're asking yourself, "What?" That's just a fancy way of saying that some artifacts aren't created by the malware, but are instead created as a result of the malware's interaction with the infected host. For example, some malware creates a Windows service to ensure its persistence; as a result, when the service is launched, Windows will create subkeys under the HKLM\System\CurrentControlSet\Enum\Root key that refer to the service name, prepended with "Legacy_*" (see Figure 6.1).

This is an interesting artifact, but how is it useful? Well, several analysts have noted that the LastWrite time for the Legacy_*\0000 keys closely approximates to the last time that the service was launched, while the LastWrite time for the Legacy_* (again, where the "*" is for the service name) closely approximates to the first time that the service was launched. This information was developed largely through observation and testing, and has been extremely useful in determining when a system was initially infected.

WARNING

Malware Evolution

One aspect of analysis that examiners need to keep in mind is that malware authors may learn of our analysis methods and attempt to use those processes against us. For example, the ZeroAccess rootkit (a.k.a., Smiscer or Max++), which was reverse-engineered by Giuseppe Bonfa, was found to delete its Legacy_* service keys that the operating system created beneath the HKLM\System\CurrentControlSet\Enum\Root key. The write-up that includes the discussion of the Legacy_* service key being deleted can be found at *http:// resources.infosecinstitute.com/zeroaccess-malware-part-2-the-kernel-mode-device-driver-stealth-rootkit*.

Another example of artifacts created by the operating system is prefetch files, specifically as a result of application prefetching performed by the operating system.

> **TIP**
>
> Application Prefetching
>
> As was mentioned, Windows 2003 and 2008 are capable of performing application prefetching, although it is not enabled by default. Enabling this functionality as part of incident preparedness planning may provide useful artifacts during incident response and analysis.

Prefetch files are found in the "C:\Windows\Prefetch" directory on Windows systems where application prefetching is enabled; by default, Windows XP, Vista, and Windows 7 have application prefetching enabled (Windows 2003 and 2008 are capable of application prefetching, but this functionality is not enabled by default). Details regarding the creation and analysis of these files was covered in Chapter 4, but suffice to say here that prefetch files have provided useful indications of malware being executed, even after that malware has been deleted from the system.

> **TIP**
>
> Prefetch and Data Exfiltration
>
> Prefetch files can contain significant data with respect to data exfiltration. For example, some intruders may use "rar.exe" to archive stolen data prior to shipping it off of the system; as such, the prefetch file for "rar.exe" may contain references to the directory paths and filenames of the data that were included in the archive. See Chapter 4 for a discussion of parsing prefetch files.

Malware artifacts can also be based on the version of Windows that the malware infects/installs itself on, or based on the permissions under which the malware is installed. There is malware, for example, that when it infects a system via a user account with Administrator privileges, it uses the Run key in the Software hive for persistence, and files may appear in the "C:\Windows\Temp" directory. However, if the account through which the system is infected is a normal user (i.e., lower-privilege account), the malware will use the Run key in the user's hive for persistence and write files to the Temp directory in the user profile. As such, when an analyst looks at the entries in the Run key within the Software hive, he won't see anything that would indicate an infection by that particular malware, and should also be sure to check (all of) the user profiles.

Determining the characteristics that we've discussed when attempting to locate malware within an acquired image can often have a significant impact on your examination. For example, some families of malware may have different file-names or propagation mechanisms associated with each variation within the family, but there will also be characteristics that are consistent across all variants. For example, while the malware family known as Conficker (family description

found at *http://www.microsoft.com/security/portal/Threat/Encyclopedia/Entry.aspx?
name = win32%2fconficker*) had differences across all variants, the malware had a
consistent persistence mechanism, using a random name for a Windows service that
started as part of "svchost.exe." As such, Conficker infections could be determined
by locating the persistence mechanism, and from there locating the dynamic linked
library (DLL) file that comprised the infection. Understanding these characteristics, in particular the persistence mechanism and artifacts, can also assist in helping
to locate malware that is not identified by antivirus (AV) scanning applications, as
locating the artifacts can lead you to the malware itself.

DETECTING MALWARE

Detecting malware within an acquired image is perhaps one of the most amorphous
and ethereal tasks that an analyst may encounter. Many analysts have cringed at
receiving instructions to "find all of the bad stuff," because the question remains,
how do you go about doing this effectively, and in a timely manner? The answer
to that is simple: you don't, and you can't. After all, isn't "bad" a relative term?
Without context, a good deal of effort can be dedicated to finding something that is
actually normal activity, or isn't the "bad" thing you're looking for. I know of one
analyst who was told to "find bad stuff" and found hacker tools and utilities, as well
as indications of their use. After reading the report, the customer stated that those
tools were actually part of the employee's job, which was to test the security of specific systems within the infrastructure. Sometimes, we have to take a moment to get
a little context and find out just what "bad" is, so that we have a better understanding of what to look for.

The goal of detecting malware within an acquired image should be one of data
reduction. Malware authors are sometimes lazy, but they can also be very insidious, and take great pains to protect their files from detection. There are a number
of techniques that malware authors can and do use to hide their programs from
detection, even going so far as to make their programs look as much like a normal
Windows program as possible. Malware authors will use specific techniques (e.g.,
giving the file a "normal"-looking name, placing the file in a directory where such
a file would be expected to be found, etc.) to hide their programs, sometimes even
based on the techniques used by analysts to detect these files.

Given the challenge of finding one (or a small number) of well-disguised files
on an image containing thousands of files, the best approach that an analyst can
take is to use a thorough, documented process to reduce the number of files that
need to be analyzed to a more manageable number. Having a documented process
allows the analyst, as well as other analysts, to see exactly what was done, what
worked, and what needs to be done to improve the process, if anything.

The following sections of this chapter lay out some steps that analysts can use
as a methodology and include in their analysis process to detect the presence of
malware within an acquired image, or provide a thorough process for ensuring that

malware does not exist with an image. However, while each section will describe that particular step thoroughly, this is not intended to be an all-inclusive list. Some of these steps are sure to be familiar, while others may be new, but given enough time, someone will very likely come up with additional steps.

Log Analysis

One of the first steps in detecting malware within an acquired image is to determine what AV application, if any, was already installed and/or run on the system. If the system did have AV installed, the analyst would need to determine if it was running at the time that the system was acquired (or when the incident occurred; some malware actually disables AV and other security products on Windows systems) and when that application was last updated. This can be done easily by examining logs generated by AV applications; many maintain logs of updates, as well as the results of regularly scheduled and on-demand scans. Some AV applications even write their events to the Application Event Log. However, in some cases, this may be a configurable option, and may be disabled or simply not enabled; therefore, if you check the event sources for the various Application Event Log records and do not see an indication of an AV application (McAfee AV products use the source "McLogEvent"), do not assume that one hasn't been installed.

WARNING

Application Event Logs

When analyzing a system, keep in mind that Application Event Logs, like the other Event Logs on Windows systems, do not simply keep recording events ad infinitum. Instead, once the logs have reached their specified size, older events are discarded to make room for new ones. The maximum size of the Event Logs can be controlled by modifying a Registry value, but in my experience, this is not something that's done very often, particularly on desktop systems. As such, analysts should look for both Application Event Log records and AV application log files, as the AV log files may have considerably more historical data available.

One of the first things I will usually look for on a Windows system is the log file for Microsoft's Malicious Software Removal Tool (MRT). MRT is a targeted microscanner that is installed in the background on Windows systems, and is updated with signatures on an almost-monthly basis. The term *microscanner* refers to the fact that MRT is not a full-blown AV application, but is instead intended to protect Windows systems from very specific threats. Microsoft Knowledgebase (KB) article 890830 (found on the Microsoft Support site at *http://support.microsoft.com/kb/890830*) provides information about installing and running MRT (there are command line switches that can be used to run scans), as well as an up-to-date list of the threats that MRT is intended to detect. MRT logs the results of its scans to the file "mrt.log," which is located in the "C:\Windows\debug" directory. The log contains information such as the version of MRT run (usually following an update), when the scan started, when the scan completed, and the results of the scan. An example of an entry from the MRT log file retrieved from a Windows XP SP3 system appears as follows:

```
Microsoft Windows Malicious Software Removal Tool v3.15, January
  2011
Started On Wed Jan 12 21:50:26 2011
Engine internal result code = 80508015
Results Summary:
----------------
No infection found.
Microsoft Windows Malicious Software Removal Tool Finished On Wed
  Jan 12 21:51:29 2011
Return code: 0 (0x0)
```

This information can be very useful to an analyst, particularly when claims are made of particular malware being found on a system; for example, I've received a number of images along with the statement that the systems had been infected with Zeus. According to Microsoft KB article 890830, detection of Win32/Zbot (also known as "Zeus" or "Wnspoem") was added in October 2010. If an analyst receives an acquired image and there is a suspicion that this particular malware had infected the system, then this is one artifact that can be used to determine whether there were any indications of particular malware on the system. As I include AV log analysis as part of my methodology for these types of examinations, I document my findings with respect to when MRT was updated, and what I find in the "mrt.log" file. This helps address issues of what malware may or may not be on the system.

TIP

MRT Registry Key

Whenever MRT is updated, the "Version" value of the Microsoft\RemovalTools\MRT Registry key in the Software hive is updated with a globally unique identifier (GUID) that indicates the version of MRT, as illustrated in Figure 6.2.

Name	Type	Data
(Default)	REG_SZ	(value not set)
EULA2	REG_DWORD	0x00000001 (1)
Version	REG_SZ	258FD3CF-9C82-4112-B1B0-18EC1ECFED37

FIGURE 6.2

MSRT "Version" value.

This GUID can be looked up in Microsoft KB article 891716 (found at *http://support .microsoft.com/kb/891716*) and used in conjunction with the LastWrite time to determine when the MRT was last updated and which threats it should detect.

Later versions of Windows (starting with Vista) tend to have Microsoft's Windows Defender application installed, although this program can also be installed on Windows XP. Windows Defender is a program that reportedly protects Windows systems from pop-ups, spyware, and "unwanted programs." As such, it may also be worthwhile to examine the application logs to see if there are any indications of unusual or suspicious activity.

TIP

Windows Defender Logs

Microsoft KB article 923886 (found at *http://support.microsoft.com/kb/923886*) provides very useful information regarding Windows Defender logs. The article describes where to go within the file system and which files and other data to collect when seeking support assistance with respect to Windows Defender. The article also describes the command you can use on Windows XP, Vista, and Windows 7 to automatically gather all pertinent information into a compressed .cab file, to be sent to Microsoft Support for analysis.

During an examination, you may find that other AV applications may have been installed and run on the system. Check the Registry, Program Files directory, and even the prefetch files for indications of these applications and their use. Often, both home user and corporate employee systems may have AV applications installed; home user systems may have freely available AV scanners installed, and corporate systems will likely have an enterprise-scale commercial AV scanner installed. As such, you may need to determine if the logs are maintained on the local system or in a central location. I have received a number of hard drives and acquired images that indicate that shortly after an incident or malware infection was suspected, the administrator logged into the system and either updated the installed AV and ran a scan, or installed and ran an AV application. Like other examiners, I've also clearly seen where more than one AV scanner was run on the system. What you would want to do is locate the logs (if possible) from these scans and determine what, if anything, these scanners may have found. Even if the administrator installed the AV application, ran a scan, and then deleted the application, you may still be able to find indications of scan results in the Application Event Log.

So why is it so important to determine which AV applications have already been run on a system? Within the information security industry, and specifically within the digital forensics and incident response (DFIR) community, it's understood that just because a commercial AV scan didn't find any malware on a system, that doesn't definitively indicate that there was no malware on the system. As such, many of us rely on a methodology, rather than one specific commercial AV application, to attempt to detect malware within an acquired image. Along those lines, what an analyst does not (and I mean *not*) want to do is hinge his findings on one AV scan, and in particular, one done using the same AV application that had been installed on the system. And to answer the question that just popped into your mind, yes, I have seen reports that have indicated that no malware was found on a system based on a single AV scan, and when the analyst went back and checked later, he found that the AV application used was the same version and malware signature file as what had been installed on the system. What is the point of redoing something that was already done, especially when it didn't provide findings of any significance?

As such, the first step of any malware detection analysis should be to determine what, if any, anti-malware or anti-spyware applications were already installed on the system, what were the versions of these applications, and when they were last updated. The version of the application itself can be very important, as AV vendors have stated that the reason why known malware hadn't been detected on a customer's infrastructure was that while the signature file was up to date, the scanning engine itself was out of date and was not properly utilizing the signatures.

Once this information has been documented, determine if there are any logs available, and if so, examine them for any indication that malware had been detected. I've had a number of opportunities to examine systems onto which malware had originally been detected and quarantined by the AV application when it was first introduced to the system. The intruder later returned to the system and uploaded a new version of the malware that the AV application did not detect, but used the same filename for the new version of the malware. As such, a search for the filename originally detected by the AV application turned up the version of the malware that the AV application didn't detect.

I've also seen instances in which an AV application detected the presence of malware, but that application had been specifically (however unintentionally) configured to take no action other than to record the detection event. As such, the logs (as well as the Application Event Log) provided clear indication that there was in fact malware on the system (including the full path to the files) but that it hadn't so much as been quarantined by the AV application. In one instance, the AV application logs indicated that the creation and subsequent deletion of malware files (presumably, after the intruder was done with them) had been detected, but again, no action other than to record these events had been taken. This proved to be extremely valuable information that provided insight into other actions taken by the intruder.

In other instances, AV scanning applications have additional functionality beyond the traditional signature-based detection. For example, McAfee AV products can detect and/or block (i.e., they can be configured to detect but not block) suspect actions, such as trying to run an executable file from a Temp directory or from a web browser cache directory. So, while malware itself may not be explicitly detected by an AV product, the actions taken to download and install that malware may be detected, and possibly even prevented or simply inhibited.

WARNING

Mixing Protection Mechanisms

I once responded to an incident in which a user's system was thought to have been infected with some form of malware. The organization used a network monitoring product that watched for DNS queries for "known-bad" malware/botnet sites, and reported on these as an indication of an infected system. As it turned out, the organization also had rolled out a campus-wide installation of a host-based anti-spyware application to all of their user systems, one which "blackholed" known malicious sites by modifying the hosts file (found in the "C:\Windows\system32\drivers\etc" directory, and described in Microsoft KB article 172218, found at the Microsoft Support site at *http://support.microsoft.com/kb/172218*) to redirect the queries for the domains and hosts to the local host (i.e., 127.0.0.1). The final result of the engagement was that the user had installed an additional anti-spyware application on his system, one which extracted all of the host names from the host files and issued DNS queries for each one, regardless of the fact that they were blackholed. The combination of these three tools, while thought to be providing overlapping layers of protection, actually triggered what was thought to be a significant incident.

Dr. Watson Logs

Another source of potentially valuable data is the Dr. Watson log file. Dr. Watson is a user-mode debugger found on Windows XP (but not Windows 7) that launches and generates a log file when an error occurs with a program. This log file ("drwtson32 .log") is located in the "All Users" profile, in the "\Application Data\Microsoft\ Dr Watson\" subdirectory, and when subsequent application errors occur, data are appended to the file. The appended data include the date, the application for which the error occurred and a list of loaded modules for the application, and a list of the processes that were running at the time of the error. I've looked to the information in this file to not just help determine if malware had been installed on the system, but also reviewed the list of processes (as well as modules loaded in the "offending" or crashed process) to see if the malware process was running at the time that the information in the log was captured. This has been very useful when attempting to verify the "window of compromise" (how long the system had been compromised) during data breach investigations.

Antivirus Scans

Once you've determined and documented which, if any, AV applications had been installed and/or run on the system prior to acquisition, another step you may decide to do is to mount the image as a volume on your analysis workstation and scan it with other AV products. Not all AV applications seem to be created equal; in some instances, I've run multiple big-name AV applications across a mounted image and not found anything. Then after running a freely available AV application, I got a hit for one of the files associated with the malware, and was able to use that as a starting point for further investigation. So, it doesn't hurt to use multiple AV applications in your detection process.

Mounting an acquired image is relatively straightforward, using a number of freely available tools. For example, the ImDisk virtual disk driver (*http://www .ltr-data.se/opencode.html/#ImDisk*) installs as a Control Panel applet and allows you to mount Windows images (NTFS or FAT) as read-only on your Windows system. AccessData's FTK Imager version 3.0 (*http://accessdata.com/support/ adownloads#FTKImager*) includes the capability to mount images, as well. As mentioned in Chapter 3, the "vhdtool.exe" program (available from Microsoft) will allow you to convert a copy of your image to a virtual hard drive (VHD) file and mount it read-only on your Windows 7 system. Regardless of the tool used, the purpose is to make the file system within the image accessible as a drive letter or volume (albeit in read-only mode) on your analysis system.

Once you've mounted the image as a volume, you can scan it with AV scanners in the same manner as you would a "normal" file system. Many AV products allow scans to be configured to only be run against specific volumes or drive letters (some even allow you to scan specific directories), making it relatively simple and straightforward to scan only the mounted volume(s). If you do not have access to commercial AV products, there are a number of free AV products available for download and use (be sure to read the license agreement thoroughly!!), several of which are simply limited (in the sense that they provide scanning but no other capabilities, such as real-time monitoring, etc.) versions of the full commercial AV products. For example, there is a free version of the AVG scanner available at *http://free.avg.com*, and you have the option to upgrade to a full version of the application that provides additional protection, while downloading files or chatting online. Other AV products such as Eset (producer of the NOD32 AV product, available at *http://www.eset.com*) provide a limited-time trial version of their software; again, be sure that you read and understand the license agreement before using any of these options.

There are a number of other AV products available for use, and many (such as Microsoft's Defender product, mentioned earlier in this chapter) are freely available, while other vendors provide limited-time trial versions of their full, professional products. This part of the chapter is not intended to provide a breakdown or "shootout" among the various available products, but to instead demonstrate that there are options available. The point is that it's always better to run a scan using an AV product that had not been installed on or run on the system, and it's not usually a bad idea to run multiple AV scans using disparate products.

One free, open-source AV product that is very useful and includes a portable (run from a thumb drive) version is ClamWin (see Figure 6.3), found at *http://www .clamwin.com*.

ClamWin can be installed on, updated, and run from a thumb drive, making it a useful option for using among multiple systems without having to install the full application on your analysis system.

Another option available, particularly when specific malware variants are suspected, is micro-scanners. These are not general-purpose AV scanning products, but are instead targeted scanners to look for specific malware variants. One such product is McAfee's AVERT Stinger product, available at *http://www.mcafee.com/us/ downloads/free-tools/how-to-use-stinger.aspx*. Downloading the file and running it on your analysis system opens the user interface (UI) illustrated in Figure 6.4.

If you click on the purple "List Viruses" button in the Stinger UI (see Figure 6.4), a dialog listing all of the malware that the microscanner is designed to detect will be listed. Again, while not as comprehensive as a more general AV product, microscanners offer a useful capability. At the same time, don't forget other scanner

FIGURE 6.3

Partial ClamWin v.0.97 portable GUI.

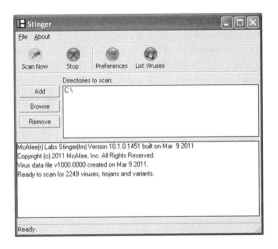

FIGURE 6.4

McAfee's Stinger UI.

products, such as those specifically designed to detect spyware and adware, as these can also provide some useful coverage. Finally, be sure to document the applications that you do use, as well as their versions and results. Both pieces of information will help demonstrate the thoroughness of your detection process.

AV Write-ups

There's something that I think is worth discussing with respect to malware write-ups from AV vendor companies. These write-ups provide descriptions and a wealth of information about the malware that these companies have found, been given access to, and analyzed. However, there's very often a gap when it comes to what incident responders and forensic analysts need to know about malware, and what's provided by the AV companies. This gap is due in large part to the fact that AV companies are not in the business of supporting incident responders; rather, they're in the business of supporting their business.

Now, don't take this as an indictment of AV companies, because that's not what I'm doing. What I am saying here is that malware write-ups from AV companies are a good resource, but should be considered within that context, as sometimes they are not complete and do not provide a comprehensive or completely accurate picture of the malware. For example, there is malware that infects files that are "protected" by Windows File Protection (WFP), but often there is no reference to WFP or the fact that it was subverted in the malware write-up. While WFP is not intended as a security or AV mechanism and is easily subverted (code for this is available on the Internet), this fact is important to know as it may help us detect the malware where the AV product fails since AV products are most often based on signatures within the malware files themselves, and not on specific artifacts on the system.

Another aspect of malware write-ups that can be confusing is that there's often no differentiation between artifacts produced by the malware infection and those produced by the ecosystem (e.g., operating system, installed applications, etc.) that the malware infects. One example of this is the MUICache key within the Registry; several years ago I found a number of malware write-ups that stated that the malware added a value to this key when it infected a system, when, in fact, the value was added by the operating system based on how the malware was executed in the test environment. Another example is the ESENT key within the Registry on Windows XP systems. When someone asked what this key was used for, Google searches indicated that there were malware samples that modified this key when executed. It turned out that Windows XP systems were mistakenly shipped with a checked (or debug) version of the "esent.dll" file, and the key itself (and all of its subkeys and values) were a result of that debug version of the DLL being deployed on production systems. As such, it wasn't the malware infecting the system that caused the Registry modifications as much as it was the result of the debug version of the DLL. This could be confusing when an analyst was examining a Windows Vista or Windows 7 system and found the malware in question, but did not find a corresponding ESENT key within the Registry.

WARNING

Googling

Analysts should beware of conclusively identifying any malware sample as a particular virus based on the name or location of the malicious file, a Registry key used for persistence, etc. There are literally hundreds of thousands of malware samples and variants floating around, and a relatively limited number of autostart/persistence locations, innocuous-looking filenames, etc. that tend to get used and reused by malware authors. Analysts should not base their analysis on "I Googled the filename and this is what I found," as doing so can easily lead to a misidentification of the malware, and an incorrect report of the malware's capabilities provided to a customer.

Remember, the customer is very likely going to have to make some tough business decisions regarding risk and compliance based on your findings, and providing incorrect information about the nature of the malware found on their systems will lead to the wrong decisions being made. In some cases, all it would take is for the intruder to design his malware to use the same filenames and locations as some very well-known malware (perhaps something known to be fairly innocuous) that has completely different functionality and poses a completely different set of risks to infected systems. This would have a significant impact on the information provided to the customer, if the analyst relied on the Googling to identify the malware.

Digging Deeper

Windows systems contain a lot of executable files, many of which are completely legitimate, and it's neither productive nor efficient to examine each and every one of those files to determine if it's malicious. While these files can be hashed and comparisons can be run, this method of identifying "known-good" files can be cumbersome, particularly on Windows systems, as software installations and system patches tend to change a number of files, so that while they are still completely legitimate, they may trigger false positives in the hash comparison tool that you're using. Also, system administrators and home users rarely maintain an accurate set of system file hashes for you to use as a baseline for comparison.

There are a number of other techniques available to analysts, beyond log analysis and AV scans, that allow us to perform some significant data reduction and considerably narrow the field of interesting files. We can use these techniques to help us detect malware within an acquired image that would be missed by other detection means. We'll discuss several of these techniques throughout the rest of this chapter, but there are a couple of things that should be clear. First, this should not be considered a complete list; I will attempt to be comprehensive, but there may be techniques discussed in which you may find limited value, and you may have your own techniques. Second, these techniques will be discussed in no particular order; do not assume that a technique presented first is any more valuable than another. Finally, whichever techniques you decide to use should be included in a documented malware detection process. A sample checklist is provided as an MS Word document along with the additional materials provided with this book (available at *http://code.google.com/p/winforensicaanalysis/downloads/list*).

Packed Files

Compression or "packing" is a means for reducing the size of a file, but more importantly, portable executable (PE) files can be packed to hide their true nature, and to "hide" from AV scanners. However, it is uncommon—albeit not unheard of—for legitimate files to be packed. Therefore, any packed files found during a scan would bear closer inspection. One tool that is freely available for checking for packed files is PEiD, available at *http://www.peid.info/* (version 0.95 is available at the time of this writing; as of April 4, 2011, the project appears to have been discontinued). The PEiD UI is illustrated in Figure 6.5.

Choosing the "Multi Scan" button on the PEiD UI allows you to run a scan of files within a directory, as well as recurse through subdirectories, and only scan PE files, as illustrated in Figure 6.6.

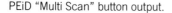

FIGURE 6.5

PEiD UI.

FIGURE 6.6

PEiD "Multi Scan" button output.

PEiD also supports command line switches (be sure to read the "readme" text file that comes as part of the distribution), but the difference from other command line interface (CLI) tools is that running the application via command line switches sends the output to GUI dialogs, as seen in Figure 6.6. Without an option for redirecting the output to files, PEiD cannot effectively be incorporated into batch files. Regardless, this is still an invaluable tool to have available.

NOTE

Using PEiD

PEiD's capability for detecting packed files is signature-based, and the configuration file that ships with the tool ("userdb.txt") contains only one signature. As such, users will need to provide their own signatures; fortunately, Jim Clausing has provided a list of packer signatures, which is available via the SANS Incident Handler's site (*http://handlers.sans .org/jclausing/userdb.txt*).

```
D:\tools>sigcheck -e -u -q c:\windows
c:\windows\PSEXESUC.EXE:
        Verified:        Unsigned
        File date:       3:39 PM 10/4/2010
        Publisher:       Sysinternals
        Description:     PsExec Service
        Product:         Sysinternals PsExec
        Version:         1.60
        File version:    1.60

D:\tools>
```

FIGURE 6.7

"Sigcheck.exe" tool.

If you would prefer a CLI tool, you might consider the Yara project, found at *http:// code.google.com/p/yara-project/*. Yara started out as an open-source project to help identify and classify malware samples, but the author's (Victor Manuel Alvarez of Hipasec Sistemas) work has expanded the project. While it remains open-source and based on Python, a Windows executable file is available for download, making it much more accessible to a wider range of users. Yara is a rules-based scanner, in which users can define their own sets of rules, based on strings, instruction patterns, regular expressions, etc., to detect and classify malware. The Google Code site for the Yara project includes a wiki page with sample rules files for packers as well as a limited set of rules to detect some malware. The packer rules are based on some of the same signatures used by PEiD, which means that those rules can be used to run PEiD functionality (packer scans) from a batch file, using a command similar to the following:

```
C:\tools>yara packer.txt C:\Windows > d:\case\yara-packer.txt
```

In this Yara command, the file "packer.txt" is simply a file that contains a limited number of rules for detecting packers, available on the Yara project wiki (i.e., copy and paste the rules into a file). The book *Malware Analyst's Cookbook and DVD* (Ligh et al., 2011) contains several "recipes" (i.e., Python scripts) for converting ClamAV (note: this is not the ClamWin AV product discussed earlier in this chapter, and is instead available at *http://www.clamav.net*) antivirus signatures and the full set of PEiD packer signatures to Yara rules files. If you work with or encounter malware at all, having a copy of the *Malware Analyst's Cookbook and DVD* available can be quite valuable.

Digital Signatures
Examining executable image files for valid digital signatures using a tool such as "sigcheck.exe" (available from the SysInternals site on MS TechNet, at http://technet.microsoft.com/en-us/sysinternals/bb897441) is a valuable approach for detecting malware. This is an excellent technique to use, in that an analyst can scan systems for executable files that do not have digital signatures, as illustrated in Figure 6.7.

As with many CLI tools, simply typing "sigcheck" at the command prompt will display the syntax for the various command line switches. Figure 6.7 illustrates a scan of just the "C:\Windows" directory, looking for unsigned executable files, regardless of their extension. CLI tools are very useful in that they can be very easily included in batch files to facilitate scanning and processing of the results. For example, adding appropriate switches will tell "sigcheck.exe" to recurse through subdirectories, and send the output to comma-separated value (CSV) format, which is suitable for ease of analysis. This is illustrated in the following command line:

```
C:\tools>sigcheck -e -v -u -q -s c:\windows > d:\case\dig_sig.csv
```

However, it's worth noting that like many methods used by responders and analysts, someone is going to find out about them and find a way to use that method against the responders and analysts. In June 2010, malware known as "StuxNet" was publicly mentioned and described, and one of the notable aspects of the malware was that it contained a valid digital signature. On July 16, 2010, a post to the Microsoft Malware Protection Center (MMPC) blog titled "The StuxNet Sting" (found at *http://blogs.technet.com/b/mmpc/archive/2010/07/16/the-stuxnet-sting .aspx*) stated that the StuxNet malware files had been signed with a valid digital signature belonging to Realtek Semiconductor Corp. This digital signature quickly expired, but other examples of the StuxNet malware that were discovered were found to use other valid signatures. As with other techniques, scanning for valid digital signatures should not be considered a "silver bullet" solution, but should instead be considered as part of an overall detection process.

Windows File Protection

WFP is a process that runs in the background on Windows systems and monitors for file change events that occur on the system. When such an event is detected, WFP determines if the event is related to one of the files it monitors, and if so, WFP will replace the modified file from a "known-good" version in its cache, which in many instances is the "C:\Windows\system32\dllcache" directory. A more comprehensive description of WFP can be found at *http://support.microsoft.com/ kb/222193*.

Many times, an attacker will get malware on a system that temporarily disables WFP and replaces or infects a "protected" file, after which WFP is reenabled. WFP does not poll or scan files, but instead "listens" and waits for file change events, so once it has been reenabled, the modified file goes undetected. Sometimes, only the file that does not reside in the cache is modified, and other times, analysts have found that both the file in the cache as well as the one in the "runtime" portion of the file system (i.e., the "system32" directory) were modified.

One means for detecting attacks where only the noncached copy of a "protected" file was modified is to compute cryptographic one-way MD5 hashes of all of the files in the cache directory, and then locate the noncached copies of those files, hash them, and compare the hashes. I wrote an application called "WFP Checker" several years ago (2008) that does exactly that, and writes its output to a

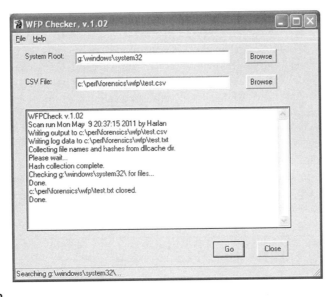

FIGURE 6.8

WFP Checker UI.

CSV-formatted file so that it can be easily viewed in a spreadsheet program or easily parsed via a scripting language. The UI for WFP Checker (following a scan of a mounted volume) is illustrated in Figure 6.8.

WFP Checker is a pretty straightforward tool for scanning live systems for indications of "protected" files that have been modified in the manner described earlier in this section. Keep in mind, however, that following hashing the files in the "dllcache" directory, only those corresponding files in the "system32" directory are hashed and compared (it should be noted that depending on the source of the files, cached copies may be maintained in other directories). Some application installers may place files in other directories, and to maintain a relatively low "noise" level (I didn't want to introduce more data to be analyzed) and reduce false positives, the rest of the volume is not searched. As you can see in Figure 6.8, a log file of the application's activity is maintained along with the output file.

Alternate Data Streams

Alternate data streams (ADSs) are an artifact associated with the NTFS file system that have been around since the implementation of NTFS itself. ADSs were originally meant to provide compatibility with the Macintosh Hierarchal File System (HFS), providing the ability to store resource forks for files shared between Windows NT and Mac systems. ADSs have been covered in great detail in other resources (Carvey, 2009), but suffice to say, ADSs can be particularly insidious based on how they can be created and used, and the fact that an analyst may be unaware of or unfamiliar with them.

Windows systems contain all of the necessary native tools to create and manipulate ADSs, as well as launch executables and scripts "hidden" in ADSs; however, until recently, Windows systems did not contain any native tools for locating arbitrary ADSs created within the file system. By "until recently," I mean to say that it wasn't until Vista was released that the *dir* command, used with "/r" switch, could be used to view arbitrary ADSs. There are also a number of third-party tools that you can add to your system or toolkit that will allow you to view ADSs, including Frank Heyne's command line "lads.exe" (available from heysoft.de), "streams .exe" (available from Mark Russinovich's site at Microsoft), and the GUI-based "alternatestreamview.exe" (available from nirsoft.net). Any of these tools can be run against a mounted image file, but keep in mind these artifacts are specific to NTFS. If the file system of the imaged system is FAT-based, there's really no point in checking for ADSs.

NOTE

Poison Ivy RAT

Poison Ivy is a GUI-based client-server remote administration tool (RAT) that is freely available on the Internet. The Poison Ivy GUI provides a point-and-click interface for configuring and creating a custom version of the "tool." One of the configuration options allows the tool to be installed within an ADS. An intruder with no programming skills simply has to select a checkbox to use this mechanism to hide their malware on the computer of an unsuspecting victim.

So why are ADSs an issue? Well, there are a number of files on systems; in many cases, thousands of files. Even when an acquired image is loaded into a commercial forensic analysis application (several of which will highlight ADSs in red font), ADSs may not be immediately visible to the analyst without digging within the directory structure. As we've mentioned, they're definitely not easy to detect on the live system, as the native tools for doing so are very limited. Therefore, while ADSs are simple and were never intended for malicious purposes, like anything else they can be particularly insidious if an analyst or system administrator simply isn't familiar with them, and doesn't even know to look for them.

WARNING

Knowing What's Possible

Knowing what to look for when performing digital forensic analysis is important, and this is where having a documented malware detection process (or checklist) can be so valuable. I've been to a number of conferences and given many seminars and presentations where I will ask the attendees (analysts, administrators, etc.) about things like ADSs, and will not be surprised at all when no one indicates that they're aware of them. That's why we have professional education and development, and that's also why it's so important for analysts to share information with each other.

The trap you want to avoid is basing your findings or conclusions on assumptions and speculation. We've all seen where something "new" has been discussed and this suddenly becomes the *cause célèbre*, as incidents are attributed to this "new" artifact or finding. Be sure to follow your documented analysis process, and if you rule out four items based on your analysis, don't simply assume that the issue is the fifth item. Run that scan or perform that analysis. What you want to avoid is stating that the issue has to do with ADSs, only to have someone come back later after having run the appropriate scan and determined that there were no ADSs within the acquired image. Don't assume that just because something is possible, that's what happened—check it.

On September 20, 2011, an interesting post regarding the creation of "stealth ADSs" appeared on the Exploit-Monday.com web site (the post can be found at *http://www.exploit-monday.com/2011/09/stealth-alternate-data-streams-and.html*). The post outlines, in part, how to add an ADS to a file that was first created using specific names (e.g., NUL, CON, etc.; part of the device namespace in Windows). These files can be created by appending "\\?\" to the file path. The author of the post found that neither "streams.exe" (available from Microsoft at *http://technet .microsoft.com/en-us/sysinternals/bb897440*), nor the use of "dir /r" (command line switch available on Windows starting with Vista) included the capability of detecting ADSs "attached" to these files, unless the file path was specifically pre-pended with "\\?\." The blog post also illustrated how Windows Management Instrumentation (WMI) could be used to launch executables from within these stealth ADSs, illustrating the risk associated with this capability. Michael Hale Ligh (also known as "MHL," one of the coauthors of *The Malware Analyst's Cookbook and DVD*), quickly followed with a blog post of his own (found at *http://mnin .blogspot.com/2011/09/detecting-stealth-ads-with-sleuth-kit.html*) that illustrated the use of "tsk_view.exe" (see his blog post for a link to the tool) to detect these stealth ADSs.

PE File Compile Times

Another check that we can run against individual files (this may take a little bit of programming to automate) is to take advantage of metadata embedded within PE files to attempt to detect suspicious files. The compile date is a 32-bit value (the number of seconds since December 3, 1969 at 4:00 pm), which is a time date stamp that the linker (or compiler for an object file) adds to the header of a PE file, as illustrated in Figure 6.9.

As illustrated in Figure 6.9, the compile date appears as "2006/08/01 Tue 21:10:42 UTC." The created and modified time stamps within the file's metadata are often modified (referred to as "timestomped") to disguise the malicious file and make it blend in with legitimate operating system and application files. While the compile time stored in the PE header could be similarly modified (e.g., using a hex editor), it is not often seen in practice. Therefore, comparing the compile time from the PE header with the created and modified times from the file metadata and looking for anomalies may allow you to identify malware.

pFile	Data	Description	Value
00000064	014C	Machine	IMAGE_FILE_MACHINE_I386
00000066	0005	Number of Sections	
00000068	44CFC352	Time Date Stamp	2006/08/01 Tue 21:10:42 UTC
0000006C	00000000	Pointer to Symbol Table	
00000070	00000000	Number of Symbols	
00000074	00E0	Size of Optional Header	
00000076	010F	Characteristics	
	0001		IMAGE_FILE_RELOCS_STRIPPED
	0002		IMAGE_FILE_EXECUTABLE_IMAGE
	0004		IMAGE_FILE_LINE_NUMS_STRIPPED
	0008		IMAGE_FILE_LOCAL_SYMS_STRIPPED
	0100		IMAGE_FILE_32BIT_MACHINE

FIGURE 6.9

Compile time in PE file header seen in PE view.

On "normal," uninfected systems, the PE files provided by Microsoft will generally be from the installation medium and have the dates of when the original OS binaries were compiled. There are a number of PE files, of course, that may be updated by patches and Service Packs, and will subsequently have compile dates associated with when the patches were built.

However, consider this example: In November 2009, a malware author creates a PE (.exe or .dll) file, and shortly thereafter, deploys it to compromised systems. As part of the infection mechanism, the file metadata times are "stomped"—in this case, the file times are copied from a file known to be on all Windows systems. This is usually done to hide the existence of the file from responders who only look at those times. One file from which malware authors seem to prefer to copy file times, noted by malware analysis conducted by AV vendors and reverse engineers, is "kernel32 .dll," found in the "system32" directory. So, if the compile time of the suspicious PE file is relatively "recent" (with respect to your incident window), but the creation time of the file is before the compile time, you may have found a suspicious file.

You might also find suspicious files by considering the executable file's compile time in isolation. For example, if the values were all zeros, this might indicate that the malware author directly edited the values. Another example of a suspicious compile time might be one that predates modern versions of Windows, such as anything before 1993.

As with other techniques, you may find that you'll have a number of possible false positives. For example, legitimate system files on Windows systems get updated through the Windows Update mechanism, but may have creation dates from the original installation media (consider the discussion of file system tunneling from Chapter 4). Consider that these may be false positives and not explicit indicators of malware infections. As such, be sure to correlate your findings from other techniques.

MBR Infectors

A great deal of malware runs from within the file system of the infected system itself; that is, the malware or a bootstrap mechanism for the malware exists some place within the file system. The malware may be an executable PE file on the system (it may be encrypted), or instead of the malware itself, a downloader may exist on the system that, when activated, downloads the latest and greatest malware and launches it. However, malware has been seen to exist on the disk, albeit originate from outside the active volumes; these are often master boot record (MBR) infector malware.

Perhaps the first known MBR infector was "Mebroot." According to the Symantec write-up (found at *http://www.symantec.com/security_response/writeup .jsp?docid = 2008-010718-3448-99*) this MBR infector was first written in November 2007 and later modified in February 2008. Once this malware was discovered, analysts determined just how insidious it was, in that an MBR infector allows the malware author to infect a system very early during the boot process, before most protection mechanisms have been initiated. In particular, artifacts of an Mebroot infection included the finding that sectors 60 and 61 of the disk (on many, albeit not all, systems, the MBR is found at sector 0 and the first partition begins at sector 63) contained kernel and payload patcher code, respectively, and that sector 62 contained a preinfection copy of the MBR. Now, this may not be the case for all variants of Mebroot, but it is important to note that on a normal Windows system these sectors are usually full of zeros (and more importantly do not contain copies of the original MBR!).

About two months after the Symantec description of Mebroot was published, an article titled "MBR Rootkit, a New Breed of Malware" appeared on the F-Secure blog (found at *http://www.f-secure.com/weblog/archives/00001393.html*) and provided some additional information about Mebroot. Then, in mid-February 2011, another article titled "Analysis of MBR File System Infector" was posted to the F-Secure blog (found at *http://www.f-secure.com/weblog/archives/00002101.html*) that described yet another bit of malware named "Trojan:W32/Smitnyl.A" that modifies or infects the MBR. The description of Smitnyl.A includes such artifacts as a copy of the original MBR copied to sector 5, and the infector payload starts at sector 39. According to the description, there is also apparently an encoded executable located in sector 45.

So how does this help us, as forensic analysts, in detecting the presence of MBR infectors in an acquired image? Well, one check that we can run programmatically (which is a fancy way of saying, "we can write code to do this for us") is to determine where the first partition starts (we can confirm this by running "mmls.exe" from the TSK tools against the image), and then to run from sector 0 to that sector (usually, though not always, 63) and locate any sectors that do not contain all zeros.

Let's take a look at an example; Figure 6.10 illustrates the output of "mmls.exe" (one of the Sleuthkit tools) run against an acquired image of a Windows system. As we can see in Figure 6.10, the first 63 sectors are "Unallocated," and the first NTFS partition for this system (in this case, the C:\ volume) starts at sector 63. Sample Perl code to check the sectors with a raw/dd image for any content other than zeros might look like the following:

```perl
my $file = shift;
my $data;
open(FH,"<",$file) || die "Could not open $file: $!\n";
binmode(FH);
foreach my $s (0..63) {
```

```
         Slot    Start        End          Length        Description
00:      Meta    0000000000   0000000000   0000000001    Primary Table (#0)
01:      -----   0000000000   0000000062   0000000063    Unallocated
02:      00:00   0000000063   0097482419   0097482357    NTFS (0x07)
03:      00:01   0097482420   0488263544   0390781125    NTFS (0x07)
04:      -----   0488263545   0488281249   0000017705    Unallocated
```

FIGURE 6.10

Output of "mmls.exe."

```perl
seek(FH,0,$s * 512);
read(FH,$data,512);
my $str = unpack("B*",$data);
if ($str != 0) {
print " Sector ".$s."\n";
}
}
close(FH);
```

When I ran this code against an image that I had already checked manually (by opening the image in FTK Imager and tabbing through sectors 0–63 in the hex view pane), I found that as expected, sectors 0, 10, and 63 contained something more than zeros. At this point, I've reduced the amount of data I need to look at (data reduction through coding is a wonderful thing) from a total of 64 sectors to just one, as sector 0 contains the MBR and sector 63 contains the beginning of the C:\ volume. Running this same code against a system infected with either of the discussed MBR infectors would produce markedly different results, but still only have to dig into about half a dozen (as opposed to 64) sectors.

However, our coding doesn't need to stop there ... and because this really rocks, I didn't stop with just the previous sample code. I ended up writing "mbr.pl," a Perl script that provides much more functionality than the previous sample code (the code for "mbr.pl" is a bit too lengthy to list here), which not only tells the analyst which 512-byte sectors are nonzero, but will also provide other capabilities. For example, we can see just the sectors that contain something other than zeros using the following command line:

```
C:\Perl>mbr.pl -f f:\case\disk0.001 -s
Sector 0
Sector 10
Sector 63
```

If we want to see more, we can remove the "-s" switch (stands for "summary") and have the script print out the nonzero sectors in a hex editor–like format, as illustrated in Figure 6.11.

Finally, the script allows also us (via the "-d" switch, for "dump") to dump the raw contents of the 512-byte sectors to files on the disk. This allows us to run *diff* commands on the sectors, or generate MD5 or ssdeep hashes for the sectors; the raw sectors or the hashes can be uploaded to sites like VirusTotal for a modicum of

FIGURE 6.11

Sample "mbr.pl" output.

analysis. Further, file hashes generated using Jesse Kornblum's "ssdeep.exe" (freely available at *http://ssdeep.sourceforge.net/*) can be compared to determine if any of the hashes are similar, as some MBR infectors (albeit not all) will copy the original MBR to another sector.

Other checks can be added to this code; for example, we could check the first 2 bytes of the sector for "MZ," which is just a quick-and-dirty check for the *possibility* that the sector is the beginning of a PE file. The "mbr.pl" script is provided as part of the materials associated with this book.

TIP

Coding Skills

Having some ability to program, whether it's writing batch files or via a scripting language like Python or Perl, can prove to be an extremely valuable skill. Programming requires the ability to compartmentalize a task into smaller subtasks, to think methodically, and to spell; if you misspell your variable names in Perl (and don't use the "use strict" pragma) you're going get unexpected results. All of these skills are valuable to an analyst, as is the ability to have the computer system do the bulk of the "heavy lifting" for you, allowing you to automate repetitive tasks.

Registry Analysis

Earlier in this chapter, we discussed persistence mechanisms and malware artifacts, and how both can be found in the Registry. In Chapter 5, we discussed various tools and techniques for parsing data from the Registry, and we can use those to detect the presence of malware on systems. Registry analysis can be an extremely important and revealing technique when looking for the presence of malware in an image. For example, as new variants of Conficker were released, they weren't immediately detected by installed AV products on a good number of systems, but one thing did remain constant across the variants: The malware used a random service name, running as part of the "svchost.exe" process, as its persistence mechanism. In many instances, within malware families that use the Registry for persistence, there is some consistency across the family.

In addition to persistence mechanisms, malware will many times also have other artifacts that you can look for that will indicate the presence of malware when AV scanner applications do not do so. Consider some of the artifacts discussed earlier in this chapter, such as values beneath the MUICache key, prefetch files, processes listed in the Dr. Watson log file, etc.; these (and others) can provide indications of malware on a system that may be missed by AV products.

Internet Activity

Many analysts look to a user's Internet activity to determine web sites that they've visited, often as part of a wider examination. However, the same technique can be used to check for the presence of malware, as well as potentially identify the source of the malware (from whence it came). Many times, when an intruder gets malware onto a system, she does so with elevated privileges; for example, if the intruder gains Administrator-level access to a system, she can use those privileges to create a scheduled task or a Windows service, both of which will run with elevated, System-level privileges. If the malware running with elevated privileges uses the WinInet API (also used by Internet Explorer) to communicate off of the system, there will be artifacts of this communication, including entries in the Temporary Internet Files (TIF) "index.dat" file for the "Default User" user.

On November 15, 2006, Robert Hensing (a Microsoft employee who used to lead their incident response team) posted to his TechNet blog (*http://blogs.technet .com/b/robert_hensing*) about malware "hiding" in the "Default User" user profile. Robert had seen some of the same odd entries in a user profile's Web history that I'd seen during examinations, and had gone so far as to test his theories by launching Internet Explorer as a scheduled task (so that it would run with System-level privileges). After surfing to several sites using this "super IE," Robert then found Web history in the "Default User" profile. It's also important to note that Robert had actually posted to his blog much earlier (January 27, 2005, with a post titled "Anatomy of a WINS Server Hack") with respect to finding the artifact of content in the Temporary Internet Files directory in the "Default User" profile.

An analyst has a number of means available to parse the Internet history from within an image. I have found that ProDiscover (both the IR and Basic editions; I mention these two specifically as they are the ones to which I have access) is very good at parsing these data; simply open the project file and navigate to your image via the Content view. Navigate through the tree to the user profile directory, and then right-click to reveal the dropdown menu illustrated in Figure 6.12. Select "Find Internet Activity..." and allow the application to populate the Internet History Viewer, as illustrated in Figure 6.13.

Christopher Brown released ProDiscover (Incident Response Edition) 6.10.0.1 on May 5, 2011, and one of the updates that he included in this version is the ability for ProDiscover to also parse Internet history from the Chrome and Firefox

FIGURE 6.12

ProDiscover dropdown menu.

FIGURE 6.13

Populated ProDiscover Internet History Viewer.

browsers. (Note: ProDiscover version 7.0.0.3 was released in September 2011, and included additional functionality.)

I have also seen Internet history for the LocalService account during analysis, and in a manner similar to what Robert was able to demonstrate, have been able to trace these artifacts back to malware that was making use of the WinInet API and was installed as a Windows service, running under the Local Service account. Examination of the malware indicated that it did, in fact, use the WinInet APIs, and testing of the malware in a lab environment illustrated that the malware did communicate off of the infected system through the use of HTTP requests.

Another way to quickly check for the potential presence of this type of malware artifact is to navigate to the Temporary Internet Files directories for the profiles in question and quickly check to see if the "index.dat" files contain any entries. You can do this by checking the size of the file and seeing if it contains all zeros (I've seen this before), or extract strings from the files. As we will discuss in more detail in Chapter 7, you can also use a Perl script that uses the Win32::UrlCache module to parse the contents of the "index.dat" file. The method or tool you use to perform a check like this is really up to you, as the examiner, but the important point of this section is to understand that Internet history is not something that we normally expect to see in association with the "Default User" or "LocalService" user profiles on a Windows system, and as such, this is something worth checking for, and something I do for most cases that are suspected to involve some type of malware.

Additional Detection Mechanisms

In addition to the various detection techniques we've discussed so far, there are a number of other locations within an image that you can look for indications of a malware infection. For example, looking for unusual scheduled tasks, either the actual .job files in the Tasks directory or listed in the scheduled tasks log file ("SchedLgU.txt").

TIP

AT Jobs

Scheduled tasks created using the native "at.exe" utility are often used by intruders to install malware on or execute other processes on a system. While Administrator privileges are required to create these scheduled tasks, the tasks themselves run with elevated privileges. Within most infrastructures, "at.exe" is not commonly used for routine system administration, and as such, the existence of scheduled tasks named "at1.job," "at2.job," etc. would merit a closer look.

We've discussed malware that uses a Windows service as a persistence mechanism, and other artifacts associated with services. Another place you might want to look is to examine the System Event Log (discussed in detail in Chapter 4) for indications of services being started (event ID 7035) with a user security identifier (SID), rather than a system SID. Services are usually started by LocalService (SID: S-1-5-19) or NetworkService (SID: S-1-5-20) or similar accounts (depending on their configuration), so services (particularly the PSExecSvc service) started by a user account are definitely worth a closer look. Also, services usually start when the system is booted; services that are started hours or days after a system start may also indicate something suspicious.

Another location within the file system that you may find indications of malware includes Temp directories, either the Windows Temp directory ("C:\Windows\Temp") or the Temp directory within the user profile. Further, the Tasks folder ("C:\Windows\Tasks") is often used to store malware or a location from which to conduct operations, as this is one of the "special" Windows folders in which the true contents are not visible when viewed via Windows Explorer. The same is true for the Fonts ("C:\Windows\Fonts") folder, as well as the Recycle Bin. With these folders, the true contents can be seen via the command line, using the *dir* command.

As with many of the techniques that we've described so far in this chapter, none of them provides us with 100% guaranteed detection of malware. However, we can correlate the output from multiple techniques, and use these techniques to perform data reduction and address the potential for malware being on the system you're analyzing. Remember that there are no silver bullets in information security and digital forensics, but by automating the use of multiple techniques to look for different artifacts of malware, from different perspectives, the goal is to provide enough coverage to minimize the chance of the malware avoiding detection. We should never expect to completely eliminate the possibility of a system being infected, but what we can do is continually improve our process and checklist, and perform as complete and thorough of an assessment as we can.

Seeded Sites

Not long ago an excellent question was posed in an online forum as a hypothetical event. Essentially, someone is found to have contraband images and videos on her system, potentially as a result of using a P2P sharing network. During the examination of the system, several instances of malware are found, and the claim is made that the purveyor of the contraband materials purposely "seeded" his site with malware to provide his customers with a plausible excuse, and that this was actually part of the "contract" for accessing the site.

Given something like this (and you'd think that this will be something that we'd need to address), what could an analyst do to address the issue? As we've discussed in this chapter, running an AV scan on a system and locating files identified as malware is simply one step of several in the process of addressing the "Trojan defense." Once the malware files have been identified, the game isn't over. Just because malware files were found on a system, it doesn't immediately follow that those files were responsible for downloading the contraband. The first thing that an analyst would want to do is determine and document where the malware files are located within the file system, particularly with respect to the contraband files. Were the files identified as malware found in the P2P download directory, or were they located in the web browser cache directory? This can be a very important factor, as the presence of malware on a system does not immediately lead to that malware being responsible for populating the system with contraband images.

A next step would be to determine if the malware had ever actually executed. After all, just because the malware files were located on the system doesn't mean that the "Trojan defense" can effectively be employed (the operative word being "effectively"). If the malware files were written to the file system, but the malware was never executed (and this fact can be proven), then the defense is nullified. What are the file times for the malware files? What are other artifacts of the identified malware? Does the malware modify Registry keys or values when run? Are other files created as a result of the malware executing? What is the malware's persistence mechanism (e.g., Run key, Windows service, etc.), and does that mechanism exist on the system? Remember, *the absence of an artifact where one is expected is itself an artifact*. As such, the analyst may be able to build a thorough case demonstrating that while the malware files were found on the system, there were no indications that the malware had actually been executed, and completely obviate the "Trojan defense."

> **TIP**
>
> **Did Malware Run?**
>
> An excellent example of determining whether malware had run occurred during an exam that involved the Coreflood bot. When this malware actually executes and infects a system, there are several Registry keys and values created, and files containing configuration information and collected data are also created. Finding the Registry artifacts allowed me to identify unique instances of the infection, and differentiate those from detection events, where the installed AV product detected the file and deleted it before the system could be infected. This not only allowed me to identify how many times (and when) systems had been infected, but also see where the malware had been modified to avoid detection, only to be detected and deleted later following a subsequent AV update.

Finally, did the identified malware have the capability to download contraband, as well as the functionality to place the contraband within the file system where they were found? This may require a modicum of reverse-engineering skill to determine, but sometimes it's as simple as opening the malware .exe or .dll file in a tool such as PEView (found at *http://www.magma.ca/~wjr/*) and looking at the import address table (IAT) to see if it imports any DLL functions that allow for network or off-system communications (remember our discussion in this chapter regarding the WinInet APIs). Determining whether the identified malware could have downloaded contraband files may simply be an additional step to further address the "Trojan defense." In one malware examination, I was able to locate actual indications of off-system communications after our malware reverse engineer succeeded in running the malware and providing me with unique strings that were specific to the malware. I ended up locating several instances of the keywords within the pagefile extracted from the system, and examining the surrounding bytes, was able to see HTTP GET request headers and responses, which included time stamps.

> **NOTE**
>
> **Digging Deeper**
>
> Once you've located the malware, and used the four characteristics discussed earlier in this chapter to gather further information about the malware, there may be a need to find out just a little bit more about it. At this point, you've very likely documented the malware, including where within the file system you found it, how you found it (e.g., suspicious Registry value, AV scan, etc.), any other associated artifacts, etc. There may be additional work you can do, and do quickly, to add a bit more information about the malware to your documentation. This section is not intended to teach malware reverse engineering, as this topic would (and has) filled a book of its own; however, there are other excellent books already available that provide comprehensive coverage of this topic, in particular, the *Malware Analyst's Cookbook and DVD* (Ligh et al., 2011).

SUMMARY

Detecting malware on a system can be difficult, and detecting potential malware within an acquired image even more so. However, this is something analysts in law enforcement and in the public and private sectors have to deal with, and as such, need the knowledge, skills, and process to accomplish this task. AV scanning applications may prove insufficient for this task, and analysts may have to look for artifacts of a malware infection, rather than the malware itself, to locate the malware. As such, it is important for analysts to understand the characteristics of malware to understand the types of malware artifacts that may be present on a system, as well as where and how to locate those potential threats. Analysts should always document their activities, and developing a checklist of malware detection techniques can be very valuable, particularly when the analyst fills in that checklist with the results of each technique, or a statement or justification for not using the technique.

In the next chapter, we will walk through the process of creating a timeline of system activity for analysis; this is a technique that can be used to determine a great deal of additional information about not just the infection vector used to get the malware on the system, but also actions that occurred in association with the malware following the infection. This analysis technique has a number of other uses, and as such deserves a chapter of its own.

References

Carvey, H. A. (2009). *Windows forensic analysis* (2nd ed.). Burlington, MA: Syngress Publishing.

Ligh, M. H., Adair, S., Hartstein, B., & Richard, M. (2011). *Malware analyst's cookbook and DVD*. New York: Wiley.

Timeline Analysis

INFORMATION IN THIS CHAPTER

- Timelines
- Creating Timelines
- Case Study

INTRODUCTION

I've mentioned several times throughout the book thus far that there are times when commercial forensic analysis applications simply do not provide the capabilities that an analyst may need to fully investigate a particular incident. Despite all of the capabilities of some of the commercial applications, there's one thing I still cannot do at this point; that is, load an image and push a button (or run a command) that will create a timeline of system activity. Yet the ability to create and analyze timelines has really taken the depth and breadth of my analysis forward by leaps and bounds.

Throughout the day, even with no user sitting at a computer, events occur on Windows systems. Events are simply things that happen on a system, and even a Windows system that appears to be idle is, in fact, very active. Consider Windows XP systems; every 24 hours, a System Restore Point is created, and others may be deleted, as necessary. Further, every three calendar days a limited defragmentation of the hard drive is performed; as you would expect, sectors from deleted files are overwritten. Now, consider a Windows 7 system; Volume Shadow Copies (VSCs) are created (and as necessary, deleted), and every 10 days (by default) the primary Registry hives are backed up. All of these events (and others) occur automatically, with no user interaction whatsoever. So even as a Windows system sits idle, we can expect to see a considerable amount of file system activity over time. When a user does interact with the system, we would expect to see quite a bit of activity: files are accessed and Registry keys and values are created, modified, or deleted, etc. When malware executes, when there is an intrusion, or when other events occur, an analyst can correlate time-stamped data extracted from the computer to build a fairly detailed picture of activity on a system.

TIMELINES

Creating timelines of system activity for forensic analysis is nothing new, and dates back to around 2000, when Rob Lee (of SANS and Mandiant fame) wrote the "mac-daddy" script to create ASCII timelines of file system activity based on metadata extracted from acquired images using The Sleuth Kit (TSK) tools. However, as time has passed, the power of timeline analysis has been recognized and much better understood. As such, the creation of timelines has been extended to include other data sources besides just file system metadata; in fact, the power of timelines as an analytic resource, using multiple data sources, potentially from multiple systems, is quickly being recognized and timeline analysis is being employed by more and more analysts.

Throughout this chapter, we will discuss the value of creating timelines as an analysis technique, and demonstrate a means for creating timelines from an acquired image. The method we will walk through is not the only means for creating a timeline; for example, Kristinn Gudjonsson created log2timeline (*http://log2timeline .net/*), described as "a framework for [the] automatic creation of a super timeline."

This framework utilizes a number of built-in tools to automatically populate timelines with data extracted from a number of sources found within an acquired image.

NOTE

Log2timeline

Kristinn's log2timeline framework is a valuable resource for analysts, and is comprised of various Perl modules that can be used to parse different data sources for time-stamped data. Currently, log2timeline supports modules to parse various structures discussed in this chapter, as well as history files from common web browsers, metadata from some common document types, and log data from widely used applications such as Apache, IIS, or Squid.

This framework can be extremely useful to an analyst. While the approach and tools that I use (which will be described throughout the rest of this chapter) and Kristinn's log2timeline may be viewed by some as competing approaches, they are really just two different ways to reach the same goal. Log2timeline allows for a more automated approach to collecting and presenting a great deal of the available time-stamped data, whereas the tools I use entail a much more command line–intensive process; however, at the same time, this process provides me with a good deal more flexibility to address the issues that I have encountered.

NOTE

Approaches to Timelines

From my perspective, there are two schools of thought at opposite ends of the spectrum when it comes to creating timelines. This is not to say that one is any better or any more correct than another, as it's simply a matter of the goals of your analysis, and of your preference. I refer to one school of thought as the "kitchen sink" approach, where everything possible is included in a timeline and the analyst begins to sort things out from there. Personally, I find this cumbersome, but I do understand why some analysts might prefer this approach. I tend to take a minimalist approach, building my timeline a layer at a time, based on the goals of my analysis and adding specific data sources to bring the available context into focus.

For example, when addressing an issue of contraband images on a system, the question was posed as to whether or not someone logged into the system remotely and somehow added the images. I saw from the Security hive data that auditing of both successful and failed logins was enabled, so as part of my analysis, I created a timeline of just the remote login events available in the Security Event Log (for Windows XP, event ID 528 and 540 events). This way, I had something concise that I could create and refer to quickly, rather than having to open a much larger timeline file composed of a bunch of data sources that had little if anything to do with the question I was trying to answer.

During another examination, I was confronted with a Windows system that had been compromised through SQL injection; as the web server and database server (both components are required for SQL injection) had both been installed on the same platform, I was only analyzing a single system. I started by taking an iterative approach to locating the SQL injection statements in the web server logs. I located what appeared to be indicators of SQL injection in the logs and sorted those by source IP address. I then removed those

---

attempts that, based on the source IP address, appeared to originate from a legitimate scanning service that had been engaged by the customer, and performed searches for all requests originating from the remaining IP addresses. I was able to "see" (using a mini-timeline of just the pertinent web server log entries) clusters of activity on specific dates; when I added these events to the file system metadata, I was able to see not just the commands sent to the system via the SQL injection statements, but also the effect they had on the file system. In the end, I was able to build a complete picture of what happened on the system, and when it happened, using only two data sources.

Again, the approach that any particular analyst uses should be based primarily on the goals of their examination, but will likely also include their preference, how comfortable they are with their knowledge of the data and tools, and any documented processes and procedures they employ.

Data Sources

The early days of digital forensic analysis included reviewing file system meta-data: metadata that is associated with the time stamps from the $STANDARD_ INFORMATION attributes within the master file table (MFT). As we know from Chapter 4, the time stamps within this attribute are easily modified via publicly accessible application programming interfaces (APIs); if you have the necessary permissions to write to a file (and most intruders either get in with or elevate to System-level privileges), you can modify these file times to arbitrary values (this is sometimes referred to as *timestomping*, from the name of a tool used to do this). However, in many cases, rather than "stomping" the file times, the intruder or malware installation process will simply copy the file times from a legitimate system file, such as "kernel32.dll," as this is simply much easier to do, requires only a few API function calls, and leaves fewer traces than "stomping" times.

TIP

Timestomping Artifacts

"Timestomp.exe" (a description of the tool can be found at *http://www.forensicswiki .org/wiki/Timestomp*), developed by James C. Foster and Vincent Lui (at the time of this writing, I could not locate a reliable site from which to download a copy of "timestomp .exe"), reportedly has a 32-bit granularity with respect to its ability to modify file times (as opposed to the 64-bit granularity used in the common Windows FILETIME structure), and it modifies only the time stamps found in the $STANDARD_INFORMATION attribute within the MFT. As such, the use of a tool such as this would be easy to detect, by first checking the granularity of the time stamp within the MFT to see if the lower 32 bits are all zeros, and then comparing the creation dates in the two attributes ($STANDARD_INFORMATION and $FILE_NAME).

As the Windows operating systems developed and increased in complexity, various services and technologies were added and modified over time. This made the systems more usable and versatile, not only to users (desktops, laptops) but also to system administrators (servers). Many of these services and technologies (e.g., the Registry, application prefetching, scheduled tasks, Event Logs, etc.) not only maintain data, but also time stamps that are used to track specific events. Additional services and applications, such as the Internet Information Server (IIS) web server, can provide additional time-stamped events, in the form of logs. This concept also applies to various client applications; for example, the Firefox web browser "bookmarks.html" file (as of Firefox 3, Mozilla moved to the use of a SQLite database for storing bookmark information) is an XML-formatted file that contains information about bookmark links, including the date each was added and when they were last modified. An example of the format of a folder in the "bookmarks.html" file appears as follows:

```
<DT><H3 ADD_DATE="1200093363" LAST_MODIFIED="1200093398"
 ID="rdf:#$RS6tu">WFP</H3>
```

As you can see and imagine, Windows systems are rife with timeline data sources, many of which we've discussed throughout the book (particularly in Chapter 4). Also, in Chapter 3 we discussed how to get even more time-stamped data and fill in some analytic gaps by accessing VSCs. Overall, Windows systems do a pretty decent job of maintaining time-stamped information regarding both system and user activity. Therefore, it's critical that analysts understand what data sources may be available, as well as how to access that time-stamped information and use it to further their analysis.

Time Formats

Along with the variety of data sources, Windows systems maintain time-stamped information in a variety of formats. The most frequently found format on modern Windows systems is the 64-bit FILETIME format (the structure definition is available at *http://msdn.microsoft.com/en-us/library/ms724284(v=vs.85).aspx*), which maintains the number of 100-nanosecond intervals since midnight, January 1, 1601, in accordance with Universal Coordinated Time (UTC, analogous to Greenwich Mean Time or GMT). As we saw in Chapter 4, this time format is used throughout Windows systems, from file times to Registry key LastWrite times to the "ShutdownTime" value within the Registry System hive.

Every now and again, you will see the popular 32-bit Unix time format on Windows systems, as well. This time records the number of seconds since midnight on January 1, 1970 relative to the UTC time zone. This time format is used to record the "TimeGenerated" and "TimeWritten" values within Windows 2000, XP, and 2003 Event Log records (a description of the structure is found at *http://msdn .microsoft.com/en-us/library/aa363646(VS.85).aspx*).

Other time-based information is maintained in a string format, similar to what users usually see when they interact with the system or open Windows Explorer, such as "01/02/2010 2:42 PM." These time stamps are often recorded in local system time after taking the UTC time stamp and performing the appropriate conversion to local time using the time zone and daylight savings settings (maintained in the Registry) for that system. IIS web server logs are also maintained in a similar format (albeit with a comma between the date and time values), although the time stamps are recorded in UTC format.

Yet another time format found on Windows systems is the SYSTEMTIME format (the structure definition is available at *http://msdn.microsoft.com/en-us/library/ms724950(v=vs.85).aspx*). The individual elements within the structure of this time format record the year, month, day of week, day, hour, minute, second, and millisecond (in that order). These times are recorded in local system time after the conversion from UTC using the time zone and daylight savings settings maintained by the system. This time format is found within the metadata on Windows XP and 2003 scheduled tasks (.job files), as well as within some Registry values, particularly on Vista and Windows 7 (refer to Chapter 5).

Finally, various applications often maintain time stamps in their own time format, particularly in log files. For example, Symantec AV logs use a comma-separated, text-based format in six hexadecimal octets (defined at *http://www.symantec.com/business/support/index?page=content&id=TECH100099&locale=en_US*).

So, it's important to realize that time stamps can be recorded in a variety of formats (to include UTC or local system time), and we will discuss later in this chapter tools and code for translating these time stamps into a common format to facilitate analysis.

Concepts

When we create a timeline of system activity from multiple data sources (i.e., more than simply file system metadata), we achieve two basic concepts (credit goes to Cory Altheide for succinctly describing these to me awhile back); we add *context* to the data that we're looking at, and we *increase our relative level of confidence* in that data.

Okay, so what does this mean? Well, by saying that we add context to the data that we're looking at, I mean that by bringing in multiple data sources, we begin to see more detail added to the activity surrounding a specific event. For example, consider a file being modified on the system, and the fact that we might be interested in what may have caused the modification; that is, was it part of normal system activity? Was the file modification part of an operating system or application update (such as with log files, etc.)? Or was that file modification the direct result of some specific action performed by a user? By using time-stamped information derived from multiple data sources, normalizing the data (i.e., reducing the time stamps to a common format), and incorporating them into an overall view, we can "see" what additional activity was occurring on the system during or near that time. I've used timelines to locate file modifications that were the result of a malware infection (see Chapter 6), and could see when a file was loaded on a system, and then a short while later the file (i.e., with a "suspicious" name or in a suspicious location) of interest was modified.

When we say that timelines can increase our relative level of confidence in the data that we're analyzing, what this means is that some data sources are more easily mutable than others, and we have greater confidence in those that are less easily mutable (or modified). For example, we know that the file time stamps in the $STANDARD_INFORMATION attribute of the MFT can be easily modified through the use of open, accessible APIs; however, those in the $FILE_NAME attribute are not as easily accessible. Also, to this date, I have yet to find any indication of a publicly available API for modifying the LastWrite times associated with Registry keys (remember Chapter 5?) to arbitrary values. These values can be updated to more recent times by creating and then deleting a value within the key, but we may find indications of this activity using tools and techniques described in Chapter 5.

The point is that all data sources for our timeline have a relative level of confidence that the times associated with those sources are "correct," and that relative level of confidence is higher for some data sources (Registry key LastWrite times) than for others (file times in the $STANDARD_INFORMATION attributes of the MFT, log file entries, etc.). Therefore, if we were to see within our timeline a Registry key associated with a specific malware variant being modified on the system and saw that a file also associated with the malware was created "nearby," then our confidence that the file system metadata regarding the file creation was accurate would be a bit higher.

We also have to keep in mind that the amount of relevant detail available from time-stamped information is often subject to *temporal proximity*. This is a *Star Trek*–sounding term that I first heard used by Aaron Walters (of the Volatility project) that refers to being close to an event in time. This is an important concept to keep in mind when viewing time-stamped data; as we saw in Chapter 4, some time-stamped data are available as metadata contained within files, or as values within Registry keys or values, etc. However, historical information is not often maintained within these sources. What I mean by this is that a Registry key LastWrite time is exactly that; the value refers to the last time that the key contents were modified in some way. What is not maintained is a list of all of the previous times that the key was modified.

The same holds true with other time-stamped information, such as metadata maintained within prefetch files; the time stamp that refers to the last time that particular application was launched is just that—the last time this event occurred. The file metadata does not contain a list of the previous times that the application was launched since the prefetch file itself was created. As such, it's nothing unusual to see a prefetch file (for MS Word, Excel, the Solitaire game, etc.) with a specific creation date, a modification date that is "close" to the embedded time stamp, and a relatively high run count, but what we won't have available is a list of times and dates for when the application had been previously launched. What this means is that if your timeline isn't created within relative *temporal proximity* to the incident, some time-stamped data may be overwritten or modified by activities that occurred following the incident but prior to response activities, and you may lose some of the context that is achieved through the use of timeline analysis. This is an important consideration to keep in mind when performing timeline analysis, as it can explain an apparent lack of indicators of specific activity. I've seen this several times, particularly following malware infections; while there are indicators of an infection (e.g., Registry artifacts, etc.), the actual malware executable (and often, any data files) may have been deleted and the MFT entry and file system sectors overwritten by the time I was able to obtain any data.

Benefits

In addition to providing context and an increased relative confidence in the data that we're looking at, timelines provide other benefits when it comes to analysis. I think that many of us can agree that a great deal of the analysis we do (whether we're talking about intrusions, malware infections, contraband images, etc.) comes down to definable events occurring at certain times, respective to each other or to some external source. When we're looking at intrusions, we often want to know when the intruder initially gained access to a system. The same is often true with malware infections; when the system was first infected determines the window of compromise (i.e., how long the system was infected) and directly impacts how long sensitive data may have been exposed. With respect to payment card industry (PCI) forensic assessments, one of the critical data points of the analysis is the "window of exposure"; that is, answering the question of when the system was compromised or infected and how long credit card data was at risk of exposure. When addressing issues of contraband images, we may want to know when the images were created on the system to determine how long the user may have possessed them, what actions the user may have performed in relation to those images (e.g., launched a viewing application), and when those actions occurred.

These examples show how analysis of timeline data can, by itself, provide a great deal of information about what happened and when for a variety of incidents. Given that fact, one can see how creating a timeline has additional benefits, particularly when it comes to triage of an incident, or the exposure of sensitive data is in question. One challenge that has been faced by forensic analysts consistently over the years has been the ever-increasing size of storage media. I can remember the days when a 20-megabyte (MB) hard drive was a big deal; in fact, I can remember when a hard drive itself was a big deal! Over time, we've seen hard drive sizes go from MB to gigabytes (GB) to hundreds of GB, even into terabytes. But it's not just hard drives, it's all storage media. External storage media (e.g., thumb drives and external hard drives) have at the same time increased in capacity and decreased in price. The same is true for digital cameras, smart phones, etc.

Where timelines can be extremely beneficial when dealing with ever-increasing storage capacity is that they are created from text-based metadata, rather than file contents. Consider a 500-GB hard drive; file system metadata (discussed later in this chapter) extracted from the active file system on that hard drive will only comprise tens of kilobytes. Even as we add additional data sources to our timeline information (such as data from Registry hives, or even the hive files themselves), and the data themselves approach hundreds of kilobytes, it's all text-based and can be compressed, occupying even less space. In short, the relevant timeline data can be extracted, compressed, and provided or transmitted to other analysts far more easily than transmitting entire copies of imaged media.

To demonstrate how this is important, consider a data breach investigation where sensitive data (such as PCI) was possibly exposed. These investigations can involve multiple systems, which require time to image, and then time to analyze, as well as time to search for credit card numbers. However, if the onsite responder were to acquire images, and then extract a specific subset of data sources (either the files themselves or the metadata that we will discuss in this chapter), these data could be compressed, encrypted, and provided to an offsite analyst to conduct an initial analysis or triage examination, all without additional exposure of PCI data, as file contents are not being provided.

The same can be said of contraband image investigations. Timeline data can be extracted from an acquired image and provided to an offsite analyst, without any additional exposure of the images themselves; only the filenames and paths are provided. The images themselves do not need to be shared (nor should they) to address such questions as how or when the images were created on the system, or whether the presence of the images is likely the result of specific user actions (as opposed to malware). While I am not a sworn law enforcement officer, I have assisted in investigations involving contraband images; however, the assistance I provided did not require me (thankfully) to view any of the files. Instead, I used time-stamped data to develop a timeline, and in several instances was able to demonstrate that a user account had been accessed from the console (i.e., logging in from the keyboard) and used to view several of the images.

In short, it is often not feasible to ship several terabytes of acquired images to a remote location; this would be obviated by the time it would take to encrypt the data, as well as by the risks associated with the data being lost or damaged during shipment. However, timeline data extracted from an acquired image (or even from a live running system) can be archived and secured, and then provided to an offsite analyst. As an example, I had an image of a 250-GB hard drive, and the resulting timeline file created using the method outlined in this chapter was about 88 kilobytes (KB), which then compressed to about 8 KB. In addition, no sensitive data was exposed in the timeline itself, whereas analysis of the timeline provided answers to the customer's questions regarding malware infections.

Another aspect of timeline analysis that I have found to be extremely valuable is that whether we're talking about malware infections or intrusions or another type of incident, in the years that I've been performing incident response and digital forensic analysis as a consultant, it isn't often that I'm able to get access to an image of a system that was acquired almost immediately following the actual incident. In most cases, a considerable amount of time (often weeks or months) has passed before I get access to the necessary data. However, very often, creating a timeline using multiple data sources will allow me to see the artifacts of an intrusion or other incident that still remains on the system. Remember in Chapter 1 when we discussed primary and secondary artifacts? Well, many times I've been able to locate secondary artifacts of an intrusion or malware/bot infection, even after the primary artifacts were deleted (possibly by an AV scan, or the result of first-responder actions). For example, during one particular engagement, I found through timeline analysis that specific malware files had been created on a system, but an AV scan two days later detected and deleted the malware. Several weeks later, new malware files were created on the system, but due to the nature of the malware it was several more weeks before the portion of the malware that collected sensitive data was executed (this finding was based on our analysis of the malware, as well as the artifacts within the timeline). By locating the secondary artifacts associated with the actual execution of the malware, this allowed us to specify the window of exposure for this particular system to a more accurate and narrow timeframe, for which the customer was grateful.

Finally, viewing data from multiple sources allows an analyst to build a picture of activity on a system, particularly in the absence of direct, primary artifacts. For example, when a user logs into a system, a logon event is generated but it is only recorded in the Security Event Log if the system is configured to audit those events. If an intruder gains access to or is able to create a domain administrator account and begin accessing systems (via the Remote Desktop Protocol), and that account has not been used to log into the systems previously, then the user profile for the account will be created on each system, regardless of the auditing configuration. The profile creation, and in particular the creation of the NTUSER.DAT hive file, will appear as part of the file system data, and the contents of the hive file will also provide the analyst with some insight as to the intruder's activities while he was accessing the system. I've had several examinations where I was able to use this information to "fill in the gaps" when some primary artifacts were simply not available.

Format

With all of the time-stamped information available on Windows systems, in the various time-stamp structures, I realized that I needed to create a means by which I could correlate all of it together in a common, "normalized" format. To this end, I came up with a five-field TLN (which is short for "timeline") format to serve as the basis for timelines. This format would allow me to provide a thorough description of each individual event, and then correlate, sort, and view them together. Those five fields—time, source, system, user, and description—and their descriptions follow.

Time

With all of the various time structures that appear on Windows systems, I opted to use the 32-bit Unix time stamp, based on UTC as a common format. All of the time-stamp structures are easily reduced to this common format, and the values themselves are easy to sort on and to translate into a human-readable format using the Perl *gmtime()* function. Also, while Windows systems do contain a few time values in this 32-bit format, I did not want to restrict my timelines to Windows systems only, as in many incidents valuable time-stamped data could be derived from other sources as well, such as firewall logs, network device logs (in syslog format), and even logs from Linux systems. As I did not have access to all possible log or data sources that I could expect to encounter when I was creating this format, I wanted to use a time-stamp format that was common to a wide range of sources, and to which other time-stamp structures could be easily reduced.

For example, Andreas Schuster (maintainer of the *int for(ensic) {blog;}* blog, found at *http://computer.forensikblog.de/en*) created Perl code (that he allowed others to copy and use) that translates the 64-bit FILETIME time stamp into a 32-bit Unix epoch format when he began delving into Windows memory parsing and analysis; an example of that code appears as follows:

```
sub getTime($$) {
my $lo=shift;
my $hi=shift;
my $t;
if ($lo==0 && $hi==0) {
  $t = 0;
}
else {
  $lo -=0xd53e8000;
  $hi -=0x019db1de;
  $t=int($hi*429.4967296+$lo/1e7);
};
$t=0 if($t<0);
return $t;
}
```

This takes the lower and upper 32-bit portions (respectively) of the 64-bit FILETIME time structure and returns a 32-bit Unix epoch format time stamp.

NOTE

Granularity

When developing this format for representing events, I felt that grouping events within 1-second intervals would provide sufficient granularity and that there was really no need to break events out in millisecond or 100-nanosecond intervals. Some analysts have suggested that the granularity of the original time-stamp format is required; however, we often find ourselves mixing 64- and 32-bit time stamps due to the data that we're including in our timelines.

For translating other time formats to a common structure, the Perl DateTime module comes in very handy. If you're using the ActiveState ActivePerl distribution (mentioned in Chapter 1), this module is easy to install using the Perl Package

Manager (PPM) command *ppm install datetime* at the command line. Once this module is installed, the provided HTML documentation includes sample code for translating various time values into a Unix epoch time.

Perl code that uses the DateTime module to parse the time-stamp structure found in AV logs and translate it into something human-readable appears as follows:

```
sub parseDateAsEpoch {
  my $li_time=shift;
  my $yr=hex(substr($li_time,0,2))+1970;
  my $mon=hex(substr($li_time,2,2));
  my $day=hex(substr($li_time,4,2));
  my $hr=hex(substr($li_time,6,2));
  my $min=hex(substr($li_time,8,2));
  my $sec=hex(substr($li_time,10,2));
  my $dt=DateTime->new(year => $yr,
    month=>$mon+1,
    day=>$day,
    hour=>$hr,
    minute=>$min,
    second=>$sec);
    return $dt->epoch;
}
```

Perl code that translates the SYSTEMTIME structure into a human-readable time structure (albeit not specifically reduced to UTC format) appears as follows:

```
sub parseDate128 {
my $date = $_[0];
my @months = ("Jan","Feb","Mar","Apr","May","Jun","Jul",
              "Aug","Sep","Oct","Nov","Dec");
my @days = ("Sun","Mon","Tue","Wed","Thu","Fri","Sat");
my ($yr,$mon,$dow,$dom,$hr,$min,$sec,$ms) = unpack("v8",$date);
$hr = "0".$hr if ($hr<10);
$min = "0".$min if ($min<10);
$sec = "0".$sec if ($sec<10);
my $str = $days[$dow]." ".$months[$mon-1]." ".$dom."
  ".$hr.":".$min.":".$sec." ".$yr;
return $str;
}
```

Remember that the SYSTEMTIME structure is based on the local system time for the system being examined, taking the time zone and daylight savings settings into account. As such, you would first need to reduce the value to the 32-bit time format, and then make the appropriate adjustments to convert local time to UTC (86,400 seconds/hour times the "ActiveTimeBias" value from the Registry, for that system, and for that time of year).

TIP

Registry Analysis

As we will discuss later in this chapter, there may be some modicum of Registry analysis that needs to occur prior to creating a timeline. For example, if we know that we're going to be working with a number of time stamps in the SYSTEMTIME object format, we'll want to examine the system's time zone settings (found beneath the Control\TimeZoneInformation key within the appropriate ControlSet) so that we can properly translate these to UTC format.

Source

The source value within the TLN format is a short, easy-to-read identifier that refers to the data source within the system from which the time-stamped data were derived. For example, as we'll see later in this chapter, one of the first places we often go to begin collecting data is the file system, so the source would be "FILE." For time-stamped data derived from Event Log records on Windows 2000, XP, and 2003 systems, I use the "EVT" (based on the file extension) identifier in the source field, whereas for Vista and Windows 7 systems, I use the "EVTX" identifier for events retrieved from the Windows Event Logs. I use "REG" to identify data retrieved from the Registry, and "SAV" or "MCAFEE" to identify data retrieved from Symantec AV and McAfee AV log files, respectively.

You might be thinking, what is the relevance of identifying different sources? Think back to earlier in this chapter when we discussed the *relative level of confidence* we might have in various data sources. By using a source identifier in our timeline data, we can quickly see and visualize time-based data that would provide us with a greater level of relative confidence in the overall data that we're looking at, regardless of our output format. For example, let's say that we have a file with a specific last modified time (source FILE). We know that these values can be modified to arbitrary times, so our confidence in these data, in isolation, would be low. However, if we have a Registry key LastWrite time (source REG) derived from one of the most recently used (MRU) lists within the Registry (such as the RecentDocs subkeys, or those associated with a specific application used to view that particular file type) that occurs prior to that file's last modified time, we've increased our confidence in that data.

I do not have a comprehensive list or table of all possible timeline source identifiers, although I have described a number of the more frequently used identifiers. I try to keep them to eight characters or less, and try to make them as descriptive as possible, so as to provide context to the data within the timeline. A table listing many of the source identifiers that I have used is included along with the materials associated with this book.

System

This field refers to the system, host, or device from which the data were obtained. In most cases within a timeline, this field will contain the system or host name, or perhaps some other identifier (based on the data source), such as an IP address or even a media access control (MAC) address. This can be very helpful when you have data from multiple sources that describe a single event. For example, if you're looking at a user's web browsing activity, you may have access to the user's workstation, firewall logs, perhaps web server proxy logs, and in some cases, even logs from the remote web server. In other instances, it may be beneficial to combine time-lines from multiple systems to demonstrate the progression of malware propagating among those systems. Finally, it may be critical to an investigation to combine wireless access point (WAP) log files into a timeline developed using data from a suspect's laptop. In all of these instances, you would want to have a clear, understandable means for identifying the system from which the event data originated.

User

The user field is used to identify the user associated with a specific event, if one is available. There are various sources within Windows systems that maintain not just time-stamped data, but also information tying a particular user to that event. For example, Event Log records contain a field for the security identifier (SID) of the user associated with that particular record. In many cases, the user is simply blank, "System," or one of the SIDs associated with a System-level account (e.g., LocalService or NetworkService) on that system. However, there are a number of event records that are associated with a specific user SID; these SIDs can be mapped to a specific user name via the SAM Registry hive, or the ProfileList sub-keys from the Software hive.

Another reason to include a user field is that a great deal of time-based information is available from the NTUSER.DAT Registry hive found in each user profile. For example, not only do the Registry keys have LastWrite times that could prove to be valuable (again, think of the MRU keys), but various Registry values (think UserAssist subkey values) also contain time-based data. So, while many data sources (e.g., file system and prefetch file metadata) will provide data that are not associated with a specific user, adding information derived from user profiles (specifically the NTUSER.DAT hive) can add that context that we discussed earlier in this chapter, allowing us to associate a series of events with a specific user. Populating this field also allows us to distinguish the actions of different users.

Description

This field provides a brief description of the event that occurred. I've found that in populating this particular field, brief and concise descriptions are paramount, as verbose descriptions not only quickly get out of hand, but with many similar events analysts will have a lot to read and keep track of when conducting analysis.

So what do I mean by "brief and concise"? A good example of this comes in representing the times associated with files within the file system. We know from Chapter 4 that files have four times—last modified, last accessed, when the file metadata was modified, and the file creation or "born" date—associated with each file, usually derived from the $STANDARD_INFORMATION attribute within the MFT. These attributes are often abbreviated as MACB. As such, a concise description of the file being modified at a specific time would be "M . . . < filename >"—it's that simple. The "M" stands for "modified," the dots represent the other time stamps (together they provide the MACB description), and the filename provides the full path to the file. This is straightforward and easy to understand at a glance.

I have found that doing much the same thing with Registry LastWrite times is very useful. Listing the key name preceded by "M...," much like last modified times for files, is a brief and easy-to-understand means for presenting this information in a timeline. Registry key LastWrite times mark when a key was last modified, and by itself, does not contain any specific information about when the key was created. While it's possible that the LastWrite time also represents when the key was created, without further contextual information, it is best not to speculate and to only consider this value "as is"—that is, simply as the LastWrite time.

When populating at timeline with Event Log records, I've found that a concise description can be derived from elements of the event itself. Using the event source from the Event Log record, along with the event identifier (ID), the type (warning, info, or error), and the strings extracted from the event (if there are any), I've been able to create a brief description of the event. For example, on Windows XP and 2003 systems, event ID 520 (source is "Security") indicates that the system time had been successfully changed; from such an event record, the Description field would appear as follows:

```
Security/520;Success;3368,C:\WINDOWS\system32\rundll32.exe,v12
    mware,REG-OIPK81M2WC8,(0x0,0x91AD),vmware,REG-OIPK81M2WC8,(0x0,0x
    91AD),1/17/2008,4:52:28 PM,1/17/2008,4:52:27 PM
```

To see what each of the fields following "Security/520;Success;" refers to, see the event description found at *http://www.ultimatewindowssecurity.com/securitylog/ encyclopedia/event.aspx?eventid=520*. A Description field such as the previous example might seem a bit cryptic at first to some analysts, but over time and looking at many timelines, I've developed something of an eye for which events to look for when conducting analysis. In addition, I've relied heavily on the EventId.net web site, purchasing a new subscription every year so that when the next exam comes up I can search for and review the details of the various event sources and IDs.

TLN Format

Now that we've discussed the five basic fields that can comprise a timeline, you're probably asking yourself, "Okay, in what format are these events stored?" I have found that storing all of these events in an intermediate events file (usually named "events.txt") in a pipe ("|") delimited format makes them very easy to parse (we will discuss parsing the events file later in the chapter). As such, each individual event appears as follows in the events file:

```
Time|Source|System|User|Description
```

The use of a pipe as a separator was a pretty arbitrary choice, but I needed to use something that wasn't likely to show up in the Description field (like a comma or semicolon) and play havoc with my parsing utility. The pipe seemed like a pretty good choice.

CREATING TIMELINES

With all this talk about timelines, it's about time we created one. What we'll do is walk through a demonstration of creating a timeline from a Windows XP image, start to finish, pointing out along the way different techniques for getting similar information from Vista and Windows 7 systems, as well as some alternative techniques for obtaining the same information.

This process is going to be modular in nature, allowing us a great deal of flexibility in creating timelines. As we walk through the process, you'll notice that we're creating the timeline in stages. In some of the steps, the data that we extract will be stored in an intermediate file. We will first extract the data into an intermediate file in one format (generally whatever format is used by the tool capable of extracting our data of interest). We'll then use another tool to manipulate that data into a normalized format (TLN format) in an intermediate events file. Since our events file will contain multiple sets of unsorted, appended data, our last step will be to parse the events file and sort it into a final timeline file. This can be very beneficial, particularly if an application uses a new format to store its data, or something happened with the application that corrupted the data that we're parsing. Think of this as something of a debugging step, as checking the contents of the intermediate file can help you figure out whether something is wrong, and how to fix it.

Remember, there are no commercial forensic analysis applications that allow us to press a button and create timelines from all available data; rather, we often have to rely on multiple open-source and freely available tools to extract the necessary data. As these tools are often created by various authors with completely disparate goals in mind, we often have to extract the data into the format provided by the tool, and then manipulate or restructure the data so that we can add them more easily to our timeline format. So, starting with an acquired image, we will extract the data we want or need in whatever format is provided by the available tools, and then use or create the necessary tools to put that data into our common timeline format in an "events" file, which we will then parse into a timeline. I know that this process does seem terribly manual and perhaps cumbersome at first, but to be honest, over time I've found that having this sort of granular level of control over the information that is added to a timeline can be advantageous. Hopefully, through the course of our discussion, you will see the same thing, as well.

NOTE

Modular Approach

You will notice throughout the process that we're about to walk through that it's modular. That is, the process is not about pushing a button and having everything done for you, but about determining what data you need and using the appropriate tools to extract that data. Each tool used is separate and distinct, and in some cases, the tool provides additional capabilities beyond simply populating a timeline. Creating full timelines can generate a considerable amount of data, and I've found over time that creating mini-, micro-, or even what I refer to as nano-timelines (i.e., creating separate timelines from limited data sources) has been an extremely valuable tool. Using the tools along with the *find* command has allowed me to create distinct timelines of just remote login or AV detection events. In many cases, this has provided me with an initial event that I could then take to the full timeline and view other surrounding events and context.

Before we get started, we need to make sure that we have the necessary tools available. You should have installed ActiveState ActivePerl version 5.12 (found at *http://www.activestate.com/activeperl/downloads*). In addition to the Perl installation, you will need the timeline scripts ("tln_tools.zip," available at *http://code .google.com/p/winforensicaanalysis/downloads/list*) and TSK tools, which can be found at *http://www.sleuthkit.org/sleuthkit/download.php*. Once you've assembled this collection of tools, you will be ready to start creating timelines.

As we're going to be creating a timeline from an acquired image, you will need to have an image available so that you can follow along with and use the commands that comprise the process that we will walk through in the rest of this chapter. There are a couple of ways to obtain an image of a Windows system if you don't already have one. One is to simply use FTK Imager to acquire an image of one of your own systems. There are also a number of images available online; for example, there is the Hacking Case image available from the National Institute of Standards and Technology (NIST) web site (the image can be found at *http://www.cfreds.nist .gov/Hacking_Case.html*). Lance Mueller has posted several practical exercises to his ForensicKB.com web site, which include images that can be downloaded. For example, the scenario and link to the image for his first practical can be found at *http://www.forensickb.com/2008/01/forensic-practical.html*. In fact, an acquired image from any Windows system (Windows 2000 through Windows 7) would serve as a good learning tool as we understand how to create timelines. That being said, let's get started.

File System Metadata

One of the first sources of timeline data that I generally start with is the file system metadata. These data are most often referred to as MACB times, where the "M" stands for last modification date, "A" stands for last accessed date, "C" stands for the date that the file metadata was modified, and the "B" refers to the "born" or creation date of the file. Another way of referring to these times is MACE, where the "C" refers to the creation date and the "E" refers to when the file metadata was modified (or "entry modified"). For consistency, we'll use the MACB nomenclature. Regardless of the designation used, these data are derived from the $STANDARD_ INFORMATION attribute within the MFT (discussed in detail in Chapter 4).

> **TIP**
>
> NTFS File Times
>
> MS KnowledgeBase (KB) article 299648 (found at *http://support.microsoft.com/?kbid=299648*) provides descriptions of the effects that various operations (e.g., copy or move) have on the file system metadata associated with files and folders within the NTFS file system. This KB article should be used as a reference and support (rather than replace) analyst testing of various events and conditions.

We can use TSK tools (specifically "mmls.exe" and "fls.exe") to easily extract these data from an acquired image into what is referred to as a "bodyfile." When an image is acquired of a physical hard drive, it will often contain a partition table. Using "mmls.exe" (man page found at *http://www.sleuthkit.org/sleuthkit/man/mmls.html*) we can parse and view that partition table. The command used to view the partition table of an image acquired from a Windows system appears as follows:

```
C:\tools>mmls -t dos -i raw <image>
```

Optionally, you can save the output of the command by using the redirection operator (i.e., ">") and adding "> mmls_output.txt" (or whatever name you prefer) to the end of the command. An example of the output that you might see from this command is illustrated in Figure 7.1.

From the sample output that appears in Figure 7.1, we can see the partition table and that the NTFS partition that we would be interested in is the one marked 02, which starts at sector 63 within the image. If you downloaded the "hacking case" image from the NIST site mentioned earlier in this chapter, the output of the *mmls* command run against the image would look very similar to what is illustrated in Figure 7.1. However, if you get an error that begins with "Invalid sector address," the image you're looking at may not have a partition table (such as when an image is acquired of a logical volume rather than the entire physical disk), and you can proceed directly to the part of this chapter where we discuss the use of "fls.exe."

You may also find that the partition table isn't quite as "clean" and simple with some acquired images. Figure 7.2 illustrates the output of "mmls.exe" run against a physical image acquired from a laptop purchased from Dell, Inc.

```
DOS Partition Table
Offset Sector: 0
Units are in 512-byte sectors

     Slot    Start       End         Length      Description
00:  Meta    0000000000  0000000000  0000000001  Primary Table (#0)
01:  -----   0000000000  0000000062  0000000063  Unallocated
02:  00:00   0000000063  0312576704  0312576642  NTFS (0x07)
03:  -----   0312576705  0312581807  0000005103  Unallocated
```

FIGURE 7.1

Sample "mmls.exe" output.

In Figure 7.2, the partition we'd most likely be interested in (at least initially) is the one marked 04, which starts at sector 178176. We will need to have this information (i.e., the sector offset to the partition of interest) available to use with "fls.exe" (man page found at *http://www.sleuthkit.org/sleuthkit/man/fls.html*) to extract the file system metadata from within the particular volume in which we're interested.

Using the offset information we can collect file system metadata from the partition of interest. Returning to our first example (Figure 7.1, with the NTFS partition at offset 63), the "fls.exe" command that we would use appears as follows:

```
C:\tools>fls -i raw [-o63] -f ntfs -r -p -m C:/ <image>>bodyfile.txt
```

In this command, the various switches used all help us get the data that we're looking for. The "-m" switch allows us to prepend the path with the appropriate drive letter. The "-o" switch allows us to select the appropriate volume. (I've included the "-o" switch information in square brackets as it can be optional; if you get an error message that begins with "Invalid sector address" when using "mmls .exe," it's likely that you won't have to use the "-o" switch at all. Alternately, the value used with the "–o" switch may change, depending on the image you're using (volume or physical image) or the offset of the volume in which you're interested. For example, offset 63 would be used for the volume listed in Figure 7.1, but offset 21149696 would be used to extract information from the partition marked 05 in Figure 7.2 (and you'd likely want to use "-m D:/" as well). The "-p" switch tells "fls.exe" to use full paths for the files and directories listed, and the "-r" switch tells "fls.exe" to recurse through all subdirectories. Explanations for the other switches, as well as additional switches available, can be found on the "fls.exe" man page.

You should also notice that the listed *fls* command includes a redirection operator, sending the output of the command to a file named "bodyfile.txt." The bodyfile (described at *http://wiki.sleuthkit.org/index.php?title=Body_file*) is an intermediate format used to store the file system metadata information before translating it into the TLN event file format that we discussed earlier.

```
    Slot    Start        End          Length       Description
00: Meta    0000000000   0000000000   0000000001   Primary Table (#0)
01: -----   0000000000   0000000062   0000000063   Unallocated
02: 00:00   0000000063   0000176714   0000176652   Dell Utilities FAT (0xde)
03: -----   0000176715   0000178175   0000001461   Unallocated
04: 00:01   0000178176   0021149695   0020971520   NTFS (0x07)
05: 00:02   0021149696   0307335167   0286185472   NTFS (0x07)
06: Meta    0307335168   0312578047   0005242880   Win95 Extended (0x0F)
07: Meta    0307335168   0307335168   0000000001   Extended Table (#1)
08: -----   0307335168   0307337215   0000002048   Unallocated
09: 01:00   0307337216   0312578047   0005240832   Hidden CTOS Memdump?   (0xdd)

10: -----   0312578048   0312581807   0000003760   Unallocated
```

FIGURE 7.2

Sample "mmls.exe" output from a Dell system.

> **NOTE**
>
> Events File
>
> We discussed the use of intermediate formats earlier in this chapter; timeline data stored in the five-field, pipe-delimited TLN format is referred to as an "events file," simply because it contains the events that will comprise the timeline in their raw, unsorted form. The actual creation of the timeline originates with this file.

Using this approach allows us to not just keep track of the information output from our various tools, but to also keep that data available for use with other tools and processes that may be part of our analytic approach. To translate the bodyfile (output of "fls.exe") information to a TLN events file format (the five fields described earlier in this chapter), we want to use the "bodyfile.pl" script, which is available as part of the additional materials available with this book, in the following command:

```
C:\tools>bodyfile.pl -f bodyfile.txt -s Server > events.txt
```

This command is pretty simple and straightforward. To see the syntax options available for "bodyfile.pl," simply type the command "bodyfile.pl" or "bodyfile.pl -h" at the command prompt. The "-f" switch tells the script which bodyfile to open, and the "-s" switch fills in the name of the server (you can get this from your case documentation, or by running the "compname.pl" RegRipper plugin against the System hive, as described in Chapter 5). Also, notice that we redirect the output of the command to the "events.txt" file; as with many of the tools we will discuss, the output of the tool is sent to the console, so we need to redirect it to a file so that we can add to it and parse the events later.

At this point in our timeline creation process, we should have a bodyfile ("bodyfile.txt") and an events file ("events.txt"), both containing file system metadata that was extracted from our acquired image. However, there may be times when we may not have access to an acquired image, or access to the necessary tools, and as such cannot use "fls.exe" to extract the file system metadata and create the bodyfile. One such example would be accessing a system remotely via F-Response; once you've mounted the physical drive on your analysis system, you can then add that drive to FTK Imager as an evidence item just as you would an acquired image. You might do this to extract specific files (e.g., Registry hives, Event Log files, prefetch files) from the remote system for analysis. FTK Imager also provides an alternative means for extracting file system metadata, which we can use in situations where we may choose not to use "fls.exe."

One of the simplest ways to do this is to open the newly acquired image (or the physical disk for a remote system accessed via F-Response) in FTK Imager, adding it as an evidence item. Figure 7.3 illustrates the image examined in Figure 7.2 loaded into FTK Imager version 3.0.0.1442.

Now, an option available to us once the image is loaded and visible in the evidence tree is to select the partition that we're interested in (say, partition 2 listed in

```
Evidence Tree
  disk0.001
       Partition 1 [86MB]
       Partition 2 [10240MB]
       Partition 3 [139739MB]
       Partition 5 [2559MB]
       Unpartitioned Space [basic disk]
```

FIGURE 7.3

Image partition listing visible in FTK Imager.

```
   Obtain Protected Files...
   Detect EFS Encryption
   Export Files...
   Export File Hash List...
   Export Directory Listing...
   Exit
```

FIGURE 7.4

FTK Imager "Export Directory Listing..." option.

Figure 7.3), and then select the "Export Directory Listing..." option from the File menu, as illustrated in Figure 7.4.

When you select this option, you will then be offered a chance to select the name and location of the comma-separated value (CSV) output file for the command (as part of my case management, I tend to keep these files in the same location as the image itself if I receive the image on writeable media, such as a USB-connected external hard drive). Once you've made these selections and started the directory listing process, you will see a dialog such as is illustrated in Figure 7.5.

At this point, we should have a complete directory listing for all of the files visible to FTK Imager in the volume or partition of interest within our image. However, the contents of the file will require some manipulation to get the data into a format suitable for our timeline. I wrote the script "ftkparse.pl" specifically to translate the information collected via this method into the bodyfile format discussed earlier in this chapter. The "ftkparse.pl" script takes only one argument, which is the path to the appropriate CSV file, and translates the contents of the file to bodyfile format, sending output to the console. An example of how to use the "ftkparse.pl" script appears as follows:

```
C:\tools>ftkparse.pl c_drive.csv>bodyfile.txt
```

If you use the previous command, be sure to use correct file paths for your situation.

FIGURE 7.5

FTK Imager creating a directory listing.

WARNING

Installing Perl Modules

When running Perl scripts discussed in this chapter, you may see error messages that indicate that a particular module could not be located. If you're using the ActiveState ActivePerl distribution, you can use the Perl Package Manager (PPM) to install the appropriate modules and supporting documentation. For example, the "ftkparse.pl" script uses the DateTime module; if you need to install this module, simply open a command prompt, change to your Perl directory, and type "ppm install datetime"; PPM will take care of installing the module for you.

After running the command, if you open the resulting bodyfile in a text editor, you will notice that the file and directory paths appear with some extra information. For example, when I ran through this process on the Vista image described in Figure 7.2, the body file contained paths that looked like "RECOVERY [NTFS]\ [root]\Windows\," where "RECOVERY" is the name of the particular volume from which the directory listing was exported. To get this information into a usable format, use your text editor to perform a search-and-replace operation, replacing "RECOVERY [NTFS]\[root]\" with "C:\." Once you've completed this process with the appropriate volume information, you can then proceed with creating your timeline. The biggest difference between using the FTK Imager directory listing, as opposed to the output of "fls.exe," is that the file/directory metadata change date (the "C" in MACB) would not be available (FTK Imager does not extract the "C" time), and would be represented as a dot (i.e., ".") in the bodyfile.

Once you've completed this search-and-replace operation, you can run the "bodyfile.pl" Perl script against the "bodyfile.txt" file that resulted from running "ftkparse.pl," translating it into an events file.

In summary, the commands that you would run to create your events file for file time-stamped data from an acquired image using "fls.exe" would include:

- mmls -t dos -i raw <image>
- fls -i raw [-o 63] -f ntfs -r -p -m C:/<image>> bodyfile.txt
- bodyfile.pl –f bodyfile.txt –s Server > events.txt

If you opted to use FTK Imager to export a directory listing, the steps you would follow to create an events file for file "time-stamped data" are:

- Export directory listing via FTK Imager (dir_listing.csv)
- ftkparse.pl dir_listing.csv > bodyfile.txt
- Search-and-replace file and directory paths with appropriate drive letter
- bodyfile.pl –f bodyfile.txt –s Server > events.txt

Now, if you've created separate events files for different volumes (C:\, D:\, etc.) or even from different systems, you can use the native *type* command to combine the events files into a single, comprehensive events file, using commands similar to the following:

```
C:\tools>type events1.txt>events_all.txt
C:\tools>type events2.txt>>events_all.txt
```

Notice in the previous command that the redirection operator used is ">>," which allows us to append additional data to a file, rather than creating a new file (or overwriting our existing file by mistake).

Event Logs

As discussed in Chapter 4, Event Logs from all versions of Windows can provide a great deal of very valuable information for our timeline; however, how we extract timeline information and create events files for inclusion in our timeline depends heavily on the version of Windows that we're working with. As we saw in Chapter 4, Event Logs on Windows 2000, XP, and 2003 systems are very different from the Windows Event Logs available on Vista, Windows 2008, and Windows 7 systems. As such, we will address each of these separately, but ultimately, we will end up with information that we can add to an events file.

Windows XP

Event Log files are found, by default, on Windows 2000, XP, and 2003 systems in the "C:\Windows\system32\config" directory, and have a .evt file extension. You can normally expect to find the Application ("appevent.evt"), System ("sysevent .evt"), and Security ("secevent.evt") Event Log files in this directory, but you may also find other files with .evt extensions based on the applications that you have installed. For example, if you have MS Office 2007 (or later) installed, you should expect to find "ODiag.evt" and "OSession.evt" files. You can access these files in an acquired image by either adding the image to FTK Imager as an evidence item, navigating to the appropriate directory, and extracting the files, or by mounting the image as a volume via FTK Imager version 3 (or via ImDisk) and navigating to the appropriate directory.

Once you have access to these files, you should use the "evtparse.pl" Perl script to extract the necessary event information using the following command:

```
C:\tools>evtparse.pl -d<directory>-t >evt_events.txt
```

This command tells the "evtparse.pl" script to go to a specific directory, extract all event records from every file in that directory with an .evt extension, and put that information into the "evt_events.txt" file in TLN format, adding "EVT" as the data source. So, if you've mounted an acquired image as the G:\ volume, the argument for the "-d" switch might look like "G:\Windows\system32\config." Many times, I will extract the Event Log files from the drive or the image using FTK Imager, placing them in a files directory, so the path information might then look like "F:\<case>\files."

If you do not want to run this script against all of the .evt files in a directory, you can select specific files using the "-e" switch. For example, if you want to create an events file using only the event records in the Application Event Log, you might use a command similar to the following:

```
C:\tools>evtparse.pl -e G:\windows\system32\config\appevent.evt -t >
    app_events.txt
```

I actually use this technique quite often. As I mentioned earlier in this chapter, there are times when I do not want to create a full timeline, but would rather create a mini- or micro-timeline, based on specific data, so that I can get a clear view of specific data without having to sift through an ocean of irrelevant events. For example, I once worked an examination where the customer knew that they were suffering from an infection from specific malware, and informed me that they had installed the Symantec AV product. After running the "evtrpt.pl" Perl script (described in Chapter 4) against the Application Event Log, I noticed that there were, in fact, Symantec AV events listed in the event log (according to information available on the Symantec web site, events with ID 51 indicate a malware detection; "evtrpt.pl" indicated that there were 82 such events). As such, I used the following command to parse just the specific events of interest out of the Application Event Log:

```
C:\tools>evtparse.pl -e appevent.evt -t | find "Symantec AntiVirus/51"
    >sav_51_events.txt
```

The resulting events file provided me with the ability to create a timeline of just the detection events generated by the Symantec product, so that I could quickly address the customer's questions about the malware without having to sift through hundreds or thousands of other irrelevant events.

You'll notice that unlike the "bodyfile.pl" script, the "evtparse.pl" script doesn't require that you add a server (or user) name to the command line; this is due to the fact that this information is already provided within the event records themselves.

Windows 7

The Windows Event Logs on Vista, Windows 2008, and Windows 7 systems are located (by default) in the "C:\Windows\system32\winevt\logs" directory and end in the .evtx file extension. As discussed in Chapter 4, these files are of a different format from their counterparts found on Windows XP systems, and as such, we will need to use a different method to parse them and create our events file. Another difference is the names; for example, the primary files of interest are "System.evtx," "Security.evtx," and "Application.evtx." As with Windows XP, additional files may be present depending on the system in question; for example, I have also found the file "Cisco AnyConnect VPN Client.evtx" on a Windows 7 system that had the Cisco client application installed.

As you would expect, parsing these files into the necessary format is a bit different than with Event Log (.evt) files. One method would be to use Andreas Schuster's Perl-based framework for parsing these files; the framework is available via his blog (*http://computer.forensikblog.de/en*). Using this framework, you can parse the .evtx files and then write the necessary tool or utility to translate that information to the TLN format.

An alternate method that I've found to be very useful is to install Microsoft's Log Parser tool on a Windows 7 system, and then either extract the .evtx files I'm interested in to a specific directory, or mount the image as a volume on my analysis system. From there, I can then run the following command:

```
Logparser -i:evt -o:csv "SELECT * FROM D:\Case\File\System.evtx">
    system.csv
```

This command uses the Log Parser tool to access the necessary Windows API to parse the event records from the "System.evtx" file. The "-i:evt" argument tells Log Parser to use the Windows Event Log API, and the "-o:csv" argument tells the tool to format the output in CSV format. Not only can you open this output file in Excel, but you can use the "evtxparse.pl" Perl script to parse out the necessary event data into TLN format, using the following command:

```
C:\tools>evtxparse.pl -f system.csv -t > sys_events.txt
```

Again, this process requires an extra, intermediate step when compared to parsing Event Logs from Windows XP systems, but we get to the same place, and we have the parsed data available to use for further analysis. The one difference from "evtparse.pl" is that "evtxparse.pl" adds the source "EVTX" to the TLN-format events instead of "EVT."

WARNING

Parsing Windows Event Logs

Remember when parsing Windows Event Logs using Log Parser, you must run Log Parser on a Windows 2008 or Windows 7 system, due to the fact that Log Parser relies on the native API for accessing data within the .evtx files. Attempting to run Log Parser on a Windows XP system to parse an "Application.evtx" file extracted from a Vista or Windows 7 system will result in unusable data, as the APIs are not compatible. The opposite is also true; you cannot run Log Parser on Vista or Windows 7 to parse Event Log (.evt) files obtained from a 2000, XP, or 2003 system.

As with the other timeline events files that we've discussed thus far, you will ultimately want to consolidate all of the available events into a single events file prior to parsing it into a timeline. You can use a batch file to automate a great deal of this work for you. For example, let's say that you have an image of a Vista system available on an external hard drive, and the path to the image file is "F:\vista\disk0.001." You can mount the image as a volume on your Windows 7 analysis system (i.e., G:\) and create a batch file that contains commands similar to the following to parse the System Event Log (repeat the command as necessary for other Windows Event Log files):

```
C:\tools>logparser -i:evt -o:csv "SELECT * FROM %1\Windows\
    system32\winevt\logs\System.evtx" > %2\system.csv
```

If you name this batch file "parseevtx.bat," you would launch the batch file by passing the appropriate arguments, such as follows:

```
C:\tools>parseevtx.bat G:F:\vista
```

Running the previous command populates the "%1" variable in the batch file with your first command line parameter (in this case "G:," representing your mounted volume) and the "%2" variable with your second command line parameter (in this case "F:\vista" representing the path to where your output should be stored), and executes the command. You would then use (and repeat as necessary) a command similar to the following to parse the output .csv files into event files:

```
C:\tools>evtxparse.pl -f %1\system.csv -t>%1\sys_events.txt
```

Again, you will need to repeat the previous command in the appropriate manner for each of the Windows Event Logs parsed. An example version of "parseevtx.bat" to run against the System, Application, and Security Event Logs in this manner is included along with the additional materials available for this book.

Prefetch Files

As discussed in Chapter 4, not all Windows systems perform application prefetching by default; in fact, prefetch files are only usually found on Windows XP, Vista, and Windows 7 systems (application prefetching is disabled by default on Windows 2003 and 2008 systems, but can be enabled via a Registry modification). Also, as discussed in Chapter 4, prefetch files can contain some pretty valuable information; for the purpose of this chapter, we're interested primarily in the time stamp embedded within the file. We can use the "pref.pl" Perl script to extract the time value for the last time the application was run (which should correspond closely to the last modification time of the prefetch file itself) and the count of times the application has been run into TLN format, using the following command:

```
C:\tools>pref.pl -d G:\Windows\Prefetch -t -s Server>pref_events.txt
```

Now, we have a couple of options available to us with regards to the previous command. For example, as the command is listed, the "-d" switch tells the tool to parse through all of the files ending with the .pf (the restriction to files ending in ".pf" is included in the code itself) extension in the Prefetch directory (of an acquired image mounted as the G:\ volume); if you would prefer to parse the information from a single prefetch file, simply us the "-f" switch along with the full path and filename for the file of interest. By default, the "pref.pl" Perl script will parse embedded information from Windows XP prefetch files. However, that same information is found at different offsets within prefetch files from Vista and Windows 7 systems and can be found at different offsets within the file, so you need to add the "-v" switch, with no additional arguments, if you're working with prefetch files from those systems. The "-t" switch tells the Perl script to structure the output in TLN format, and adds "PREF" as the source. Also, you'll notice that as with some other scripts that we've discussed thus far, "pref.pl" has an "-s" switch with which you can add the server name to the TLN format; prefetch files are not directly associated with a particular user on the system, so the user name field is left blank.

Finally, at the end of the command, we redirected the output of the script to the file named "pref_events.txt." Instead of taking this approach, we could have easily added the output to an existing events file using ">> events.txt."

Registry Data

As we've discussed several times throughout this book, the Windows Registry can hold a great deal of information that can be extremely valuable to an analyst. Further, that information may not solely be available as Registry key LastWrite times. There are a number of Registry values that contain time stamps, available as binary data at specific offsets depending on the value, as strings that we need to parse, etc. As such, it may be useful to have a number of different tools available to us to extract this information and include it in our timelines.

Perhaps one of the easiest ways to incorporate Registry key LastWrite time listings within a timeline is to use the "regtime.pl" Perl script (part of the additional materials available for this book). Rob Lee originally asked me some time ago to create "regtime.pl" to parse through a Registry hive file and list all of the keys and their LastWrite times in bodyfile format; that is, to have the script output the data in a format similar to what "fls.exe" produces. I wrote this script and provided it to Rob, and it has been included in the SANS Investigative Forensic Toolkit (SIFT) workstation (found at *http://computer-forensics.sans.org/community/downloads/*), as well as Kristinn's log2timeline framework. A bit ago, I modified this script to bypass the bodyfile format and output its information directly to TLN format. An example of how to use this updated version of "regtime.pl" appears as follows:

```
C:\tools>regtime.pl -m HKEY_USER -r NTUSER.DAT -s System -u User>
    reg_event.txt
```

Similar to the "fls.exe" tool discussed earlier in this chapter, "regtime.pl" includes an "-m" switch to indicate the "mount point" of the Registry hive being parsed, which is prepended to the key path. In the previous example, I used "HKEY_USER" when accessing a user's Registry hive; had the target been a Software or System hive, I would have needed to use "HKLM/Software" or "HKLM/System," respectively. The "-r" switch allows you to specify the path to the hive of interest (again, either extracted from an acquired image or accessible by mounting the image as a volume on your analysis system). As you would expect, the "-s" and "-u" switches allow you to designate the system and user fields within the TLN format, as appropriate; the script will automatically populate the source field with the "REG" identifier.

With respect to parsing time-stamped information from within Registry values, there are two options that I like to use; one involves RegRipper, described in Chapter 5. By making slight modifications to "rip.pl" (new version number is 20110516) and adding the ability to add a system and username to the TLN output,

FIGURE 7.6

The "tln.pl" GUI.

I can then also modify existing RegRipper plugins to output their data in TLN format. For example, I modified the "userassist2.pl" RegRipper plugin to modify its output format into the five-field TLN format and renamed the plugin "userassist_tln.pl." I could then run the plugin using the following command line:

```
C:\tools>rip.pl -r D:\cases\test\ntuser.dat -p userassist_tln -s
    SERVER -u USER
```

An excerpt of the output of this command appears as follows in TLN format:

```
1163016851|REG|SERVER|USER|UserAssist-UEME_RUNCPL:SYSDM.CPL (4)
1163015716|REG|SERVER|USER|UserAssist-UEME_RUNCPL:NCPA.CPL (3)
1163015694|REG|SERVER|USER|UserAssist-UEME_RUNPATH:C:\Putty\putty.
    exe (1)
```

Clearly we'd want to redirect this output to the appropriate events file (i.e., ">> events.txt") for inclusion in our timeline.

Another means for adding any time-stamped information (other than just from the Registry) to a timeline events file is to use the graphical user interface (GUI) "tln.pl" Perl script, illustrated in Figure 7.6.

Okay, how would you use the GUI? Let's say that rather than running the "userassist_tln.pl" plugin just mentioned, we instead ran the "userassist2.pl" plugin against the same hive file, and based on the nature of our investigation we were only in the entry that appears as follows:

```
Wed Nov 8 19:54:54 2006 Z
UEME_RUNPATH:C:\Putty\putty.exe (1)
```

Opening the "tln.pl" GUI, we can then manually enter the appropriate information in to the interface, as illustrated in Figure 7.7.

Once you've added the information in the appropriate format (notice that the date format is "MM/DD/YYYY," and a reminder even appears in the window title bar; entering the first two values out of order will result in the date information

FIGURE 7.7

The "tln.pl" GUI populated with data.

being processed incorrectly) and hit the "Add" button, the information added to the designated events file appears in the status bar at the bottom of the GUI.

I wrote this tool because I found that during several examinations, I wanted to add specific events from various sources to the events file, but didn't want to add all of the data available from the source (e.g., Registry, etc.), as doing so would simply make the resulting timeline larger and a bit more cumbersome to go through when conducting analysis. For example, rather than automatically adding all UserAssist entries from one or even several users, I found that while viewing the output of the "userassist2.pl" RegRipper plugin for a specific user, there were one or two or even just half a dozen entries that I felt were pertinent to the examination, and added considerable context to my analysis. I've also found that including the creation date from the MFT $FILE_NAME attribute for one or two specific files, depending on the goals of my exam, proved to be much more useful than simply dumping all of the available MFT data into the timeline.

Additional Sources

To this point in the chapter, we've discussed a number of the available time-stamped data sources that can be found on Windows systems. However, I need to caution you that these are not the only sources that are available; they are simply some of the most common ones used to compile timelines. In fact, the list of possible sources can be quite extensive (a table listing source identifiers, descriptions, and tools used to extract time-stamped data is included in the materials associated with this book); for example, Windows shortcut (.lnk) files contain the file system time stamps of their target files embedded within their structure. Earlier we mentioned that the Firefox "bookmarks.html" file might contain useful information, and the same thing applies to other browsers, as well as other applications. For example, Skype logs might prove to be a valuable source of information, particularly if there are indications that a user (via the UserAssist subkey data) launched Skype prior to or during the timeframe of interest.

Speaking of UserAssist data from user Registry hive files, another data source worth mentioning is VSCs. As illustrated and discussed in Chapter 3, a great deal of time-stamped data can be retrieved from previous copies of files maintained by the Volume Shadow Copy Service (VSS), particularly on Vista and Windows 7 systems. One of the examples we saw in Chapter 3 involved retrieving UserAssist data from the hive file within a user's profile. Consider an examination where you found that the user ran an image viewer application, and that application maintains a MRU list of accessed files. We know that the copy of the user's NTUSER.DAT hive file would contain information in the UserAssist key regarding how many times that viewer application was launched, as well as the last date that it was launched. We also know that the MRU list for the viewer application would indicate the date and time that the most recently viewed image was opened in the application. As we saw in Chapter 3, data available in previous versions of the user's NTUSER.DAT hive file would provide not just indications of previous dates that the viewer application was run, but also the dates and times that other images were viewed. Depending on the goals of your examination, it may be a valuable exercise to mount available VSCs and extract data for inclusion in your timeline.

So, this chapter should not be considered an exhaustive list of data sources, but should instead illustrate how to easily extract the necessary time-stamped data from a number of perhaps the most critical sources. Once you have that data, all that remains is to convert them into a normalized format for inclusion in your timeline.

TIP

Data Volume

The only drawback to using multiple data sources (and the benefits far outweigh any drawbacks) is the potential volume of timeline data. While a timeline of less than 100 KB is much less data to go through than a 250-GB hard drive, it can still be a great deal of data. For example, I've seen a number of Windows XP systems where there was simply a lot of file system activity when System Restore Points were created and deleted. One way to address this is to parse the resulting events file with tools such as *grep -v*, which specifies inverse matches, or selects nonmatching lines. Writing a regular expression that parses through the events file, looking for and removing all of the file system activity for the Restore Points directory can reduce the volume of data that you then need to analyze. I would suggest, however, that techniques such as this are used wisely; depending on the nature of your investigation and the syntax of your *grep* command, you could inadvertently exclude pertinent data from your timeline.

Parsing Events into a Timeline

Once we've created our events file, we're ready to sort through and parse those events into a timeline, which we can then use to further our analysis. So, at this point, we've accessed some of the various data sources available on a Windows system and created a text-based, pipe-delimited, TLN-format events file. The contents of this file might appear as follows:

```
1087549224|FILE|SERVER||MACB [O] C:/$Volume
1087578198|FILE|SERVER||MACB [O] C:/AUTOEXEC.BAT
```

```
1087578213|FILE|SERVER||..C. [194] C:/boot.ini
1087576049|FILE|SERVER||MA.. [194] C:/boot.ini
1087549489|FILE|SERVER||...B [194] C:/boot.ini
1087578198|FILE|SERVER||MACB [0] C:/CONFIG.SYS
1200617554|FILE|SERVER||.A.. [56] C:/Documents and Settings
1087586327|FILE|SERVER||M.C. [56] C:/Documents and Settings
1200617616|EVT|SERVER|S-1-5-18|Service Control
  Manager/7035;Info;IMAPI CD-Burning COM Service,start
1200617616|EVT|SERVER|N/A|Service Control Manager/7036;Info;IMAPI
  CD-Burning COM Service,running
1200617616|EVT|SERVER|N/A|Service Control Manager/7036;Info;IMAPI
  CD-Burning COM Service,stopped
1200617621|EVT|SERVER|N/A|EventLog/6006;Info;
1087585113|PREF|SERVER||AGENTSVR.EXE-002E45AB.pf last run(1)
1087602543|PREF|SERVER||CACLS.EXE-25504E4A.pf last run(2)
1200617562|PREF|SERVER||CMD.EXE-087B4001.pf last run(3)
```

TIP

Creating Events Files

Just a reminder, albeit an important one—we don't always have to throw everything and the kitchen sink into a timeline. Sometimes, particularly based on the goals of our analysis, we may not want to start with everything, and instead start with specific items. For example, if information about logins to a Windows system is important to my examination, I will start by using RegRipper to parse the Security Registry hive to determine the audit policy; if logon/account logon events are not being audited, then it doesn't necessarily make sense to attempt to parse the Security Event Log for those events. Even so, I will also use the "evtrpt.pl" Perl script to parse the Security Event Log and see if there are any events related to logons available, just to be sure.

We should be ready to parse the events file into a timeline, the purpose of which is to sort through the events within the events file, grouping those that occur within the same time together, and then sorting them and presenting them in an understandable format. I've written a script for this purpose, aptly named "parse.pl," and the simplest, most basic way to use this script is to run it against your events file using a command line similar to the following:

```
C:\tools>parse.pl -f D:\case\events.txt>D:\case\tln.txt
```

This command produces an ASCII-based timeline file with all of the times sorted with the most recent time first, and with all events within the same time grouped together. The output looks like the following:

```
Time
  Src System User Description
  Src System User Description
Time
  Src System User Description
```

An example of what this might look like in a "real" timeline file appears as follows:

```
Fri Jun 18 19:16:02 2004 Z
  FILE SERVER - MACB [12864] C:/WINDOWS/Prefetch/DFRGNTFS.EXE-
  269967DF.pf
Fri Jun 18 19:16:01 2004 Z
  FILE SERVER - MACB [8622] C:/WINDOWS/Prefetch/DEFRAG.EXE-273F131E.
  pf
Fri Jun 18 19:15:52 2004 Z
  FILE SERVER - .A.. [99328] C:/WINDOWS/system32/dfrgntfs.exe
  FILE SERVER - .A.. [51200] C:/WINDOWS/system32/dfrgres.dll
  PREF SERVER - DFRGNTFS.EXE-269967DF.pf last run(1)
```

It should be easy to see from this timeline format how the five-field TLN format plays right into not just collecting and correlating the events, but also displaying them for analysis. Again, the times are formatted in a human-readable format, based on UTC. Normalizing the times to this format allows us to incorporate data from multiple sources independent of time zone or location, and present the information in a uniform manner. All of the events that occurred within that second are then listed below the time value, slightly indented. This text-based format allows you to browse through the timeline using any text editor (as opposed to requiring a specific editor or viewer). I use UltraEdit, as it's very good at handling large files, and if I find some text of interest that I want to search on, I can highlight the text and hit the F3 key to automatically jump to the next instance of that text.

The "parse.pl" Perl script also provides some additional capabilities that can be very useful to you. For example, if you know that you're looking for all events that occurred within a particular time window, you can use the "-r" switch to specify a time window for the events that will be displayed within the timeline. For example:

```
C:\tools>parse.pl -f events.txt -r 02/12/2008-03/16/2008 > tln_
short.txt
```

This command line will parse the events file, but only place events that occurred between 00:00:00 February 12, 2008 and 23:59:59 March 16, 2008 into the timeline file.

Another option that I recently added to "parse.pl" is the ability to output the timeline information to CSV format, which would allow you to open the output file in a spreadsheet application such as MS Office Excel or OpenOffice Calc. When the information is written to the timeline file, all five fields are included on each line, separated by commas, so each row in the spreadsheet application begins with a time value in the "YYYYMMDDhhmmss" format. Spreadsheets have long been used to view and analyze this sort of time-stamped information, although in the past the information was populated manually. One of the aspects of this approach that I really think is useful to a lot of analysts is that the analyst can highlight specific events with color coding, and can even add notes into a sixth column (e.g., adding Microsoft KB articles as references, notes, etc., to clarify the information that is available in the timeline).

So now that we have a timeline, how do we go about analyzing it? I think that the best way to do this is with an example. An excerpt from a timeline created from a system that had experienced a malware infection (trimmed to make it easier to view, and with slight modifications) appears as follows (times removed to make the information easier to view):

```
FILE SYSTEM - ...B [720] C:/WINDOWS/system32/irrngife.dat
FILE SYSTEM - ...B [506] C:/WINDOWS/system32/msgsvuc.dat
FILE SYSTEM - ...B [2700] C:/WINDOWS/system32/kbdrxyl.dat
FILE SYSTEM - ...B [0] C:/Documents and Settings/user/Local
  Settings/Temp/~~x103D.tmp
REG SYSTEM - - M... HKLM/Software/Classes/CLSID/{GUID}
REG SYSTEM - - M... HKLM/Software/Classes/CLSID/{GUID}/
  InprocServer32
REG SYSTEM - - M...
HKLM/Software/Microsoft/Windows/…/ShellIconOverlayIdentifiers/
  msgsvuc
```

Other portions of the timeline appeared similar to what you see here, with specific Registry keys being created and grouped along with specific .dat files being created (remember, the "B" refers to the "born" date) within the "system32" directory. By looking for groupings similar to this throughout the timeline, you can distinguish between infections and other events where the installed AV product detected a malicious file and deleted it before any further actions could occur.

Thoughts on Visualization

I've talked to a number of analysts, and read questions posted to online forums regarding the use of visualization tools and techniques with timeline analysis. Most of these questions seem to center around entering all of the available event data into some sort of visualization model or tool, so that the analyst can then perform analysis. This isn't something that, at this point, I can see being entirely feasible or useful toward furthering analysis.

Yes, I know that having some sort of visualization tool seems as if it would make things much easier for the analyst, but we have to keep in mind that Windows systems are extremely verbose, even when they're just sitting there, apparently idle. By themselves, Windows systems will perform housekeeping functions, creating and deleting System Restore Points and VSCs, installing updates, performing limited defrags of the hard drive, etc. Once you include some of the applications and their automated functions (Java and Apple products, among others, automatically look for updates), it becomes clear that there's a lot that goes on on Windows systems when no one's around. So if you think back to Chapter 1 where we discussed least frequency of occurrence (LFO), it quickly becomes clear that any sort of visualization mechanism for representing the abundance of time-stamped data available on a Windows system will quickly not simply overwhelm the analyst, but also completely mask the critical events of interest.

What this really comes down to is how an analyst uses timelines for analysis; even so, once analysis has been performed, the analyst's job isn't complete—her findings still need to be reported and presented to the "customer." Most often pertinent excerpts of timelines are included in the report as a narrative or encapsulated in a table, although there are templates for spreadsheet applications that will allow you to create visual timelines; these should only be used after the pertinent events have been clearly identified, otherwise, everyone (the analyst, the customer, etc.) will be overwhelmed by the sheer volume of available data.

CASE STUDY

After all of this discussion, it would be a good idea to do a complete walk-through of the process for creating a timeline from an acquired image. As such, this will require an image to use, and a great place to go online to get one is Lance Mueller's first forensic practical posted via his blog (*http://www.forensickb.com/2008/01/forensic-practical.html*). The first thing you will need to do is to download the 400-MB expert witness format (EWF, also known as "Encase" format) image, and then open it in FTK Imager (get version 3 from the AccessData downloads page if you don't already have it) and reacquire the image into a 1.5-GB raw/dd image file named "xpimg.001." We'll be using this name throughout the rest of this case study; if you use a different name, use that name. Also, from the scenario that Lance provided on his blog, this appears to be a malware-related issue, so this would likely be a good opportunity to develop a timeline.

Once you have the raw/dd image available, you'll see when you run the *mmls* command described earlier in this chapter that you get the "Invalid sector address" error message, which is an indication that a partition table wasn't found. As such, you can proceed directly to using the *fls* command without the need for an offset to a specific partition. You can use the following command to create the bodyfile from the file system metadata within the image:

```
D:\tools\tsk>fls -i raw -f ntfs -r -p -m C:/ d:\case\xpimg.001>d:\
  case\bodyfile.txt
```

We can then use FTK Imager version 3 to mount the image on our analysis system (as the F:\ volume) and use "rip.pl" to obtain the system name, using the following command:

```
C:\tools>rip.pl -r f:\[root]\windows\system32\config\system -p
  compname
```

From this command, you will see that the system name is "REG-OIPK81M2WC8." You can then use the following command to parse the bodyfile into the events file:

```
C:\tools>bodyfile.pl -f d:\case\bodyfile.txt -s REG-OIPK81M2WC8>d:\
  case\events.txt
```

FIGURE 7.8

Adding an event to the events file with "tln.pl."

At this point, you've created your initial events file, and you can then go about adding Event Logs records and prefetch file metadata as additional data sources using the following commands:

```
C:\tools>evtparse.pl -d f:\[root]\Windows\system32\config -t>>D:\
    case\events.txt
C:\tools>pref.pl -d f:\[root]\Windows\Prefetch -s REG-OIPK81M2WC8 -t
    >>D:\case\events.txt
```

As part of your process for detecting malware, you run RegRipper against various hive files available within the image, including the NTUSER.DAT hive for the "vmware" user. When examining the RegRipper output file from this hive for malware autostart locations (something you remember from Chapter 6), you notice an unusual value in the CurrentVersion\Run key and enter that single entry into your events file using "tln.pl," as illustrated in Figure 7.8.

Based on this, you then decided to add the UserAssist subkey information for that user to your events file using the following command:

```
C:\tools>rip.pl -r "f:\[root]\Documents and Settings\vmware\ntuser.
    dat" -u vmware -s REG-OIPK81M2WC8 -p userassist_tln >> D:\case\
    events.txt
```

You then run "regtime.pl" against the System and Software hives from within the image to add the time-stamped data from these Registry hives to your events file using the following commands:

```
C:\tools>regtime.pl -r f:\[root]\Windows\system32\config\software -m
    HKLM/Software -s REG-OIPK81M2WC8>>D:\case\events.txt
C:\tools>regtime.pl -r f:\[root]\Windows\system32\config\system -m
    HKLM/System -s REG-OIPK81M2WC8>>D:\case\events.txt
```

At this point, you have a pretty comprehensive events file compiled, and you decide to parse it into a timeline. Using this technique, you can take an iterative approach, by adding additional events as necessary to the events file and regenerating the timeline file, as necessary. To create your timeline file, you can use the following command:

```
C:\tools>parse.pl -f D:\case\events.txt > D:\case\tln.txt
```

You then open your newly created timeline file in a text editor and search for "inetsrv\rpcall.exe" within the timeline and find the following entries:

```
Fri Jun 18 23:49:49 2004 Z
  FILE REG-OIPK81M2WC8 -..C. [524288] C:/Documents and Settings/
  vmware/NTUSER.DAT
  FILE REG-OIPK81M2WC8 -MACB [21396] C:/WINDOWS/Prefetch/SMS.EXE-
  01DC4541.pf
  FILE REG-OIPK81M2WC8 -...B [15870] C:/WINDOWS/Prefetch/RPCALL.EXE-
  394030D7.pf
  FILE REG-OIPK81M2WC8 -M.C. [152] C:/WINDOWS/system32/inetsrv
  FILE REG-OIPK81M2WC8 -.A.. [16384] C:/WINDOWS/system32/ping.exe
  PREF REG-OIPK81M2WC8 -PING.EXE-31216D26.pf last run (1)
  PREF REG-OIPK81M2WC8 -RPCALL.EXE-394030D7.pf last run (2)
  PREF REG-OIPK81M2WC8 -SMS.EXE-01DC4541.pf last run (2)
  REG REG-OIPK81M2WC8 vmware -UserAssist -UEME_RUNPATH:C:\System
  Volume Information\...\RP2\snapshot\Repository\FS\sms.exe (1)
  REG REG-OIPK81M2WC8 vmware -HKCU\..\Run -RPC Drivers-> C:\
  WINDOWS\System32\inetsrv\rpcall.exe
  REG REG-OIPK81M2WC8 -M... HKLM/Software/Microsoft/Windows/
  CurrentVersion/Run
  REG REG-OIPK81M2WC8 -M... HKLM/Software/Microsoft/Windows/
  CurrentVersion/RunServices
  REG REG-OIPK81M2WC8 -M... HKLM/System/ControlSet001/Services/
  SharedAccess/Parameters
  REG REG-OIPK81M2WC8 -M... HKLM/System/ControlSet001/Services/
  SharedAccess/Parameters/FirewallPolicy
  REG REG-OIPK81M2WC8 -M... HKLM/System/ControlSet001/Services/
  SharedAccess/Parameters/FirewallPolicy/StandardProfile
  REG REG-OIPK81M2WC8 -M... HKLM/System/ControlSet001/Services/
  SharedAccess/Parameters/FirewallPolicy/StandardProfile/
  AuthorizedApplications
  REG REG- OIPK81M2WC8 -M... HKLM/System/ControlSet001/Services/
  SharedAccess/Parameters/FirewallPolicy/StandardProfile/
  AuthorizedApplications/List
```

Noticing the entries at the end of the listing that point to the firewall settings on the system (from the System hive), you then run RegRipper against the System hive, and looking at the firewall settings output for the report file, find the following:

```
C:\WINDOWS\System32\inetsrv\rpcall.exe -> C:\WINDOWS\System32\
  inetsrv\rpcall.exe:*:Enabled:RPC Drivers
```

So at this point in your analysis, you have likely found a good candidate for the malware thought to be on the system; in this case, the "rpcall.exe" file. Not only that, you have additional context available regarding how the malware was activated on the system; specifically, from the above timeline listing, you see the following:

```
vmware - UserAssist - UEME_RUNPATH:C:\System Volume
    Information\...\RP2\snapshot\Repository\FS\sms.exe (1)
```

This indicates that "sms.exe" was run from the "vmware" user context, but the path indicates that the executable file itself was found within a System Restore Point (RP2). You know that users should not normally be able to access this directory path, let alone launch executable files. An additional search of the timeline indicates that the tool "cacls.exe," which can be used to modify permissions of various objects (e.g., files, directories, Registry keys) on Windows systems, was run shortly before the timeline listing we just saw.

While this is a brief case study, my hope is that it serves to demonstrate how powerful and beneficial timeline analysis can be, and that it encourages analysts to explore the use of this as a viable analysis technique. Not only does it demonstrate how timelines can be used to detect the presence of malware within an image (often much faster than or even in lieu of AV) but it also illustrates the concept of context that we discussed earlier in this chapter, as well as how timelines can provide an increased level of relative confidence with respect to the various data sources used to populate the timeline. Finally, while the original image file was 1.5 GB in size, the resulting timeline file is just under 6 MB, and compresses down to 511 KB.

SUMMARY

Properly employed, timelines can be an extremely valuable analysis tool. The nature of our complex operating systems, applications, and various other data sources almost necessitates an open-source approach to creating tools for parsing time-stamped data and converting them into a normalized format. Timelines can provide and facilitate a level of visibility into examinations that analysts have not seen using commercial forensic analysis applications, in cases ranging from malware infections, to suspected intrusions, to violations of acceptable use policies and contraband image cases, as well as the more "advanced" incidents that have been discussed in the media.

The open-source approach also means that an analyst isn't restricted to a specific analysis platform; many of the available tools and scripts, including those discussed in this chapter, can be run on Linux and Mac OS X platforms, often without any modification.

However, analysts should keep in mind that as versatile and powerful a technique as this is, it's still just a tool and isn't necessarily something that would or should be employed in every situation. Be sure that you fully understand the goals of your analysis before you decide to employ any particular tool, including timeline analysis.

Application Analysis

INFORMATION IN THIS CHAPTER

- Application Analysis

INTRODUCTION

So far in this book, we've discussed a number of artifacts and resources that analysts can turn to within a Windows system to help address the issues and goals they are facing. Many of the artifacts we've discussed up to this point (e.g., Registry keys, jump lists, etc.) have been generated by the operating system as a result of either user or malware interaction with the environment. What we haven't discussed is what an understanding of applications can provide to the analyst.

Application analysis can be a very important part of an examination, and as such, a very important technique for analysts to understand. Within the world of digital forensic analysis, and even restricting that world to just the analysis of Windows systems, there are a great number of applications that users may install and use. Many times when analyzing an acquired image, analysts look to certain artifacts, often without understanding how the application functions, or how the application receives user input, what the application does on its own, and when the application requires user interaction to perform a task.

Application analysis is, in some ways, similar to malware analysis, as some of the same techniques can be used to gather information regarding the effect that an application has on the environment, either through installation or normal user interaction. However, neither this book nor this chapter addresses malware analysis (or malware reverse engineering), as there are other resources that are much better suited to and address that topic in far better detail than could be addressed here. Perhaps the best resource available that addresses the topic of malware analysis is the recently published book *Malware Analyst's Cookbook and DVD* (Ligh et al., 2011).

There are a lot of applications out there that allow users to perform a great variety of tasks and activities: web and file browsers, gaming applications, servers, desktop managers for mobile devices, office suites, peer-to-peer (P2P) file sharing clients, image viewing and manipulation applications, etc. The list is just too long to provide a complete view of what's available, and it keeps growing. However, analysts and investigators often need to know detailed information regarding the artifacts left by the use of these applications, and often those questions center around what the user, the operating system, or the application itself may have done to generate an artifact.

WARNING

Assumptions

We've all heard the adages about "assumptions"—how it's spelled, what they lead to, etc. However, we often catch ourselves making assumptions about what happened on a system to create an artifact that we may be interested in. One example of this is the existence of a prefetch file for "defrag.exe" (this applies to both Windows XP and Windows 7 systems). We've all seen where an analyst was looking for something that she couldn't find, and made the statement that the user deleted whatever it was and then ran the defrag utility to cover his tracks. Most (albeit not all) times I've heard this, further examination of the system provides no indication that the user ran the utility, and instead the prefetch file is an artifact of a regularly scheduled system process. The point of all this is that it's far too easy to make assumptions about why we're seeing (or not seeing) various artifacts and those assumptions can have a severely detrimental impact on our overall analysis. It's far better to do some testing and verification, or to simply state that we don't know, than it is to make assumptions.

Many of the techniques and tools discussed in this chapter can be used to analyze applications (e.g., P2P file sharing, etc.) and malware, as well. In many ways, malware can be viewed as being similar to an application, albeit with less-than-honorable intentions. Like applications, malware needs to execute and interact with its environment, and often uses some means to remain persistent on the system across reboots and logins. As such, many of the techniques that an analyst may use to determine and verify artifacts of user application usage can be used in malware analysis.

TIP

Timeline Analysis

In Chapter 7 we discussed timeline creation and analysis, and we also discussed how timeline analysis can be used in conjunction with other analysis techniques. Using techniques discussed in this chapter can help you perform timeline analysis, by providing context to a particular artifact or set of artifacts. It is often helpful to understand what actions caused or led up to the creation or modification (the extreme case of modification is deletion) of an artifact, and if those actions were the result of user interaction with the application or of normal application function. Timeline analysis can often help you determine this by providing context to the observed artifacts.

LOG FILES

One of the first aspects of application analysis that analysts should keep in mind is log file analysis. Any application that creates and maintains log files is going to be of great value and interest to an analyst. Antivirus (AV) applications are great for this, because many times not only do they write their logs to the Application Event Log, but they also keep a text-based archive of the logs, which very often contains considerably more historical data than what appears in the Application Event Log.

For example, when examining Windows XP systems with the McAfee AV application installed, I usually find the logs in the "All Users" profile path in the "\Application Data\McAfee\DesktopProtection" folder. On Windows 7, Microsoft Defender logs are located in the "ProgramData\Microsoft\Windows Defender\ Support" directory. These logs often contain information regarding updates to the scanning engine or the signature database, as well as records of scans and detected malware (as well as any actions taken). I've examined systems on which one AV scanner had been installed, and then at some point later, another had been installed, and that system contained the full logs from both AV scanners.

However, AV applications are not the only applications that maintain logs of application activity. Applications such as web servers tend to be capable of maintaining some very comprehensive logs of activity. Like many analysts, I've been involved in several engagements over the years in which homegrown applications that were designed and written internally to an organization have been found to maintain some pretty detailed logs, which have been extremely helpful in not only scoping the engagement, but in the overall analysis of the incident, as well. Many commercial server applications (e.g., FTP servers, database servers, etc.) also have the ability to maintain considerable information via logs by default, and even more detailed information when the configuration is modified accordingly.

TIP

Incident Preparation

Referring back to Chapter 2, if you're reading this chapter and your role at your organization is that of internal IT staff, consider reviewing the applications that are deployed and in use throughout your enterprise, with a specific view toward logging capability. Consider various scenarios such as malware infections and intrusions, and then consider what could be done with respect to the logging capability afforded by the applications to make response to such incidents more effective. Would you be able to address these incidents in a more comprehensive and timely manner if the logging level were turned up or if the logs were maintained in a central location (either through log forwarding or through a regularly scheduled retrieval process)?

DYNAMIC ANALYSIS

There are times when, to answer specific questions about application usage and any artifacts that may be created through that usage, the only option available to an analyst is to execute and interact with the actual application. One option available is to use a copy of the acquired image from the system to create a virtual instance of the system itself, and then log into it and launch the application. In fact, there have been a number of times when analysts (particularly those supporting law enforcement) have done just that, as illustrating a screen capture of what the user "saw" on his desktop tends to be much clearer to a jury (or prosecutor, or any other audience) than trying to describe it in a report. A very useful application for doing this is LiveView (*http://liveview.sourceforge.net/*). Pointing LiveView at a copy of an acquired image, as illustrated in Figure 8.1, will allow an analyst to create a working virtual machine that can then be accessed, and the analyst can then access the system just as the user did.

TIP

Logging into a VM

If you've decided to perform some analysis of a system by creating a virtual instance of a *copy* of the acquired image via LiveView, and need to log into that system, there are a couple of options available to you. One is to use the System and SAM hives from the acquired imagve to dump and crack the passwords. Another is to boot the virtual instance first using a utility that allows you to change passwords on the system, and then reboot the virtual instance to the operating system so that you can log in using the new password. Both of these techniques are described in Chapter 3 of *Windows Registry Forensics* (Carvey, 2011).

FIGURE 8.1

Portion of LiveView user interface.

Clicking the "Start" button in the LiveView interface starts the process of creating the VMWare configuration files and launching (with VMWare Workstation or Player installed) the virtual machine.

Another way to go about testing an application is to set up a system (real or virtual) with a version of the relevant operating system (Windows XP, Vista, Windows 7, etc.—whichever version is running on the system that you're analyzing), install monitoring tools into that environment, and then install the application (the correct version, if available) that you want to analyze. Using a virtual environment such as VMWare (*http://www.vmware.com*), Workstation allows you to create your installation environment complete with monitoring tools, and then take a "snapshot" of the system (prior to installing the application to be tested) so that you can always revert to a known-good "clean" state for your environment.

TIP

VirtualBox

VMWare isn't the only virtual environment for Windows systems that is available. While VMWare Player and Server are freely available, the Workstation version, which allows for the convenience of virtual machines and management of snapshots, is not. VirtualBox (*http://www.virtualbox.org/*) is a virtual environment that is freely available from Oracle Corporation (part of Oracle's Sun Microsystems acquisition) and includes the ability to create and manage snapshots, as well (*http://www.virtualbox.org/manual/ch01.html#snapshots*). Be sure to consult the VirtualBox documentation for instructions regarding how to boot an acquired image as a virtual machine.

Once you have determined which of these two methods you plan to use to go about analyzing the application, there are essentially two methods for monitoring changes to a system during application installation, as well as while running and using those applications. The first method involves making and comparing snapshots of the system; essentially, make a snapshot of the system, do something with the application (perform some atomic action), take another snapshot, and then compare the two to look for differences.

There are freely available applications that allow you to do this sort of comparative analysis with specific components of the operating system. For example, RegShot (*http://sourceforge.net/projects/regshot/files/*) allows you to compare snapshots of the file system and Registry. Using open-source tools such as "fls.exe" (part of the Sleuthkit tools, available at *http://www.sleuthkit.org*), you could easily create your own tool for performing differential analysis of file system metadata from within an acquired image. However, when you're referring to executing and using an application, there very often can be much more to the analysis of that application (with respect to artifacts) than simply modifications to the Registry and file system.

Fortunately, Microsoft provides an excellent and comprehensive solution for this approach to application analysis; in fact, the Attack Surface Analyzer (ASA; still in beta at the time of this writing and available at *http://www.microsoft.com/download/en/details.aspx?id=19537*) was specifically written for this purpose. From the Overview section of the application download page:

> *Attack Surface Analyzer is developed by the Security Engineering group, building on the work of our Security Science team. It is the same tool used by Microsoft's internal product groups to catalogue changes made to operating system attack surface by the installation of new software.*

Tools such as this can be very useful, as you can snapshot the system, perform an "atomic action" such as installing the application that you're interested in, create another snapshot of the live system, and compare them to determine the "attack surface." From that point, you can perform other atomic actions, performing one function at a time or changing one variable at a time, all the while creating snapshots at specific points along the way. Then you can determine the difference between any of the snapshots at any point.

Once you've downloaded and installed ASA, you'll want to also have a copy of the application that you want to install. As with all snapshot tools, you do not want to run a scan of the system as soon as you install the tool; the reason for this is that while this does create a baseline, you do not know how much activity will occur on the system before you run your second scan for comparison. As such, you should minimize any chance for additional changes to occur to the system, and run your first scan just prior to installing your application. When you run ASA, you'll be presented with the name of a CAB (Microsoft cabinet file) file to generate, based on the system name, as well as the date and UTC time of when you launched ASA (e.g., "ENZO_5.1.3._2011-08-19_21-40-20.cab," when ASA was launched at 5:40 pm EST on August 19, 2011). When you run a scan, ASA runs through a data collection phase, during which it collects a good deal of security-specific information

Please select an action:
- ○ Run new scan
- ◉ Generate attack surface report

Select options:

Baseline Cab	C:\Users\harlan\Attack Surface Analyzer\ENZO_5.1.3_2011-08-19_21-4(▾ [Browse...]
Product Cab	C:\Users\harlan\Attack Surface Analyzer\ENZO_5.1.3_2011-08-19_21-5 ▾ [Browse...]
Report Filename	C:\Users\harlan\Attack Surface Analyzer\ENZO_5.1.3_2011-08-19_21-51-0 [Browse...]

FIGURE 8.2

Generating an attack surface report.

from the live system, enumerating such information as autorun tasks, threads, desktops, handles, services, memory information, network ports, etc.

Once the initial scan is complete, you can minimize the ASA window on the desktop and install your application. As an example, I thought it would be a good idea to install an application that many people use and are familiar with: iTunes version 10. Once the installation was complete, I opted to associate audio files with iTunes as the default application to use when launching those files.

Once I completed the iTunes setup, I closed the application and ran another ASA scan. Once that scan was complete, I selected the "Generate attack surface report" ASA option, as illustrated in Figure 8.2.

Once the snapshot comparison analysis is complete, the "report.html" page opens in your default browser with three tabs: Report Summary, Security Issues, and Attack Surface. This report presents a great deal of valuable information regarding changes to the system, including Registry changes such as modifications to the firewall rules on the system. The Security Issues tab provides information similar to what you would expect from a security assessment scan of the system.

However, as with many tools not written or designed by analysts, ASA has weaknesses or gaps in what we might expect such a tool to provide. For example, nothing in the report clearly indicated security issues with respect to file system changes (i.e., files added or modified); specifically, no information was provided regarding a scheduled task (see Chapter 5 for a discussion of scheduled tasks) that had been added to the system (e.g., to check for software updates on a regular basis). Scheduled tasks provide an effective persistence mechanism for intruders or malware. Now, missing the scheduled task being added to the system does not necessarily mean that tools such as ASA do not have their uses; in fact, tools such as this can be used to create periodic snapshots of the system for a "security health checkup." For example, the Attack Surface tab of the report clearly showed that three new services had been added to the system as a result of the installation, and two of those services were set to auto-start, and the third was set to start on demand. This can be very valuable information when part of a regular scan, as well as when used to assess an application installation.

> **NOTE**
>
> Tool Usability
>
> I see Microsoft's Attack Surface Analyzer tool, while being a "beta," not quite ready for primetime with respect to completely meeting the needs of digital forensic analysts. For one, it is intended for Vista and later systems; this isn't a huge issue, as Windows XP is being phased out as a desktop operating system. Also, just from the little interaction I had with the tool, it clearly missed identifying what could have been a fairly significant item.
>
> However, in Microsoft's defense, ASA was never billed as a tool for forensic analysts. It does appear to be useful to some extent, but as with other tools, it also seems to have its strengths as well as its weaknesses.

A drawback of using this snapshot-based approach to application analysis is that if an application creates an artifact, such as a file or Registry key, and then deletes it between the two snapshots, the fact that the file was created and then deleted may not show up in your differential analysis of the snapshots. The same would be true with existing files and Registry keys (including volatile Registry keys) that are simply accessed and not modified or changed in any way during the process; such activity may not show up when you compare snapshots. As such, the second method for monitoring an application is to use real-time monitoring applications.

An application monitoring tool that you might consider is Capture-BAT (*https://www.honeynet.org/node/315*). Capture-BAT was designed to monitor a system (including monitoring of network activity) while executing applications or "processing" documents; according to the web page, one example use case involves determining the behavior of a maliciously crafted MS Word document when it is opened in the application. Once you've downloaded and installed Capture-BAT, you'll need to reboot your system, and when it comes back up, you'll find the tool in the "C:\Program Files\Capture" directory. From there, typing "capturebat –h" at the command prompt provides the following usage information:

```
Usage: CaptureClient.exe [-chn] [-s server address -a vm server id
  -b vm id] [-l file]
-h Print this help message
-s address Address of the server the client connects up to. NOTE -a
  & -b
must be defined when using this option
-a server id Unique id of the virtual machine server that hosts the
  client
-b vm id Unique id of the virtual machine that this client is run on
-l file Output system events to a file rather than stdout
-c Copy files into the log directory when they are modified or
  deleted
-n Capture all incoming and outgoing network packets from the
  network adapters on the system and store them in .pcap files in
  the log directory
If -s is not set the client will operate in standalone mode
```

From this, you can see that it's fairly straightforward to run the Capture-BAT in standalone mode. For example, most analysts would want to run Capture-BAT with the following command line:

```
C:\Program Files\Capture\capturebat -l logs\output.txt -c
```

This command line would start Capture-BAT monitoring the system and sending logged system events to the "output.txt" file in the "logs" subdirectory, while copying files that are deleted or modified. If you have the necessary WinPCap drivers (available at *http://www.winpcap.org/*) installed on your system, adding the "-n" switch would allow you to capture network traffic, as well. If you opt to do this, you might consider using tools mentioned in the "Network Captures" section later in this chapter in your analysis.

There are other free tools available for monitoring system activity, and perhaps the best known is Process Monitor (available online from Microsoft at *http://technet .microsoft.com/en-us/sysinternals/bb896645*). Process Monitor (ProcMon) performs real-time monitoring of file system, Registry, and process/thread activity on the system.

One of ProcMon's greatest strengths—and potential weaknesses—is that it captures so much data; a vast amount of activity normally occurs on a Windows system, even when the system is "idle." Fortunately, ProcMon includes a detailed and flexible filter system. Filters can be set prior to starting a capture (to limit the amount of data collected), or after a capture is complete (to limit the amount of data displayed). One nice advantage of ProcMon or similar "active" monitoring tools is that monitoring processes during execution of an application will allow you to see any child processes that were launched and then exited; using a snapshot-based approach will only show you the before and after and will miss events that occurred during.

NETWORK CAPTURES

Many times when performing application analysis, you may want to determine if the application attempts to "phone home" or perform any network communications during the installation process, or if any other network communications occur at any point (e.g., accepting a terms of use policy, registration process, etc.). If you're analyzing an application being installed in a VM, then you'll want to incorporate some sort of network capture capability on the host system; that way, the network capture capability will not interfere with, or be interfered with, the application installation process.

WARNING

Looking for Security Functionality

There may be applications that, during the installation process, examine the environment that they're being installed and running in, to attempt to disable security functionality. For example, there is malware that is "VM-aware"; that is, it can determine that it is running in a VM, and either disable itself or follow another execution path. There is other malware that has the ability to disable security measures such as AV applications, firewalls, etc.

Tools you will want to consider using to capture and analyze network traffic include Wireshark (*http://www.wireshark.org/*) and NetworkMiner (*http://www .netresec.com/*). Installing Wireshark on your host system (if you're analyzing the application installed in a VM) will allow you to capture network traffic as it leaves the VM, as well as conduct analysis of the captured traffic. Wireshark allows you to view the captured packets, as well as reassemble network streams to view the entire "conversation" between systems. NetworkMiner is capable of passively identifying operating systems, as well as reassembling transmitted files (e.g., images, etc.) from the capture pcap files.

Another tool to consider using on your analysis system (the system or virtual machine on which you're testing the application) is Microsoft's own Port Reporter (available via MS Knowledgebase article 837243at *http://support.microsoft .com/kb/837243*), a tool that acts as something of a "netstat-as-a-service" on Windows systems. Port Reporter does not have a full packet capture capability, the way Wireshark and other network sniffer tools do, but it does provide information regarding outbound (and possibly inbound) network communications, and associates network connections with the processes using them, in much the same way the "netstat" utility does. Port Reporter installs as a service and writes its logs to the Windows\system32\Logfiles\PortReporter folder, as well as writing to the Application Event Log. MS Knowledgebase article 837243 provides examples of the contents of the logs produced by Port Reporter.

If you install Port Reporter, you might also consider adding the Port Reporter Parser tool (described and available via MS Knowledgebase article 884289 at *http://support.microsoft.com/kb/884289*). This parser allows you to cull information from the Port Reporter logs using various filters.

TIP

Understanding Network Communications

When performing incident response (and this applies to forensic analysis, particularly where logs from network devices and applications are included), it is important to have an understanding of network communications. I've told a number of analysts how important it is to understand that TCP/IP communications is initiated by a three-stage handshake; if any of that fails, the communications channel is not established. Another aspect is the specific process used by Windows hosts to perform name resolution, which is addressed in MS KnowledgeBase article 172218 (*http://support.microsoft.com/kb/172218*).

I once responded to an incident that included unusual network communications; in this case, DNS name queries for hosts and domains associated with bots and possibly other suspicious activity had been detected emanating from one specific host system. Analysis revealed that the issue was a result of two anti-spyware applications that had been installed on the system; one application modified the hosts file to "blackhole" name lookups (so that if the system were infected with known malware, attempts to communicate with command and control channels would resolve to the local host), and the other read the hosts file and performed network lookups of the names it found, regardless of the IP address to which it was directed. A network monitoring application alerted on the name queries, indicating a possible incident.

> Using application analysis techniques outlined in this chapter, we were able to empirically demonstrate that the observed activity was the result of the interaction between the two applications, and not the result of a malware infection that had not been detected by either of the anti-spyware applications or the installed AV application.

APPLICATION MEMORY ANALYSIS

I've mentioned a number of times in this book that a detailed discussion of the analysis of physical memory is beyond the scope of this book, and this continues to be the case. To really do the topic justice, even focusing solely in Windows memory, would require a book all its own. That being said, one of perhaps the most overlooked aspects of application analysis is understanding what exists (e.g., data, network connections, open handles, etc.) in memory while the application is running. While this section will not be a tutorial on installing and using memory analysis tools, these tools will be mentioned as a means for extracting information from Windows memory, and are best employed by an analyst with a thorough understanding of their use.

I mention this because, like many other analysts, I've responded to a number of data breaches in which we found that sensitive data were encrypted while in transit on the network, as they moved among systems. But we also found that during the time that the data were actually on the systems, they were available in clear text in the memory used by the process that was processing and managing the data. As such, as you might assume, an attacker had loaded software on the system (referred to by some as a "RAM scraper") that would dump the contents of process memory to a file, and then parse through the file looking for and culling out that sensitive data.

Collecting and analyzing memory from a Windows system has come a long way since the Digital Forensics Research Workshop (DFRWS) 2005 Windows memory analysis challenge. For example, there are now a number of freely available tools that allow you to collect memory from Windows systems, including FTK Imager (available from AccessData at *http://accessdata.com/support/adownloads#FTKImager*) and DumpIt from MoonSol (*http://www.moonsols.com/2011/07/18/moonsols-dumpit-goes-mainstream/*). If you're using a virtual environment, you may be able to suspend the VM and collect the contents of physical memory from a file. Using VMWare Workstation, the file containing the contents of physical memory ends with the .vmem extension. You can then analyze the contents of the physical memory dump using freely available tools such as "strings .exe" (*http://technet.microsoft.com/en-us/sysinternals/bb897439*) and the Volatility Framework (version 2.0, including a standalone version for Windows systems; *http://code.google.com/p/volatility/*).

Once you have the contents of memory to examine, to see what information is available, the easiest thing to do is to run "strings.exe" against the exported file containing the memory contents. If you set up and configured the application on a system that you own and control (such as on a standalone system or virtual machine), and you used an account that you created, you may find information such as passwords, configuration settings, etc. Using Volatility, you can get a much more granular view of what the application is doing, including dumping the process information, including loaded modules, open file and Registry handles, network connections, etc. You can then correlate what you learned from application analysis on a virtual system to what artifacts you might expect to find in the acquired image.

TIP

Other Sources of Memory

If you're analyzing an image acquired from a Windows system, in particular a laptop, you may find valuable memory data in a hibernation file ("C:\hiberfil.sys"). The Volatility framework incorporates Matthieu Suiche's work on accessing the contents of this file, and being able to analyze it as if it were a physical memory dump from a live system.

SUMMARY

Analysts will often come across artifacts during an examination of an acquired image, and need to identify means by which those artifacts were created and/or modified. In most cases, this is not self-evident, and some form of additional analysis may be required to identify the circumstances that may have lead to the creation or modification of those artifacts. One means of doing this is to boot a copy of the acquired image into a virtual machine; another may be to create a system (or perhaps a virtual machine) on which to install the version of the application being examined, and monitor its behavior on that system. With available tools and techniques, application analysis is an investigative technique that analysts can employ to obtain clear and perhaps even decisive answers to their questions.

References

Carvey, H. A. (2011). *Windows registry forensics*. Burlington, MA: Syngress Publishing.
Ligh, M. H., Adair, S., Hartstein, B., & Richard, M. (2011). *Malware analyst's cookbook and DVD*. New York: Wiley.

Index

A